THE DOOR

*My twenty-six years working inside
Canada's prisons*

VERN THIBEDEAU

BOOKSIDE Press

BookSide Press
877-741-8091
www.booksidepress.com
orders@booksidepress.com

Contents

Preface

I started this memoir at the urging of my family, for which I am forever grateful. I also wish to give my heartfelt thanks to my brother, Dan, who, even though he was ill at the time, spent hours editing *The Door*.

First, I would like to say that I sincerely hope I haven't offended anyone. I imagine a few staff may be upset with me, but I have tried to be honest; so what can I say?

I want everyone to know that, except for one officer, I haven't used last names; however, there are several first names I didn't change. All inmate names have been changed except for those of three or four notorious criminals who received countrywide publicity.

I hope I don't sound overly bitter; I'm not. Just as in any job, there were ups and downs, but usually, corrections treated me fairly, and it was a very good career. I also had the pleasure of working side by side with some very accomplished and dedicated staff.

There are a couple of things I hope this book will accomplish. I realize that penitentiaries are a mystery to the average citizen, and that is certainly understandable. I hope this will alleviate some of that mystery and perhaps help people understand a little of what goes on within them.

Second, I hope everyone comes to understand some of what the people employed in a correctional setting must deal with. I must admit this pertains mostly to correctional officers, but it does relate to all staff.

In my mind, almost all correctional officers are heroes. About the few who don't meet this standard, well, what can I say? They know who they are. I must insist, though, that almost all staff in the prison system do an excellent job in extremely adverse circumstances and almost never receive any recognition for their efforts.

I hope this memoir will demonstrate that a correctional officer is usually an average person working in an extremely stressful and difficult environment with people who, for the most part, are emotionally immature and in some cases mentally unstable, and some of whom can and do become dangerous. In addition, long after most of the public have forgotten murderers like Olson, Bernardo, and Williams, correctional staff still must deal with them day in and day out, usually for years.

All the incidents I have written about did happen. Because of the time that has elapsed and lack notes, there may be some minor variations from actual events. Also, the chronological order may not be exact. I should also mention that I have not covered all the situations I was involved in or know about. To do that would take a better memory than I possess and more paper and ink than I can afford.

In closing, I sincerely wish to give a tip of the hat to correctional officers and their families. *The Door* was written for them.

I hope you find it interesting.
Vern Thibedeau

Glossary

AOD: Absent on duty.

Bingo: A slang term signifying that the institutional count is correct.

CBI: Collin's Bay Institution, also called "the Bay" or "Disney World."

CCO: Chief of correctional operations.

CMO: Case management officer.

CO: Correctional officer.

CX: A pay grade, also used as a rank.

CX 1: A correctional officer in a minimum—or medium-security institution.

CX 2: A correctional officer in a maximum-security institution.

CX 3: A senior correctional officer in a minimum—or medium security institution.

CX 4: A senior correctional officer in a maximum-security institution.

CX 5: A supervisor in a minimum—or medium-security institution.

CX 6: A supervisor in a maximum-security institution.

Dissociation: A secure area within segregation, also called "diss" or "hole."

D/W: Deputy warden, also referred to as the "2 I/C" of an institution.

ECA: Environmental control area, also known as segregation.

ETA: Escorted temporary absence, usually for a doctor appointment or similar.

FPS: Finger print system, a number assigned to convicted persons.

Hanger: A person who has attempted to hang him—or herself.

Haven: Millhaven Institution, also called "the Mill."

IDB: Inmate disciplinary board, chaired by a lawyer.

IERT: Institutional emergency response team.

IPSO: Institutional preventive security officer.

JI: Joyceville Institution, also called "the Ville."

Jug up: Inmates' meal time.

Keeper: Correctional supervisor, CX 5 or 6.

KP: Kingston Penitentiary.

OP: Off privileges.

OPP: Ontario Provincial Police.

PC: Protective custody.

P4W: Prison for women.

Pen Squad: OPP squad that investigates crime in penitentiaries in the Kingston area.

QPP: Quebec Provincial Police.

Range: A large hallway in a cell block or living unit that contains cells.

RTC: Regional treatment center, also called TC, an area inside KP.

Seg: Segregation, a secure area inside an institution.

SHU: Special handling unit, a highly secured unit for inmates who havecommitted a serious crime while under sentence.

Slasher: A person who has cut him—or herself to gain attention or commitsuicide.

UM: Unit manager.

UTA: Unescorted temporary absence, classed as a rehabilitation escort.

V&C: Visits and Correspondence, the department responsible for all visitations and mail going in and out of correctional institutions.

Chapter 1

My first day at Collin's Bay Penitentiary.

I first saw the Door on April 10, 1973.

I don't recall the exact time, but I remember the weather: it was damp, with angry black clouds crashing into each other, and I was vehemently hoping this was not a sign of my future. And my emotions—they were a mixture of extreme excitement and a large dose of very real apprehension. You do tend to have mixed emotions when you are embarking on a unique career. You have no way of knowing if you are going into a tailspin or flying to the moon. But because I was stepping into a very weird and unusual environment, you can bet I was the owner of a large dose of fear.

When I first stood in front of the Door, I didn't realize the impact it would have on my family and me. I also did not visualize the drastic changes it would make in my life. If I could have had an insight into those changes, I might very well have turned around and run from the Door.

The Door was immense. Most doors are made to allow one or two people to enter or leave at one time. Doors also usually have an aura around them that says, "Welcome." The Door seemed to scream a warning to leave.

With my heart hammering in my chest, I hesitantly placed my hand around the immense handle and gave it an experimental tug. And nothing, absolutely nothing, happened! By now, every fibre in my being was screaming at me to turn around and leave. The long drive back to my home and normal routine was becoming more appealing to me with each passing moment. I was beginning to believe it had been an enormous error of judgment to even think about embarking on this new life. Suddenly, there was a click. This click, to my ears, sounded like a crack of thunder. My shaking hand was still wrapped around the brass handle, so I gave it another exploratory tug. My tentative tug caused it to swing open. The Door really wasn't all that heavy after all, or I was a hell of a lot stronger than I thought!

With a great deal of trepidation, I stepped through the Door to begin my new life.

As soon as I entered the building, the Door automatically swung shut and closed with a reverberating clang. At the same time, a mechanical-sounding voice asked if it could help me. I couldn't see anyone in my vicinity and realized someone was speaking to me through an intercom. I informed this disembodied voice that I was here to begin employment. It instructed me to go up the stairs on my left to the next level and report to the staff training officer.

I found the office, which was empty, but because the door was open and a sign stated the staff training officer belonged there, I went in and sat down.

So here I was. I had taken the first major step toward beginning my new life. At the time, I thought—hoped—the Door would be the biggest obstacle I would face and that now that I had made it through the Door, I'd be home free. I was now a duly sworn federal peace officer and an official member of what at that time was called the Canadian Penitentiary Service. This name would soon be changed to Correctional Service Canada to better reflect the bilingual nature of Canada. I was also assigned to CBI (Collin's Bay Penitentiary) in Kingston, Ontario. This institution, and for good reason, was better known to some people as "Disney World."

This was certainly a huge step for a person born and raised in a small northern Ontario town who had never set foot inside a prison before; in fact, when I accepted the job, I didn't even know what a correctional officer was. I was soon to find out!

Within a few minutes, a man in uniform entered, introduced himself as Robert, and told me he was the staff training officer. He told me I was one of six new officers and that we would be assigned to him for training purposes for a couple of weeks. This training would include weapons instruction, a tour of the institution, issuance of uniforms, reading standing and post orders, and sundry other items. In addition, when there was an opportunity to send us, there was a twelve-week course at the Correctional Staff College that we would have to pass in order to keep our jobs. And strange as it may seem, we were to have the opportunity to work overtime during our training due to a chronic staff shortage at CBI; apparently, all five major institutions in the area were having the same staffing problem.

Rob took me to a large boardroom where several guys were sitting, introduced me to everyone, and said he would be right back with some reading material for me. I soon discovered that with one or two exceptions, these guys didn't know much more about prison life than I did. I still wonder if all of us would have stayed if we had been more knowledgeable about the future.

Rob soon returned with a stack of binders that he was nice enough (I'm being facetious here) to set down in front of me. He informed us we were to read these whenever we had the opportunity. He also stressed that the binders were confidential reading material and told us to make sure the last person who left the room locked the door. Then he told us he was leaving to set up the revolver range and would be back shortly. Once Rob left, I opened one of the binders. It had "Post Orders for Collin's Bay Penitentiary" printed on the front in large capital letters. The front of the binder also said "confidential material" in large red letters. Unfortunately, most of the words and phrases in the binder were completely foreign to me: *range, traveling bars, segregation, disassociation, Folger Adams keys, mace*, and on and on and on. I only read a few pages and knew with certainty I wouldn't be spending as much time reading as the administration wanted me to. Little did I know that within a very short time, I was going to regret that decision. I also didn't want to ask the others to explain anything; there was no way I wanted to appear as innocent as I was! Later, I realized everyone was more or less in the same boat and they didn't want to ask any questions either. Later in my career, I would be the one formulating institutional post orders.

Thirty minutes or so later, an older officer entered the room, introduced himself as Archie, and said he would be with us for a few days. He told us he was transferring back into corrections from the garage and would be assisting the staff training officer for a few days.

Archie asked us to follow him to an office to sign some papers and to fill out a next-of-kin form. In less than two years, my wife, Sheila, and I were going to discover these next-of-kin forms were a waste of time, because, at least at CBI, they were ignored. Anyway, we trooped down the hall and signed the forms and then went to the staff lounge to have a coffee break. So far this seemed like a hell of a good job—little did I know!

Within a short time, Rob returned and told us to follow him down to the staff mess for lunch. We all trooped down those same stairs, came to a large barrier, and had to stand there until it slid open. The barrier was controlled from an immense room enclosed in metal walls about four feet high. Thick glass extended up for about another five feet and disappeared into the ceiling. There were slots in the metal just below the glass, and Rob told us these small doors were gun ports. My immediate thought was, *Well, ain't that nice.*

Rob informed us this sizeable area was called the main control. He also explained that two officers were posted here on all shifts except for the morning shift (eleven to seven). Apparently, only one staff member was required on that particular shift. He also told us the glass was bulletproof and the control centre contained numerous weapons in case of an emergency. He made sure we understood the danger of inmates breaching the centre and seizing the weapons. However, I was to find that—at least back then—it practically took an act of war for weapons to be issued at the Bay. In addition to the weapons in the main control, he told us the main armoury was on the second floor just down from his office. I couldn't help but think, *Hell, there are enough firearms right here to start a small war!*

We trooped around the main control and went through another opened barrier at the other end. And there it was. The strip! This area had been called the strip for years and was known by that name throughout the region. It was basically a large hallway that must have been twenty feet wide and appeared to continue forever. Rob told us that all movement, staff and inmate, was through the strip. I must admit the strip hit me much like the Door; it made me feel small and inconsequential. It was cavernous.

At this particular time of day, the strip was almost empty. I could see only three or four people, and they were in uniform. Rob explained that all inmates were locked in their cells and being counted. I must admit this certainly made me happy. I really was not in any hurry to see a bunch of inmates. He also told us he had purposely waited until this time to take us down to the mess. I looked at my watch and noted that it was eleven thirty. I still remember thinking it was really nice of him to do this for us; however, it didn't take me very long to learn that there was a method to his madness.

As we continued our walk, he explained that staff counted the inmates several times a day, always at the same times, and this particular count was called the noon count. He informed us that we would become very familiar with counts, and from that I got the impression that counts were extremely important and highly regulated. One thing he didn't bother to inform us was that by the time we finished eating, the count would be called correct and the strip would be full of inmates going for their lunch. I guess it was just as well he didn't—I was able to enjoy my lunch!

Rob started down the strip and we, as usual, followed like obedient little sheep. We were all craning our heads around like chickens trying to see everything at once. But everything was so completely alien, my mind just couldn't accept everything I saw. I can just imagine what we must have looked like to other staff. As we followed along, he explained about the barriers and exits leading off the strip. The first exit was on the left and went to admissions and discharge. I looked into the area as we passed, but there wasn't much to see.

The next exit was also on the left and went into the gym and school area.

And then on the right I was afforded my first view of a cell block. This block, named Three Block, was separated from the strip by a large barrier made of steel bars. The barrier looked like it would hold against anything except an assault by a tank! I tried to look into the cell block, but it was difficult to see anything and I certainly didn't want to be left behind by our little procession.

A little farther down the strip on the left side was another block. This one was named One Block, and once again there was not much to see. However, emanating from this area was noise. The noise assaulted the ears and seemed to be made up of several radio stations turned as loud as they could possibly go and all tuned to different stations. Mingled with this was the sound of people yelling and other voices screaming, "Turn the fucking radios down." These commands were answered with shouts and jeers of profanity and someone screaming, "Stick the goddamn thing up your ass."

I have to mention one thing here. One of the loudest songs being played was "The Night Chicago Died" by Paper Lace. At the time this was a hit tune, and I think one of the favourite lines of the song was "about a hundred cops are dead," because every time that particular line was played, the inmates all cheered. I must admit, though, that no matter how many times I heard the song, it was one of my favourites.

Directly across from One Block was Two Block. There was not much to see in this area either. There was a large empty area leading to stairs that were closed off so you could tell they went up but not where they ended. Toward the left, there was an entrance to a range, but it was closed off by a barrier similar to the cell block barriers but on a much smaller scale. Rob informed us this had once been 2A but had been converted to segregation due to the fire in Three Block. I couldn't hear any screaming or yelling, and it was difficult to imagine there were well over a hundred men locked up in this one area.

Farther down the strip and on the left side was another cell block. This one naturally was called Four Block but was different than the other three and appeared much newer. I later found out that this cellblock had been built just a few years previously. While walking past we could tell it had one range running perpendicular to the strip and another range directly above it; also, the range barriers and cell doors were solid steel instead of bars.

As we neared the end of the strip, we began to wonder just where the hell this staff mess was hiding. At the end of the strip, which was still more than a hundred feet away, we could see still another barrier that exited to the outside. Rob told us this barrier was called the south barrier and was the only exit inmates could use to go to their work area or to the exercise yard. There was a uniformed staff member standing at the barrier, and we were told he was a keeper. I was to learn later that keeper was a fairly high rank in security and one was in charge of the prison at all times other than regular working hours. Naturally, I didn't realize it at the time, but I was to reach this dizzy height eight years later, which, at the time, was quite fast.

A few steps past Four Block and on the other side of the strip was another very solid-looking door. Rob headed for it, and we assumed we had finally reached the mess. We walked through it, with our illustrious leader, where else, but in front leading, and suddenly we were in a large room that looked similar to any restaurant I had ever seen. Rob explained that all staff received a hot lunch when they were working the day shift. Since I was in Kingston by myself and had very little money and no idea where I was going to live, you can imagine how happy I was to find out I was going to have free hot lunches.

Several staff members were sitting at tables eating, some in uniform and some in civilian clothing. Everyone looked at us, and most offered some type of greeting or at least a smile. I noticed the staff in uniform seemed to be rushing their meals. It also appeared that staff were divided by an invisible barrier—uniformed staff in one group and no uniformed staff in another. I later found out that this was a natural occurrence; correctional officers just seem to gravitate to other correctional officers. To some degree, this isolation also extends to their families. It wouldn't take long for my family and me to fit into this pattern.

During our lunch, staff continually entered and left the mess, and we could overhear some of their conversations.

One officer said, "The count's late again because of those goddamn cons in One Block."

"So what? That's nothing new," another replied.

A few minutes later an officer entered the mess and hollered, "Bingo!"

"Well," someone said, "We're one count closer to retirement."

And shockingly, it suddenly hit me; I was included in that particular statement!

Rob explained that all inmates were locked in their cells for the formal counts and not allowed out until every inmate was accounted for. He also told us that sometimes the count took longer than usual because staff counted wrong or the inmates screwed around and hid in their cells. "There are even times," Rob said, "when it's the keeper's screw-up. It's been known for a keeper to add wrong or forget to note that an inmate has left or reentered the institution."

Once the count was in, several uniformed staff jumped up and left the mess, and several more came in. And then Rob told us it was time for us to leave. He said he would take us back to the lounge area, and then we were on our own until 1300 hours, at which time he wanted us back in our meeting room. We headed for the exit, and Rob opened the door. I couldn't see out, but the blast of noise was unbelievable. When we had entered the mess earlier, the strip had been almost empty and actually, in a weird sort of way, peaceful. Now there was a loud rumbling sound intermingled with individual yells, curses, and even some laughter. It sounded as if there were hundreds of men out there and everyone was yelling, hollering, or fighting.

When I came to the door and it was my turn to step onto the strip, I almost went into shock! Christ, it was full of inmates, and they were a huge, tough-looking bunch of guys. I could have sworn there must have been two or three hundred of them. I would eventually learn that due to the control of major movement, there were no more than sixty or seventy of them. They were all bunched up and heading in the same direction, and that was toward the keeper, who was standing at the south barrier. Thankfully, he didn't appear to require any help, least of all from me.

Suddenly, it was my turn to step into the middle of this loud, laughing, arguing, and jeering mass of convicts. I didn't know much about inmates, and as far as I knew, I had never even been close to one. However, I did know by now that these guys were doing time for everything from committing break- and-enters to murdering one or more people and God only knew what else in between. Also, I suddenly realized almost all of them were a hell of a lot bigger than I was. Some had arms about the same size as my leg, and added to that were the tattoos—I had never seen so many tattoos.

So here I was in a situation I had never even considered before, my stomach flipping around, my heart pounding, and I was praying I wouldn't throw up. But I did know I had to step into this undulating sea of criminals. My only salvation was watching Rob. He just stepped into this mass, said hi to a few, and started walking; watching him made me realize this was likely an everyday occurrence. Also, I couldn't believe this was overly dangerous, or he wouldn't have been doing what he was doing. So I just started to chew on my tongue, hoped I didn't look too scared, and forced myself onto the strip.

This was one of the most difficult times I ever had in the service. I could barely see Rob, but every once in a while I noticed his hat bob up out of the crowd, and I just kept heading for it. I'm sure the inmates realized we were new to this business, and they were, to put it mildly, making very rude comments. The more comments they uttered, the tighter my stomach became. By this time I was expecting to be raped at any moment, and my stomach was tied up in a knot about the size of a golf ball. I was positive they'd be able to hear my heart thudding or at the very least see my hands shaking. But I had been around long enough to know I couldn't allow myself to show them how terrified I really was, so I just kept struggling against the flow of inmates. I was positive it took three hours to force my way through that pack of humanity. But by the time I reached Three Block, I had regained my senses and realized it had only taken a few minutes to walk that tremendous distance.

With my body in the process of reverting more or less back to normal, I began taking stock of my situation. During this episode I had reached an unshakable decision. I had decided that if God allowed me to live, I was heading back up north just as soon as I could make it to the car! However, right about then I spotted Rob, and I could tell he was carefully watching us and at the same time trying to let on that he wasn't. I was beginning to think he might have timed our exit from the mess as some kind of test, and perhaps we weren't in as much danger as I imagined. If that was the idea, I guess it worked, because the next day I found out one guy resigned right after our little walk. I certainly didn't blame him; if I hadn't been so stubborn, I would've packed it in with him and headed home.

Once we were sure we were all going to live, the bunch of us trooped up to the lounge area, had a coffee, and watched some of the staff play euchre. At 1300 hours, we reported to our classroom and waited for Rob. He made his appearance about half an hour later, told us to do some more reading, and instructed us to be back in the morning at 0800 hours ready to spend some time at the revolver range.

Chapter 2

My tour of Collin's Bay Penitentiary.

I must admit that leaving for work on my second day of employment with the penitentiary service was not nearly as traumatic as it had been the day before. However, I was still filled with doubt about whether I'd be able to survive in this alien environment. I arrived at the pen (there I was, picking up the jargon after only one day) at about 0745 hours and had to identify myself, because we hadn't been issued identification cards yet. I reported to the classroom and learned I was the last one to report. However, Rob wasn't in yet anyway. I found out later that he wasn't the most ambitious officer I would meet. However, he did know a lot about the job. Once he arrived, Rob had Archie take us to the range while he went to the armouries to pick up the revolvers. Once again we all trooped along.

Rob eventually showed up carrying several revolvers, and we spent the morning firing handguns. Shortly before lunch, we headed back to our famous room and then trooped down to the staff mess. This was a repeat of the day before; however, now it wasn't nearly as stomach-tightening or nerve-wracking. But believe me, it was still exciting.

After finishing lunch, we reported back to the classroom and once again waited for Rob. Once he arrived he informed us he had a couple of extra staff available and thought this would be a good time to give us a tour of the institution. I lucked out on this occasion, because I ended up going with Archie. This certainly worked for me, because he was one of the friendliest guys I would meet, and he knew the institution intimately. Luckily he didn't mind answering silly questions, because I had dozens of them. Another lucky item was that he didn't mind stopping for coffee and chatting with staff, because this was a learning experience in itself.

Sadly, Archie was killed shortly after he retired. I was told he had an accident up north while involved with his hobby. People tend to wonder why some of us expire before our time while some useless pukes seem to live indefinitely, but after being in this line of work, you stop wondering and just shake your head; there is no answer.

The first stop of any real interest was Three Block. The cell block barrier was locked, and a staff member had to unlock it so we could get in. I was told all barriers were to remain locked except during major inmate movement. A staff member explained that, at least in theory, if the barriers were locked and the inmates attempted to take over the cell block or the institution, it would make it more difficult for them to do so and perhaps give staff an opportunity to isolate the problem or escape. Mind you, I was also told that if a takeover was planned properly, inmates would start it during major movement. I must admit I would have preferred it if he hadn't mentioned this particular possibility. I did learn this was a very real concern and had happened several times. And about ten years later in Quebec, there was a takeover that caused the death of several staff. I know this because I ended up taking staff from Kingston Penitentiary to Quebec for the funeral services.

Just inside the cell block, we entered a large vestibule area. I was told this was common to each cell block, and during their shifts, staff spent most of the time in this area. To my left was a large office for the staff working this particular block. Crammed into this office were a large wooden desk, several chairs, and a couple of filing cabinets pushed up against the wall. A large wooden board with a list of names was attached to the wall. One of the staff explained that it was a list of the inmates, their institutional numbers, and the cells they were assigned to in Three Block. He also told me each cell block had a similar system. He continued by telling me that during counts, staff had to account for each and every inmate under their charge. He also stressed that in practice, staff working the cell blocks usually knew where the inmates were, or at least where they were supposed to be, at all times.

Archie told me Three Block was somewhat unique. There were two ranges—one on the main level and one up the stairs—and each range had fifty cells. The cells in this block had solid wooden doors, and each door had its own individual lock; however, each cell was unlocked by the same key. He picked this time to say, "If you forget everything I tell you, don't ever forget this. Never, never, *ever*, put a key down and leave it; always hook it on your belt or put it in your pocket, preferably out of sight of the inmates!" He further emphasized, "One of the things staff must ensure is that inmates never ever get their hands on any of our keys."

To this day, I am still unable to leave a key in a lock. Even carrying bags of groceries into the house, I have to unlock the door and then wait until I get the key out of the lock before going in—Sheila thinks I'm a little crazy.

Archie told me that up until a short time ago, the bottom range had been used for segregation, but segregation had had to be moved to Two Block, because an inmate had started a cell fire. He explained that when the wooden door caught fire, it warped, and the inmate almost burned to death because staff had a hard time forcing it open. Apparently cells, wooden doors, and fire are not a good combination.

As Archie and I entered the bottom range, he said we wouldn't bother going upstairs, because the upper level was almost exactly the same as the lower. I must admit, entering the range was scary. There were several inmates sitting or walking around, but to be truthful, I was pleasantly surprised. They actually seemed like normal people and not wild animals; they even spoke to us and asked how things were going. I didn't know it at the time, of course, but several years later, two staff members, one a very good friend of my wife and myself, were stabbed to death, and one of them almost decapitated, by an inmate who worked in the kitchen! And the asshole slept on this range.

The cell doors were something to behold. They were built just like a sandwich, with two sheets of thick hardwood and a metal plate between them. Once these three parts were bolted together, they formed an extremely solid door, which also had a small opening with a sliding plate so staff could look into the cell and observe the inmate. Apparently, we had to make sure they were still there and alive during counts. The cells certainly were small when compared to regular bedrooms, but each one had a single bed, a sink, a toilet without a cover or seat, a desk, and a chair. However, they were not as stark or as empty as this description implies. Some of the cells had been fixed up rather nicely. They were painted different colors and had pictures stuck all over the walls. In fact, Archie told me some of the items, including a lot of the pictures, technically weren't allowed due to the risk of fire.

To my dismay, I discovered that management tacitly allowed this excess material. This rule-bending and other laxity that management tolerated caused a lot of the staff's difficulties. To emphasize the point, Archie took me to the cell that had been burned out. The heavy cell door was charred and warped so badly it couldn't be closed; the inside of the cell still contained a cloying smell of wet ashes and burned clothing. This smell is something a person never forgets, and even after all this time, it was still difficult to breathe while standing inside. It was impossible to tell what color the walls had been. The paint was blackened and blistered. I could only imagine the heat needed to cause this much damage.

During my career, I was never able to fathom why anyone locked in a cell would start a fire; anyone in this position certainly had to understand that he was putting himself and others in extreme danger. Unfortunately, I saw so many similar instances that I eventually stopped questioning why people do horrifying things to themselves and others. It's a sad statement when a person must try to numb his own feelings to survive. And I had to try to remain that way for as long as I worked in the prison system, but at the same time, I had to switch back to being a normal person when off duty. Believe me, your head can get screwed up.

Three Block also functioned as an impromptu meeting place for staff. There was a large coffee urn in a small room off the main office, and staff working inside picked up coffee there for themselves and their partners. Naturally, they stopped to have a chat when time permitted. While we were having a break, several staff came in to pick up coffee, and Archie took the time to introduce me to most of them. Almost every staff member I met was very amiable. Several had comments to make: "Where are you from?" "Are you just starting?" "Why did you ever pick a job here?" "You should have gone to another institution." But at least they were speaking to me, and a few even gave me some useful hints.

Eventually we left Three Block and headed over to One Block. On the way, Archie told me this block was referred to as "the Ghetto." He informed me that new inmates and inmates who screwed up in the other blocks were assigned to the Ghetto. He emphasized the point that if you put several young inmates new to the prison system together and then throw in some poorly behaving inmates, you have a recipe for problems. Archie said most problems in the institution originated from inmates living in the Ghetto and that this block was one of the most difficult posts to work. I didn't know it at the time, but I was going to be assigned to B Squad during my five years at the Bay, and most of my time was going to be in One and Two Blocks. Archie's information about difficulties was to prove very true.

Entering One Block was certainly different from entering

Three Block. Physically, it was similar. There was the large vestibule, an office (this office was much smaller; barely large enough for two people and the desk), and of course the ranges. The difference here was that there were four ranges rather than two, and each range had around thirty-six cells. Two of the ranges, 1-A and 1-B, were on the bottom floor. The two upper ranges, 1-C and 1-D, were reached by stairs in the vestibule. The upper ranges had a type of narrow catwalk, and I wasn't even sure if two people would be able to walk side by side; however, it was possible to look down to the bottom floor. This was an extremely important safety factor for staff, because an officer on the bottom range could watch his partner on the upper range and vice versa.

When I was standing at the entrance looking down the range, I couldn't see the cell doors, because they were inset about six inches. However, I could see an iron bar about waist-high jutting out about a foot from each cell. Archie explained that the bars were handles for locking and unlocking the cells, and both One and Two Blocks had this type of locking system. Some people claim this system was invented by an inmate, and for all I know, that could be true. However, in most prisons, this system is being replaced by individual key locks and electronic locking devices.

This system is simple yet ingenious and also safe for staff. It consists of two flat rails that run the length of the range above the cells, a metal dowel that slides up and down into the rails, and a steel rod that sticks out from the cell door, which is used to lift the metal dowel up or down. An officer can stand outside the range and align the rails via a set of wheels, which allows the dowel to slide up, and this in turn unlocks one or all of the cell doors. As I've mentioned, this is a simple yet safe locking system, and once the inmates are locked in their cells, they are usually there until staff unlock the cells. You will note that I said usually they are there until unlocked again; this is not always the case, as I was to find out several weeks later!

The cells in this block were open-faced. In other words, bars instead of solid doors secured the fronts of the cells. The cells were about the same size as those in Three Block but were not nearly as tidy and clean; in fact, some were disgustingly filthy. Several cell fronts had blankets or pieces of cardboard attached to the bars, and it was very difficult to see into some of them. Archie said it was imperative for staff to be able to see into the cells, because each time we passed a cell, we were supposed to make sure the inmate was alive and in good health. He also stressed that this was doubly important during counts. Staff had to ensure that a living body and not a dummy was counted. Archie informed me that orders stated that cell bars were not to be covered, but naturally inmates ignored the rule and insisted on putting this crap up for privacy and to help keep the dust out. He also said this was another rule that was often ignored. I was to find that many rules were ignored. To be honest, some of the blame belonged to the line staff, but most of the blame could be laid directly at the feet of management.

We left One Block and crossed the strip to Two Block. We entered the usual vestibule, and I saw the office to the right. It was about the same size as the office in Three Block but not nearly as cluttered. There was also a door immediately to the left with a sign that informed me it was the institutional court. Within ten months, I was going to be seriously injured almost on the exact spot where I was presently standing! Luckily, I wasn't aware of this unpleasant fact.

This block had four ranges; however, the first range to the left of the vestibule was blocked by a solid wooden door. A large sign at the top of the door announced that this was the segregation unit, and no unauthorized admittance was allowed. The other range, to the right of the vestibule, was open and appeared to be a regular range. Archie told me the other two ranges were upstairs. One of the differences between Two Block and One Block was that the upper ranges in Two Block were separated from the lower ranges by a floor. In other words, you could not see the upper ranges from the lower ranges. Except for the range used for segregation, the floor between the upper and lower ranges, and appearing much cleaner, Two Block was very similar to One Block. It even had approximately the same number of cells on each range. If I had realized I was going to be working overtime in this block within a couple of days, I would have tried to understand the routine much more thoroughly.

Archie said he thought we had enough time to tour Four Block and that would be about it for the day. This certainly aroused no complaint from me; I was feeling really tired, and I was ready to pack the day in by that time. I wasn't doing any work other than some walking, but boy was I finding this environment stressful. Also, I still doubted my ability to survive in this setting. We left Two Block and walked to Four Block. This block was closer to the officer's mess and was on the opposite side of the strip from Two Block.

Four Block was different from the other cell blocks, and the first difference was the entrance barrier. It was made of solid steel and slid sideways on a track, and when open, it was parallel with the strip wall. There were only two ranges of fifty cells each, and the cells on each range faced each other. Like in Three Block, the upper range was directly above the lower range. Both range barriers and the cell doors were solid steel and slid on tracks; they also had the usual narrow openings for viewing purposes, but with thick glass rather than a sliding plate. Another good thing in this block was that the staff could look down both ranges from the office and the stairs were in clear view.

Once again, Archie decided to tour just the bottom range, because the ranges were identical. The cells in this block appeared to be a little larger than in the other blocks, and the back of each cell faced the outside, so each cell had an exterior window. The cell windows didn't have steel bars but instead had three horizontal bars made of cement. Archie explained that each cement bar had a free-floating steel rod inside. So if a person managed to saw through the cement, the saw wouldn't be able to cut the rod, because the rod would simply spin. Within a year or so, we were going to find out that this system didn't work much better than the regular bars. But we were lucky that time; the police officer wasn't shot, and we got the con back!

There appeared to be a large number of inmates in this block. However, they seemed relatively friendly and appeared to be cleaner and better dressed than the inmates in the other blocks. Archie explained that this block was the preferred place for inmates to live and that most of them attended school. In fact, he said, "Most of the inmates in this block are grade four."

I thought, *No damned wonder they're in school if they're only in grade four!* I found out later Archie actually meant the inmates were on grade four *pay*. At the time, there were five pay levels, and most of the inmates attending school were on pay level four. I don't remember what level four was worth, but it would have been around four or five dollars a day.

Four Block was the preferred block to work in. Unfortunately, this block was not on B Squad's roster, and as I mentioned, I was eventually assigned to B Squad.

By now it was becoming rather late, and Archie suggested we might as well pack it in and go home. He didn't get an argument out of me. I was tired, stressed out, and had to find a place to live. The one good thing, though, was that by the end of the day I had decided, or almost decided, that I could handle this job. I kept thinking, *If the other guys can do the job, there's no reason I can't.*

I must admit, though, that before I retired, there were several times when I wished I had quit and headed back up north.

Chapter 3

My terrifying first overtime shift.

The days flew by, and before I knew it, I was in my second week of work in a federal penitentiary, and I didn't feel nearly as stressed when reporting for duty. I had also found a place to live. It was a bedroom in a house, and even though no meals were included, it was a lot less expensive than staying in a hotel.

Once the training officer arrived, he divided us into the same groups as the previous week to do more touring and instructed us to report back after lunch.

Archie and I headed out, and he decided we would go out the south barrier and take a walk through the shops. We passed the kitchen and went through the south barrier, and from there I could see the fenced-in exercise yard and the two south towers. The exercise yard was quite large. The chain-link fence was about twelve feet high and was topped with barbed wire. One end of the fence abutted the east wall and ran perpendicular to the wall for several hundred feet. The fence then took a right angle to the south, and after several hundred feet, it connected to the south wall. This section had a small gate that allowed pedestrians to enter or leave. Archie said a few of the staff were concerned because, in their minds, the fence made it easier for inmates to reach the top of the wall and just hop over. And in the near future, this was going to happen.

One of the towers (Archie told me it was the southwest tower) had a fenced-in area beneath it that was commonly called the sally port. There were two officers assigned to this area to search vehicles.

During our walk through the shops, Archie pointed out how easy it was for inmates to manufacture weapons. This was particularly true in the machine shop and the garage. He informed me that staff had discovered zip guns, knives, bar spreaders, and even homemade silencers inside. He continued this story by saying, "Hell, it's almost common to find homemade knives and other odds and ends somewhere in the cell blocks." This certainly made me feel good about going back inside!

Believe it or not, at MI, I had to deal with an inmate who was able to insert zip gun parts into his rectum! Amazingly, this was the method he used to transport weapons for himself or for other inmates. Naturally, this was also a favorite method many inmates used to transport drugs or money, and staff couldn't do a hell of a lot about it other than locking them in a cell and shutting their water off. This was also a common method visitors used to smuggle drugs into the institutions. I guess anything to help out a loved one! Archie did tell me there were several procedures to help curtail the transportation of weapons from the shops. Inmates were to be searched by their instructors prior to leaving the shop; however, a few instructors performed this search rather haphazardly. In addition, some inmates leaving their shops for various reasons weren't searched at all. Inmates also threw contraband out the shop windows to be picked up and carried into the cell area at a later time. That's why inmates entering the cell area were supposed to be searched on a random basis, but naturally, this upset the inmates, so it wasn't encouraged by management. The same problem held true for cell searching. Inmates understandably hated having their cells searched; after all the cells were their homes, and even if the person performing the search was careful, the inmate's personal property would get messed up. And to be honest, I came to discover *some* staff were not overly careful when doing cell searches. And of course sometimes inmates had their contraband seized.

After lunch, we all went back to our classroom and just sat around chatting. Eventually, Rob came in and told us the institution couldn't fill all the posts for the night shift (three to eleven) and asked if anyone was interested in working overtime. Immediately, my stomach resumed clutching at itself all over again. In my mind, I could envision how handy an extra eight hours pay at time-and-a-half would be. Why, that came to four dollars and eighty-eight cents an hour; multiply that by eight hours, and by God I would have a whole extra thirty-nine dollars on an overtime cheque! Money certainly was a major consideration for me at the time.

The regular pay for a new officer was three dollars and twenty-five cents an hour. Certainly not a great sum of money, not even back in 1973, and I had a wife and three children who liked to eat. On top of the overtime pay, I would receive a free hot supper, and that, for someone in my position, was nothing to sneeze at either. But I had no uniform and certainly no idea how to fulfill the duties of any of the posts. Then it struck me that, having no uniform and not knowing any of the jobs, I was sure to end up in a tower or at least on a post as far away from inmates as possible. So I tepidly eased my hand up.

When Rob looked at me, I reminded him I had no uniform and had only been here a week. His reply to that was, "That's no problem; I'll take you up to SIS"—whatever that was—"and they'll issue you a uniform, and then I'll find out what position the keeper wants to put you in."

I foolishly replied, "A tower would probably be good, because I know absolutely nothing about inmates."

In no uncertain terms he stated, "It would be unlawful to put you or anyone else into an armed post without being trained and qualified on both the .303 rifle and the .38 revolver."

Now my stomach was really clutching at itself. *God, Thibedeau, when are you ever going to learn?* But there was no way I could back down in front of everyone.

So Rob, the other silly volunteer, and I headed for SIS. We walked down the strip, went into Two Block, and headed up the stairs toward the upper ranges. We trooped past 2D and C and entered a tremendously huge area that was isolated from the ranges by a wooden wall. In the not-too-distant future, inmates were going to cause a bit of a disturbance by torching this wall. While climbing the stairs, Rob explained that this area was the department that, among other things, issued clothing to both staff and inmates. We were both measured by a staff member (very quickly, I might add) who then disappeared into that cavernous area of shelving, boxes, and hanging clothing. I couldn't help wondering how in hell he would be able to find anything in that hodgepodge. However, he soon returned with our uniforms clutched in his arms and told us he would issue one set and we would collect the balance of our uniforms when the other new staff received theirs.

While the other volunteer, whose name was John, and I were having a coffee in the lounge (coffee seemed to be the life-blood of both correctional staff and inmates), Rob showed up. He told John he was assigned to the East Yard. That didn't sound too bad to me, and I kept my fingers crossed and hoped I would also be awarded with a job far, far away from any inmates. I almost fell off my chair in shock when he informed me I was going to be in Two Block! *Two Block! Christ, I couldn't get much more involved with inmates than that.* Now I was really wishing I had kept my big mouth shut. But at the same time, I knew I had to take the big step sometime, so why not now and get it over with?

We still had half an hour or so to kill, so back to the reading room we went. In addition to more reading, we listened to Rob relate some of his experiences to us. He was exceptionally good at telling stories, and I must admit we found them interesting and I don't doubt we learned a few lessons. Even at the time, though, I wondered how true they were—or if they were true, if he had been as involved in the stories as he claimed. But all in all, he was one of the good guys and willing to help us out any way he could.

Less than two years later, a senior correctional officer told me he thought I was one of the unlucky ones. He made his point by saying, "Vern, you have been involved in more dangerous crap in your two years than I have been in almost thirty. I strongly advise you to get out the hell out of the service and look for another line of work." So there I was, with less than twenty-four months in the service, being advised to get out, and I hadn't been involved in half the episodes the training officer told us he had been mixed up in.

Eventually, Rob said that everyone except for the two guys (I was thinking the two idiots) working overtime could go home for the day. So there I was, once again wishing I hadn't opened my mouth up. Just as I was going to leave, Rob looked at me and said, "Oh, Vern, personnel wants to see you in their office for a couple of minutes."

After enduring the many good-natured smirks directed at us, John headed to the lounge for a coffee, and I took off to see what personnel wanted. I found the office, and as I entered I couldn't help nervously wondering what the hell was going on now. I went up to a counter, and when I stated my name, a lady asked me where my application to join the service went. "We've been tearing the place apart looking for it and can't find it anywhere," she said.

"Well, that's easy to explain; I never filled one out."

"You had to fill one out; you can't be employed without it."

"I'm here and I know I didn't fill one out," was my reply, with a little sarcasm thrown in.

I ended up sitting at a desk, filling out an application, and back-dating it by several weeks. As you likely know, when dealing with the government, if there is no paperwork, the episode, birth, death, or whatever just did not take place!

Back to the lounge I went. We had been told that before each shift, the keeper took roll call in the lounge and everyone going on duty had to be present for it. Since John and I were early, we sat around, watched a few staff play euchre, and of course drank more coffee.

Half-way through our coffee, a senior correctional officer came in with a clipboard and started to call out names. Each officer answered when his name was called, and the senior officer told him where he would be working. When my name was called (and naturally he pronounced it wrong), everyone's eyes swung toward, me and could feel myself shriveling inside, especially when he called out, "Two Block!" Once roll call was completed, everyone started to leave the lounge, so I just followed along.

When I entered Two Block, I spotted an officer standing by the barrier. I introduced myself and informed him that he was stuck with a partner who knew absolutely nothing about working in an institution, let alone this particular cell block. He didn't appear overly upset and told me he'd heard new staff was in on training and had expected this might happen. Alex said it was quite common to put new staff to work as soon as possible. We chatted for a while, and he gave me a quick rundown on the comings and goings of the block. He made me feel a little better when he told me the nights, at least up to now, had been fairly quiet. After a short discussion, it seemed like the job was a matter of doing a few counts, walking the ranges every hour for changeovers, and hoping no fights or fires broke out. We also had to hope the inmates would go into their cells at 2300 hours for the lockup and count so we could get home on time.

Alex told me the one good thing about Two Block was that we only had three ranges to worry about. Because of the fire in Three Block, 2A had been turned into segregation, and since this area had its own staff, there was only one range on the bottom and the two upper ranges to worry about. He also informed me that Two Block, as a rule, was relatively quiet, because by the time inmates moved in here they had settled down and didn't want to get kicked back to the Ghetto. Once we had chatted for a few minutes, Alex told me we always checked the cells whenever we took over from another shift, and it was about that time.

"That's fine with me, but you'd better tell me what to do."

"Ah, it's simple. We each walk a range and make sure the inmates are quiet and behaving themselves."

I sure as hell didn't know what misbehaving would be, but I wasn't about to tell him that.

Then he added, "Just be sure to check that no inmates are sick or hanging around"—I'd been there long enough to know he meant hanging by the neck—"and make sure they're not cutting the bars or beating each other up. Also, make sure the fucking TV is off."

To me, this all sounded like I was taking part in a movie or something. Also, since I was the newest officer, I volunteered to patrol the upper ranges. So up I went. Because I came to 2D first, I decided that was the one to walk. I looked down the range and saw that it was very similar to One Block except that it had no catwalk. In fact, about the only items on the range were a few tables and chairs, and even though I had hoped there wouldn't be any, several inmates were hanging around talking. Also, there were the usual large, barred windows across from the cells and the now-familiar locking handles sticking out from the cells. And there at the end of the range sat the large television Alex was concerned about. Thankfully it was off; I wouldn't have known what the hell to do if it had been on.

Somewhat hesitantly, I started down the range, and I couldn't help but notice that most of the inmates were watching me. And then it suddenly hit me: this was my first time alone with inmates. Also, the unpleasant thought entered my head that if something happened to me, no one would be aware of it for God knew how long. But at the same time I sensed that if I showed the inmates that I was, to be blunt, scared to death, I would have a very rough time working here. So I just continued strolling down the range and looking into each cell with what I hoped was a dispassionate manner. The odd cell did have an inmate in it, but most of them were empty. But according to Alex, the cells would be filled once the inmates came back from work.

I continued down the range and noticed three inmates walking toward me shoulder-to-shoulder. They were talking back and forth, waving their arms around, and laughing, and somehow they managed to do this and still keep their eyes on me. If I had thought my stomach was flipping around earlier, it was now trying to climb out my windpipe! I was positive, or at least almost positive (I was to find that in this line of work, you could almost never be positive of anything), they were just trying to give me a hard time, but that was still just a guess on my part. I steeled myself and kept walking and checking the cells. At the same time I fervently hoped I was right and they were just testing me and I would get off the range in one piece. The closer we approached, the more I started to sweat, because they sure as hell didn't seem to be moving out of my way! We continued to draw closer, and now the sweat was literally making rivulets down my back and my heart was thumping so loudly I was sure they'd hear it. Now we were close to bumping into each other, and I didn't have a clue what the hell was going to happen. Putting it mildly, I was becoming tremendously apprehensive; in plain English, I was having the crap scared out of me! I swear to God this was the loneliest I'd ever felt in my life. We drew closer and closer, and just before we did bump into each other, they separated just enough for me to walk through. I noticed they were very careful not to touch me, and they didn't even make a comment in my direction. It was almost as if I wasn't even there, and I must admit that suited me just fine.

I finished walking to the end of the range feeling very thankful that I was still alive and not even injured. Then I simply turned around and started back toward the range entrance. That entrance looked like it was a world away, but the walk back wasn't actually bad at all; a couple of inmates even spoke to me. Mind you, it was just a quick "How you doing" and a "Good afternoon," but it was kind of nice. However, it was a hell of a lot nicer when I reached the end of the range, stepped out, and could breathe again. Now, heaven help me, I only had one more range to walk.

Just as I turned and headed toward 2C, I spotted Alex standing on the stairs. He was standing with just his head showing and I had the distinct impression he was keeping an eye out for me. Believe me, that was one good feeling. I entered the other range and did the walk like a pro; at least I thought so at the time. That walk was almost an anticlimax.

As I mentioned, seeing Alex watching my back was certainly an immense relief. I still remember that feeling; believe me, the word *partner* took on a whole new meaning. It was a meaning that stayed with me for the rest of my career.

I finished walking the last range and returned to the office, and there was Alex sitting back at the desk without a care in the world.

As I entered the office, he looked up at me and asked, "How'd it go; any problems?"

What could I say, other than that I had been scared to death? Hell, the back of my shirt was soaked, but the inmates hadn't hurt me. In fact, they hadn't even threatened me, so I just replied, "Nope, no problems. everything worked out okay."

Alex and I sat in the office and chatted for a while and at the same time kept our eyes on the barrier. I didn't really know why we were watching the barrier, but I figured if Alex was watching it then I should too. During our chat, I mentioned that I was sure that while reading post orders, I had read a paragraph stating there should always be two officers present while doing range patrols. I told him that at the time I didn't even know what a range was, but now I was wondering about it.

Alex looked at me and replied, "You're right, they do say that, but those orders are sort of pie-in-the-sky. Management write them up that way, but they never tell us where all the staff is supposed to come from. On top of that, if we did go by them, changeovers would be late, and then the shit would hit the fan. But," he added, "If we feel things are unsettled on the ranges, or if there have been problems, we certainly double up. Believe me, Vern, you're going to find several situations like this, and we know fucking well it's only to cover management's ass. And if something does go wrong and staff hasn't followed post orders, there's no doubt in our minds management will leave us swinging in the wind."

That's another thing I was going to find out about this job. Staff members usually worked with partners, and they spent a great deal of time together. As a general rule, everything was quiet and basically there wasn't a lot to do, so staff stood around and chatted with one another. Once you knew you could count on your partner, you tended to get rather close. In fact, I think there were times I knew more about an officer's personal problems than his wife did.

Alex must have noticed I was curious about the reason we were staring at the barrier, because he said normally it would be locked, but because inmates usually start dribbling back from work early, it was too much of a hassle locking and unlocking it. However, he stressed that when it was unlocked, we had to make damn sure no inmates from another block slithered in. "If we allow an outside inmate in and there's a problem, such as a fight or worse, we have to explain how he got in, and that wouldn't be very pleasant, at least not for us."

A few minutes later, I heard the roar of what sounded like a hundred voices coming from the strip. I couldn't really tell from which end of the strip the sound was originating; it seemed to reverberate from one end to the other. As soon as I heard the low rumble, which at times was punctuated by the odd yell and once in a while by a laugh and with the usual cursing, I jumped up and looked at Alex, hoping he knew what in hell was going on! The roaring seemed to grow louder, and Alex looked over at me, chuckling. "That's the cons coming back from the shops. They know we have to get the count in before they can eat, so usually they'll go straight to their cells and relax. Once the count's in they'll be sent to the kitchen when the strip boss calls for them."

"What the hell's a strip boss?" I asked.

"Oh, he's the three responsible for the cell blocks, the timing of all convict movement, and he's also the 2 I/C on back shifts. There are two threes on the night shift, and one keeper who's in charge of the prison."

Alex was right. Inmates—there didn't seem to be any end to them—started pouring into the cell block. And believe me, the noise level in the area shot way up. As they poured in, they all looked over at us, and Alex explained that inmates were always curious about who was on duty. He told me an inmate's adherence to the rules more or less depended on the staff working in the block. He also let me know that a lot of staff ignored or bent the rules. Alex picked this time to make sure I realized he was fairly strict and that the inmates were well aware of it.

Later I found out Alex was in B Squad, the same squad I would be in, and we ended up spending many, many hours working together. We both believed in a firm, fair, and friendly philosophy, with emphasis on the *firm*. This would cause some head-butting with both management and inmates, but although we didn't actually discuss it, I think we both thought it was worth the effort. But to be honest, I think management caused us, or at least me, more problems than the inmates.

Mixed in with the inmates entering the block were a couple of officers. Once they cleared the group of inmates, they came into the office, and Alex introduced us and mentioned to me that whenever there was an official count, staff from other areas came into the blocks to help. Once the inmates stopped coming in, Alex walked over to the barrier, locked it, and told me to count upper C. I replied that I'd be happy to do that if he told me how to do it.

"Oh, there's nothing to it. Just go up on the range, holler *count up* and once the cons are in their cells, walk down and make sure the cell doors are closed. When you reach the far end, turn around, and as you walk back, count how many inmates you have."

This sounded easy, so with an "Okay," I started up the stairs. Once I reached the head of the range, I yelled, "Count up." To my ears it sounded quite impressive, but most of the inmates just ignored my authoritative command; certainly none ran to their cells. Once again I hollered, "Count up," this time much louder and, I hoped, with a lot more authority. Thankfully, the inmates started into their cells, and I began my long, long walk to complete my very first count! As I came to each cell, I pushed on the cell door to make sure it was fully closed and continued down until I came to the end of the range. Once there, I turned around and started back. There were still a few inmates on the range, but because I didn't have a clue what to do about it, I just kept right on walking. Thankfully, each inmate went into a cell before I reached him. I checked each cell, and if there was an inmate in it, I counted him.

When I reached the front of the range, I took a glance back and then headed down to tell Alex how many inmates I had counted. By the time I reached the office the others were back with their counts and waiting for me. I told Alex my total; he wrote it down on a count pad, added up the count for the block, checked the count board, and stated that we should be okay. He told me to hang around the office and he'd take the count up to Three Block and give it to the keeper.

The two guys that had given us a hand left, saying they had to be on their posts before the count came in. That left little old me in the block with around ninety convicts, and I must admit I was very happy they were locked in the cells; in fact, I was ecstatic about that little fact! Alex returned within a few minutes and told me the count was in, but we had to wait until the strip boss signaled us to let the cons out for jug up.

Alex and I were just standing at the barrier waiting for the count to come in and chatting when we heard what sounded like a herd of elephants coming down the stairs from the upper ranges. We both looked over and saw a pile of inmates on their way down. Alex roared at them to get their asses back on their range, because the count wasn't in yet. The inmates, with much complaining and several derogatory remarks, retreated back up the stairs.

Once I looked at Alex's expression, I had a sinking feeling I had neglected to do something that was rather important, and then to confirm it, he asked if I'd spun the wheel when I came off the range. All I could do was throw him a blank stare and ask, "Wheel? What wheel?"

"For Christ sakes, the fucking locking wheel."

"Sorry, I didn't know I was supposed to do that."

Alex was good about it. He admitted it was his fault for not explaining it fully. He continued by saying, "I hope to hell the count's correct; if it isn't, we'll have to go up and try to push them back into their cells for a recount."

Luckily, a few minutes later someone yelled, "Bingo!" I looked at Alex with what I would guess was a quizzical expression, because before I could ask, he said, "Bingo means the count is correct."

That certainly made me feel one hell of a lot better after forgetting to lock that stupid wheel.

"I hope the count comes in as quickly at eleven," Alex said. "I'm going to play cards after work."

Within a few minutes the strip boss stuck his head in and yelled, "Jug up." Before I could say anything, Alex told me that was the signal to send them out to eat.

I followed Alex toward the bottom range, thinking, *God, how am I going to learn all this stuff? Christ, even the language is different in this place.*

I watched Alex spin the wheel to unlock the cells as he hollered, "Jug up!" Then we headed to the foot of the stairs and yelled "Jug up" for the inmates I hadn't locked up. Next we both tramped upstairs and unlocked D range, and away they trotted.

Alex told me there wasn't much more to do for a little while, and he was going to eat his lunch. Just as he said that, an officer came into the block, introduced himself as Leon, and asked how things were going. We chatted for a few minutes and then Leon said he had to get back to the keeper's office to clear an inmate going out on a pass. Just before leaving, he said he had an overtime form for me to sign. Once I accomplished that little job, he told me always to make sure I signed one every time I worked overtime. Once Leon left, Alex told me as far as he was concerned, Leon was about the best keeper at the Bay.

Within a minute or two, the strip boss came in to tell me I could head to the officer's mess to grab a bite to eat. It was a good meal and certainly a lot cheaper than if I had had to eat in a restaurant.

When I made it back to Two Block, I found Alex in the office relaxing, and he waved me over and said I might as well join him until recreation was called. He explained that recreation included the gym, weight room, and the exercise yard, or the cons could just sit on the range and watch television. "And as you would expect," he continued, "the more inmates that leave the block, the better for us. I've been here for a year or so, and I'm still uncomfortable having a bunch of cons sitting on the range making toast and boiling water for coffee."

While Alex and I were relaxing, a few inmate workers from the kitchen came into the block with loaves of bread, butter, jam. and all kinds of stuff. Apparently, this was delivered to each range every evening, and inmates were allowed to use whatever they wished. *Holy Christ*, I thought, *it's just like living in a hotel.* The main concern among staff, according to Alex, was the five-gallon containers of hot water the inmates used to make coffee. I agreed with Alex that this did seem dangerous. However, I've never heard of the hot water being used as a weapon, not even during disturbances.

While we sat in the office and chatted, Alex eating his lunch and me drinking coffee, the inmates started to dribble back from the kitchen. Most of them continued onto their ranges. However, the odd one came into the office to ask a question or two. The inmates were more or less pleasant except for one or two who were upset about one thing or another. One thing about inmates, when they're pissed off about something they certainly don't mind telling the world about it.

It didn't take very long in my career to decide that in many ways, most inmates were stuck somewhere around the emotional age of adolescence. This of course didn't refer to all inmates, but a large percentage of them did act like children or young teenagers. I found that when discussing an inmate's problem with him, everything would usually be okay unless the problem couldn't be solved immediately or you had to say no to a request. In almost all cases, when that happened, the inmate became very agitated, and often this was the point when threats were made. Most inmates didn't seem capable of mature discussion but resorted to screaming and at times to physical reactions. This was not the mentality of an adult. To put it succinctly, many of the inmates I met were really just overgrown, violent, and at times dangerous children. And believe me, when they wanted something, they wanted it immediately—and immediately meant *now*, not later in the day, not tomorrow or next week, but *now*.

And so the evening rolled on. I think it went a lot faster for me than it did for Alex. At 1800 hours, the strip boss showed up at our barrier and yelled, "Two Block, yard up."

Alex unlocked the barrier leading to the strip, and away went dozens of inmates. As with every other major movement except breakfast and work-up, the inmates all want out at the same time. And believe me, those dozens of inmates hanging around the vestibule yelling, bickering, and laughing made me extremely uncomfortable; in fact, it sent shivers up and down my back. I was very happy to see them on their way.

Alex told me recreation was from 1800 to 2230 hours and inmates could pretty well go wherever they wanted, including staying on their ranges or in their cells. The only stipulation was that they had to stay in one area for an hour, because everything was locked. However, each hour there was a changeover, and they could move to another area at that time if they wanted.

This changeover system was one of the routines that ended up causing me a great deal of difficulty. I soon learned that most staff went on the ranges to unlock and then again twenty minutes later to relock, and that was it. Alex's routine, which I adopted, was the same, except at different times he would make an extra patrol while the cells were locked. By way of explanation, Alex looked at me and said, "The cons don't appreciate this extra walk, because they consider the ranges their territory. I want to make sure they realize *I'm* in charge and they don't own fuck all."

In fact, later in my career, I came to believe that most inmates didn't mind that extra patrol, because it made them feel safer.

Once the stampede of inmates died down, Alex said it was about time to do the first lockup. He looked at me with a silly-assed grin and said, "This is really very simple. It's just a matter of walking down the range, making sure there's no more than one inmate in a cell, no cons from another block hanging around, no one's cutting bars, there are no fights, and no inmates are ill, bleeding, or worse. Also, when walking back from the end of the range, make sure the cell doors are pushed closed." And then for emphasis, and with an even wider grin, he just had to say, "And for God's sake Vern, don't forget to spin the wheel!" After all this, he said, "And make sure to yell "lockup" before starting down the range. And while you're doing this, it's also a good idea to try to get an approximate count and try to and get a *feel* if there's anything unusual happening."

"My God, you said it was simple. How in hell am I going to remember all that?"

But all joking aside, it only took a few months for me to be able to get the *feel* of a block just by going in and looking around. It was just sort of a sense that most staff developed over time.

Up I went. There were several inmates on the range, some standing around talking and some sitting on chairs watching television. I hollered, "Lockup," and started down the range for the second nerve-shattering walk of my career. My stomach still clutched at itself, but not nearly as tightly as during my first walk; hell, I could even breathe. But now my mind was spinning, trying to remember everything Alex had told me. I think I forgot just about everything he had said, and to be honest, all I wanted to do was make it down to the end of the range and get back in one piece. I did remember about the wheel; in fact, I kept saying, *wheel, wheel, wheel* to myself while I walked. Of course, the first time an inmate asked me a question, I forgot all about that fucking wheel. So down the range I went, once again wishing I was anywhere but there. I just kept walking, looking around at everything and everyone, and hoping the inmates thought I was a pro. The noise level had risen considerably, and naturally, the more inmates were there, the noisier it was.

To my immense relief, I reached the end of the range safely, turned around, and headed back. Once I reached the front of the range, I just kept right on trucking and had almost reached the other range when I remembered that God damned wheel. I rushed back, took a look down the range, and didn't see any cell doors open, so I spun the wheel and used that huge key to lock it. I headed for 2-C and did the same thing; this time I remembered to spin that wheel. As soon as I had accomplished this great feat, it suddenly stuck me that I couldn't remember if Alex had said to lock the range barriers or leave them open. So there I was, standing indecisively with all my doubts hurtling back and grabbing at me. Did I lock them, leave them open, or what? It was still locked in my mind that a mistake on my part could cause major difficulties and possible injury to staff or inmates.

While I was standing there wondering what the hell to do, an inmate came up the stairs and actually spoke to me in a pleasant manner. He gave me his name and said he realized I was new to the system and told me the place wasn't as bad as it seemed. He even asked if I had remembered the wheels this time. He must have seen my indecision, because he mentioned the range barriers and said they were never locked during the evening except during problems. This inmate and I had an extremely interesting chat, although it was much shorter than I would've liked. He kept looking around, and I had enough sense to realize he was concerned about inmates seeing him chatting with an officer (*fucking pig* in inmate terminology), so I told him I'd better get down to the office and headed for the stairs. I felt a hell of a lot better; it was a relief knowing some inmates were just ordinary guys. I've often wished I could have thanked him for that conversation. However, I think he knew what he was doing and was well aware of how much he helped me; at least I hope he was. When I made it back downstairs, Alex was standing at the main barrier, so I went over to keep him company. I also wanted to verify the information regarding the range barriers.

"Oh yeah, they're left open; cons can travel range-to-range, but they can't leave the block without permission."

I certainly didn't mention that I had taken advice from an inmate. I hadn't been there long, but you can bet it had been long enough for that to sink in. I did mention, though, that I had had an interesting chat with one.

Alex told me there was nothing wrong with that and informed me that I would be having many discussions with inmates, some good and some bad. "But," he stated in no uncertain terms, "always remember: inmates are not in here because they want to be and will milk any weakness they can find." While staring directly into my eyes, Alex continued, "Don't ever forget, convicts will usually be nice enough, but if you stand between them and the wall during an escape, one way or another, they'll go right over you!"

Alex and I just stood around and chatted. We didn't really know each other well enough to discuss anything personal, but I did pick up a lot of very useful information. We hung around the main barrier some of the time and then for a change sat in the office. Every once in a while the strip boss came around to say hi and see how things were going, and even a few staff dropped in (I think mostly to see what kind of a guy I was) and had a chat. It stayed fairly quiet. The odd inmate came out and tried to leave the block, but Alex wouldn't let them out. I got the distinct impression they really didn't expect him to bend the rules but wanted to try just for the sake of trying, and except for a couple of inmates, they didn't stand around and argue.

In what seemed a very short time, Alex glanced at his watch and said, "Hell, it's time to do our thing and unlock for changeover. We don't ever want to forget that, or people would hear the yelling and whining out on Bath Road."

Christ, here we go again. "Well, tell me what to do and I'll try and get it done."

"Nothing to it; just go to each range, spin the wheel to unlock the cells, and holler, "changeover." Once you've finished that, do a quick walk down the range and make sure anyone in a cell is okay and can get out if he wants. The cells stay open until ten after, and then we go down and lock them like we did before."

I did the two upper ranges and thankfully had no difficulty. In my mind at least, I handled myself like a pro. However, I sure as hell knew I had a lot more to learn.

Once we were back in the office, Alex looked at me and

said he had forgotten to mention something that could be kind of important. "Always check the spokes on the wheels and the cell locking handles for razor blades."

"What in hell are you talking about? What razor blades?"

Alex told me that sometimes inmates would use gum to stick tacks or broken razor blades to the back side of a handle or spoke. "You can imagine what would happen to your hand if you grabbed onto something like that. In fact, while we're on the subject, don't ever ever stick your hand or fingers into a place you can't see. You just never know what the cons will use to set us up."

I must admit this information shook me somewhat, but on the other hand, it was nice to be included in the word us. "Christ, isn't there anything we can do about stuff like this?"

"No, not really; you just have to be careful. You'll pick up several tricks as you go along. And one other thing, never ever use the word *goof* in here. That word's the worst insult you can throw at an inmate. In fact, it's practically an unwritten law that an inmate must retaliate, and that's whether it's against staff or another inmate, and the retaliation usually involves a weapon."

Well, I've learned more useful information in just a few hours working than I have since I started this crazy job. Christ, it just keeps pouring in.

By now it was time to lock the cells again. Alex and I did our thing, and I couldn't help wondering how many more times I'd be doing this same thing. I finished locking up (after very carefully inspecting the wheels) and made it back downstairs safely. Once I made it back, Alex had a bit of a surprise for me. He said we were going to wait for a few minutes and then go back on the ranges and do another walk. He also told me we'd do this one together, because it was an extra patrol and the inmates hated them. Alex also reminded me again about the ownership thing between staff and inmates and said if the inmates were up to anything, it usually took place while the cells were locked. Part of the reasoning on the inmates' part was that most staff just did the required locking and unlocking and didn't bother with the extra patrols.

This time when we stepped onto the range, the reception was just a little different from my previous one. As soon as we entered 2-B the comments started: "Get the fuck off the range," "Goddamn pigs always sticking their noses into things," and a lot of similar comments. But one thing I did notice was that the inmates were very careful to make sure we couldn't tell who was mouthing off.

During our stroll down the range, Alex told me these remarks were normal when staff did something the inmates didn't like. I know one thing: if looks could kill, we would've been dead many times over.

We did find two inmates in a cell, though. Alex stopped in front of the cell and told me to wait at the cell while he went back to unlock the wheels. "Make damn sure one or both of them come out, and keep an eye out that no other cell doors open up."

While I was waiting for Alex to unlock the cell, one of the inmates looked at me and said, "I suppose that prick's going to charge me."

"I don't know. You'll have to ask him when he gets back; this is all new to me. I know one thing though: there's only supposed to be one to a cell."

I was watching Alex, and when he waved at me I lifted the cell handle and both inmates came out. Once they were out, I shut the door and signaled Alex, and he spun the wheel to lock it again. I watched Alex coming back, and when he was close enough, one of the inmates looked over at him and said, "Hey, boss, you aren't going to charge me, are you?"

Alex looked at him and said, "No, not this time. Just consider it a warning."

As we continued our walk, Alex explained that there were several reasons for the rule of one to a cell. One of the concerns, he explained, was that inmates had been known to force another into a cell for sex. He told me homosexual activity was considered a major offence under the Penitentiary Act, and staff had to charge inmates if they were caught.

Needless to say, this bit of information just about floored me. "How could something like this happen with staff all over the place? Jesus, an inmate just has to yell for help, and we could get there in no time."

Alex told me life inside just didn't work that way. On the street a person called the police for help; but inside, one of the main concerns cons had was being known as a rat. Alex said once that happened to an inmate, he'd better get to one of the officers and have himself signed into segregation for protection. He further informed me that once an inmate did that, he usually ended up in Kingston Pen, and that was about the lowest thing that could happen to a con.

I should mention here that Kingston Penitentiary had a dual purpose at that time. All prisoners in Ontario sentenced to two years or more were sent to KP for medical evaluation, security classification, and all kinds of testing. Once that was completed, they were sent to a regular institution to begin working their way through the system toward what was loosely called rehabilitation. The second purpose of KP was to provide a protective custody environment for inmates that couldn't survive in a regular institution. Some of the reasons for being in protective custody could include having committed a particular crime, such as a sex crime or violence against a child, or having been a police or correctional officer or an informant. Another common reason was that an inmate had got himself into debt through gambling or drugs and couldn't pay it off.

An inmate who ended up in KP was known as a PC. This was such derogatory title that if an inmate was released to the street from Kingston Pen and rearrested, he was likely to be sent back to KP. This usually held true no matter how long the inmate was out or what he was rearrested for. In other words, in the prison system, a PC was the lowest of the low. I've seen inmates—big, tough, tattooed, prison-wise bikers—break down and cry because they got themselves into trouble of some kind and had to go to KP and be known as PCs.

Rather than sit in the office, Alex and I sat on a bench next to the main barrier and did some more chatting. Actually, chatting and watching seemed to be a major part of the job. I couldn't help comparing this work to my other jobs, and so far, this seemed much easier. I was to find there are various definitions of *easier*! At any rate, we discussed worldly affairs until 1950, when Alex informed me that we had to open up for the 2000 hours count. He told me staff cleared the recreation areas shortly before eight and all inmates had to return to their cells for the count. The count usually took about twenty minutes, and once it was in, the inmates were allowed out again for recreation. Alex said to go up, spin the wheels open on each range, and come back to the vestibule. "Then we just wait until the cons are all back and do a count."

I thought, *Oh sure, nothing to it.* I just hoped I would eventually be as casual about these weird things as Alex was. Just think, knowing a count was coming up and not feeling the old stomach tighten up; wouldn't that be nice? Luckily, unlocking the cells and even doing the count was uneventful. Everything went the way it was supposed to. Once the count was in, we just went to the ranges, unlocked the cells, and hollered, "Gym up." Alex had told me there was still no yard in the evenings because it was too dark.

The rest of the evening just floated along in a bit of a blur for me. We did our changeovers, walked the ranges, listened to nasty comments about us being on the ranges, and did a lot of talking to each other. Alex spoke to several inmates about things that I had no clue about, but I did listen to pick up any information that I could. Fortunately, Alex didn't mind explaining all these unknown and wonderful things to me.

At about 2245 hours, Alex said the inmates would be starting back shortly, and at 11:00 sharp we would start the last count. He said this count was the most important one for staff working the night shift. Our shift ended at 2320 hours, and if there was a miscount, we would be a little late getting out, and no one wanted to stay a minute longer than we had to. And to make me feel better, he mentioned the ribbing a guy had to take if he caused a miscount. "So, for God's sake, make sure you do a good count and keep your fingers crossed that there's nothing interesting on television. Sometimes if there's a good show on, they refuse to go in until it is over and we have to stay late."

Alex continued this explanation later by telling me that quite often inmates refused to go in for the count at 2300 hours, and management didn't do dick about it. "Most of the staff thinks the fucking TVs should be yanked off any range that causes a problem. But as usual, they refuse to do a damn thing. As far as most of us are concerned, this is just another example of management being scared of the cons."

Once the extra staff had come in and Alex didn't think any more inmates were going to straggle in, we started up for the count. I didn't feel nearly as uptight about going up as I had earlier. Mind you, I was still extremely nervous and certainly praying that I wouldn't make a mistake. I had visions of counting wrong and everyone knowing about it, and I really didn't think I needed any more stress right at that moment. Once we were all back in the office, Alex added up our count slips and told us it looked good. I was happy to hear him say that if there was a miscount, it wouldn't be Two Block's fault.

While Alex was at Three Block with the count, an officer I hadn't noticed before came into the block. He told me his name and said he was in for the morning shift. I asked him where his partner was. "I don't have one." He explained that staff on the morning shift worked each block alone. In fact, the morning shift was locked in, and the strip boss took the barrier key! My looks must have told him what I thought of that, because he explained that it really wasn't as bad as it sounded. The hope was that if the inmates did manage to get out of the cells, at least they wouldn't be able to get out of the block. "Jesus," he continued, "if that ever did happen, it would be easy for them to take over most of the prison. Just remember there are only twelve of us and five hundred and some cons. You might say we're slightly outnumbered in here."

Once Alex made it back, while we were waiting for the count to be verified, he filled the morning guy in, and then we just stood around chatting. During the conversation, Alex told our relief that there were a lot of fruit flies around the back end of B Range. "If you poke around a bit, you'll likely come up with a brew." Alex must have spotted my questioning look, and with a grin he continued, "Most brew is made out of all kinds of fruit, and believe me, this attracts fruit flies, scads of the damned things. Ergo, fruit flies usually equals brew."

Well, I thought, another little piece of knowledge.

A few minutes after Alex got back to the block, someone yelled, "Bingo," and Alex said, "There it is. Let's get the hell out of here," and we headed for the strip. Just before Alex turned away, he looked at me and said, "Hope we work together again, Vern." And then he was gone.

That simple comment made me feel great. I felt tired, more from stress than any real work, but still tired. Just before getting into the car, with a feeling of wonderment and accomplishment, I looked back at that gray, red- roofed prison and thought, *By God, I did it; I really did it!* It was at that moment I knew I was going to make it and that I had found a new career!

Chapter 4

Attempted escape in Two Block.

My time as a correctional officer rolled along. I had to finish reading standing and post orders and finish touring the institution, and in between I even worked a few more overtime shifts. During the rest of the second week, we remained on what was called orientation. During this period, everyone was issued uniforms, union booklets, information regarding our pensions, and all kinds of other information. *Pensions,* I thought. *Why do I have to worry about that? God, I'm only thirty-two.* But it's unbelievable how quickly pension time rolls around.

Two weeks flew by, and I was off orientation and much more comfortable reporting for duty. I was becoming more familiar with the routine and knew several staff by name; however, one thing I learned was just how much I didn't know. Several staff told me this was the type of job where you never stopped learning or became completely comfortable while on duty. That at least made me feel somewhat better about my lack of knowledge. It was also stressed several times that I should never become complacent on this job. I don't know how many times staff told me that even if I was bored to tears, I always needed to be aware of my surroundings. It was also drilled into my head that no matter how nice or friendly the inmates seemed, I could bet money they almost always wanted something from me. It was stressed that we could not even so much as take an inmate's letter out of the institution to mail. Archie drove that home by saying, "Cons will give you a sob story like you wouldn't believe; Christ, they can almost make you cry. But if you so much as take a letter out, he's got you. It's illegal; they know it, and they'll sure as hell use it against you. If that happens you're dragged in deeper and deeper; they're not called cons for nothing."

Several weeks shot by, and in short order, I learned just how much I hated the morning shift. Imagine tower duty on the morning shift. You're sitting in a comfortable chair, your rifle in front of you, a revolver on your hip, a two-way radio beside you, and your only job is to watch for any kind of movement. If you do see someone, you use the radio to find out if it is staff or not—and you pray to hell it is staff. This particular position was excruciatingly boring at the best of times, but the morning shift, at least for me, was absolute hell. I knew a few officers who hooked a metal cup onto a finger so if they fell asleep, the cup would hit the floor, jerking them awake (and, I imagine, sending them grabbing for their rifle). In the back of my mind there was always the fear of falling asleep and being responsible for a staff member being injured or an inmate escaping.

I used the word *quiet* to describe mornings in the cell blocks, but I sure as hell don't mean that it wasn't noisy. *Quiet* is a relative term in prisons. When you have well over a hundred guys sleeping in a cell block, it isn't quiet. People dream, yell, scream, snort, fart, talk in their sleep, and do all kinds of things. And of course all this sound recoils off stone, steel, and cement. Besides the noise, some inmates stay awake all night writing or listening to their radios or just kind of staring into space, and this can be rather unnerving. In addition, big old stone buildings—and remember, Collin's Bay was built during the thirties—make all kinds of weird noises at night. You knew it was a combination of wind, temperature changes, expanding steel, and Lord knew what else. But even so, these places were still creepy as hell, and at times you couldn't help but think of ghosts walking the ranges; there are staff to this day who insist they've seen ghosts floating around. So the term *quiet* in this setting actually just means "calm." There was no one to talk to and nothing to do except the hourly patrols. Even listening to a radio or reading a book was against post orders. Thankfully, most keepers didn't care about it on that particular shift, as long as the radio was turned low and they didn't actually see us reading. In fact, the keepers, when making a trip, rattled around enough to make sure we heard them before they reached us. On top of that, whenever a keeper left a post, the officer in that particular area always phoned ahead to give a "six up." Anytime an officer heard that warning, he knew someone in authority was around somewhere. I think staff picked the terminology up from the inmates. Whenever cons are up to something, they always post a lookout. This lookout is called the "six man." This eventually evolved to the use of "six up" as a warning, and I guess we figured if it was good enough for inmates, it was good enough for us.

Fortunately—or unfortunately—not all morning shifts were boring. Quite often staff found themselves in a bit of a bind. Most of the time we were bored almost to tears, but if we weren't, it meant we were fighting inmates, fighting fires, rushing a stabbed inmate to the hospital, arguing with inmates, searching an area, or looking into a cell and hoping to hell that form under the blanket was a breathing inmate and not a dummy.

Our orders stated that when doing a range walk, we had to ensure the object in each bed was a person and that he was, in fact, breathing, because only God could help you if a dummy was counted all night. But God also had to help you if you ever woke a con or disturbed him to make sure he was alive. Most guys, if they were concerned, just stood and watched until the inmate took a breath or moved. Believe it or not, once a staff member completed a couple of patrols in a block, even though there could be a couple hundred inmates, he could usually tell if an inmate hadn't moved for a while. Once he noticed that, it was time to be a little concerned.

After being on the roster for three weeks or so, I was posted to One Block on the morning shift. I had just finished doing my walk and was heading into the office to do some more fighting to stay awake when I heard a commotion coming from the strip. Before I could get over to the barrier, someone hollered my name, and I heard the barrier being unlocked. I ran for the barrier and saw the three unlocking it, and at the same time he yelled that there had been an attempted escape and to get over to Two Block! As I took off toward the block, I heard him relocking the barrier. It's amazing how quickly you can go from being half asleep to completely alert with your heart thumping in your throat and your stomach clutching at itself; adrenalin certainly can give you a kick.

Just as I entered Two Block, the lights came on, and I could see two or three staff members tearing up the stairs to the upper ranges. One of them yelled at me to get up to 2-C and to watch out for any loose cons! I caught up to them, and we made it to the range at the same time. The first thing I saw was a cell door open, and across from the cell the keeper and another officer had an inmate spread-eagled against the wall. So much for boredom! The harried-looking keeper glanced my way and yelled, "Check the cell doors on both sides of that open one and make damn sure they're secure and when Ted gets up here, help him lock both cells with the chains."

While I was checking the two cells, I watched the keeper carefully frisk the inmate and heard him tell the three to get another officer and get the fucker down to the hole. I attempted to lift both locking handles on the cells and at the same time looked up to check the traveling bars. That's when I noticed that the traveling bars above the open cell had been spread apart but not quite far enough to allow the cell door to be opened.

Just about that time, the keeper dashed over and asked if they were okay. "Yep," I replied, "No problem."

"Good, but we're still going to padlock those two cells." He looked up at the traveling bars and said, "It's a good thing Gord spotted that when he did. Just a little more work and he would've had a con on the range for company, and then we would likely have been in a hostage situation or something a hell of a lot worse!"

A few minutes later, an officer rushed onto the range carrying two lengths of chain and two padlocks. We wrapped a chain around each cell door and padlocked them. "Now," he said, "Just let the fuckers try to get out."

Once we had the cells secured, he looked over at me and said in a rather shaky voice, "Gord did a fucking good job spotting that; most of us would've missed it. We usually just walk along and make sure the cons are in their cells and hope to hell they're still alive in the morning. If he hadn't spotted it, the chances are good he'd be dead by now!"

While all this was going on, the staff had to practically scream to each other to be heard over the noise the inmates were making. They were banging on their cell bars and screaming at us to keep the fucking noise down and to get the hell off their range. They also kept yelling at us to leave their buddy alone and stop beating him up. I was to find out this was just common practice and started up whenever something out the ordinary happened.

While all this pandemonium was happening, I kept glancing at the keeper and noticed he was getting more agitated by the minute, and then he startled the hell out of me by suddenly bellowing, "Shut your goddamn mouths. If one more of you assholes open your fucking yap, you'll all be on OP for a month, and there'll be no fucking range goodies at night, either!"

I must admit I was stunned how quickly everything quieted down. Other staff had hollered more or less the same thing without an iota of change in the noise level except that it might have risen a little. I think it was at that time I gained an inkling of the authority a keeper possessed. Thankfully, the rest of the night was uneventful except that I had to go over to Two Block and help Gord with his patrols. This really didn't seem like a very big deal to me. It helped me stay awake, and I was still new enough to the system that it didn't seem like a lot of work.

During the night the empty cell was checked, and in the morning the whole range was searched. We were looking for some type of bar spreader that the convict had used to pry the traveling bars apart; none was ever found. I always found it amazing how inmates could make things disappear.

This little episode taught me how fast I could go from being half asleep and bored to an extremely high level of tension. To one extent or another, this was going to happen innumerable times during my career. In fact, I was never sure if I should complain about being bored or not. Being bored was a lot better than having to call the police because of an escape, attempted escape, suicide, or murder. Having to call in the IERT to contain a disturbance or hostage situation wasn't very pleasant either. And believe me, it is horrendous when you receive a phone call or hear on the two-way that a staff member has been injured and an ambulance is on the way.

Shortly before I completed my two weeks on the morning shift, I received written notice that I had to attend the twelve-week induction training course at the correctional staff college. Successful completion of the course was a job requirement. So there I was, uptight again. I immediately had visions of failing and going back home with my head down in disgrace. Luckily for me, Alex was on the same shift, and as I said, no question was too dumb for him to answer. He told me not to worry about the course. He said it wasn't really difficult and a person had to be uninterested or dumb to fail the thing. This eased my mind a lot. Alex also told me I should check into living and eating at the college. He said they had bedrooms and served three free meals a day.

The next Sunday after work I packed the car and headed to the staff college. I went up to my room, and I swear to God it was smaller than a cell; there was a desk, a chair, a lamp, a bed, and a clothes closet, and that was about it. But it was free.

While I was lugging my clothes in, I noticed the officer's mess and a sign stating that it opened at 1700 hours. I wasn't sure how the kitchen staff would know I was allowed to eat in there, so I decided to leave my uniform on and hope for the best.

I entered the mess and saw that it was like any cafeteria-type restaurant. I soon found out they served a good meal, and in addition, you could eat as much as you wanted. God, it felt like heaven.

Once I finished eating, I went into the lounge area. There were several guys sitting around talking and having a beer, and I saw several I recognized. These familiar faces made me feel a lot better. One of them waved me over, so I picked up a beer and headed for the table.

We all knew tomorrow would be a busy day, so after a little conversation we decided to head to our respective rooms and get some sleep. I must admit I didn't get a lot of sleep; I was just too keyed up about the next twelve weeks.

Chapter 5

Induction Course. A tower, drunken inmates, and a rifle.

At about 0630 hours, I was up to shave, shower, have breakfast, and start the next stage of my career. This course was something all new officers had to complete. The usual procedure was to complete it prior to reporting to an institution; however, at the present time, lack of staff made this impossible.

The course I was attending was twelve weeks long, but due to the staff shortage, I would only complete seven weeks of it. At least that was better than the other six members from the Bay; they only finished six weeks. I never did find out why they were called back a week before me, although in the grand scheme of things it doesn't really make a great deal of difference.

I found the classroom and sat at a desk, and very shortly a couple of instructors hurried in to give a general run down on what was expected of us. They informed us the college would explain the fundamentals of our job and give us the necessary tools, but it was up to us to decide individually how we wished to employ these tools. They also let us know that there were several tests and that we would be graded on our contribution in class; they certainly weren't shy about letting us know we were going to be very busy. In short, we had to learn everything from how to deal with difficult and irate people in a nonphysical manner to how to use CN gas and firearms and understand the legalities of our decisions—oh, the joys of being a peace officer. In addition, we had to learn how to apply restraint equipment, come-along holds, and first aid and how and when to fill out the numerous report forms.

During our instruction regarding the use of force, it was stressed many times that we were legally responsible for any use of force. We were told no one could order us to use force; it had to be our decision. But if there was a situation that necessitated force and we didn't use it, we were also responsible for that decision. I still remember one instructor explaining it this way: "If you are in a tower and an inmate is escaping and you don't use a firearm to stop him and he does escape, does that not make you responsible for anything he does while he is out on the street? Imagine how you would feel if this same inmate injured or killed an innocent person or child. That's something you would have to live with for the rest of your life."

Needless to say, that bit of philosophy did give us something to think about. And in less than two years, I was going to be involved in an episode that resulted in three people being shot! That situation still causes me to second guess a few decisions I made.

During our training we spent numerous hours learning about firearms. This included both safe handling and firing. We had to be proficient with the .303-caliber Lee Enfield rifle, the .38-caliber revolver, and the twelve-gauge shot gun. To qualify, we had to prove we could handle them safely, and we had to attain a specific score on the firing range. There was also an emphasis on learning how to use CN gas and mace.

Shortly after completing the course, the service upgraded the .303-caliber to a .308-caliber rifle. Several years after that, they changed over to an AR-15. That particular rifle was, in my lowly opinion, perfect for our line of work, so I would imagine they've switched to a different one by now.

I don't really think I will spend a lot of time talking about this particular time in my career. Suffice it to say that the college was a busy time, and I must admit it was certainly a necessity for this crazy profession.

Eventually, I came to realize the system did allow officers the right to make major decisions. But it was also true that we were responsible for our decisions. As I mentioned, not only did I make a decision that I am still second-guessing to this day, but at one time I had two teams of detectives investigating two decisions I had made as a supervisor with the very real chance that I would face charges of excessive force!

I did luck out in one way during my time at the college. Jim, an officer at the Bay, told me about some town houses in Amherstview. I had mentioned to him that I was planning to bring my family to Kingston and that I was looking for a place for us to live. That perked me up and gave me something to feel good about.

Once I was back at work it didn't take long to get into the swing of things. By now I was slowly developing the work ethic I would use for the remainder of my career, and among other things, I was becoming a fairly strict officer. Mind you, the inmates had a different name for it, but I don't think we have to mention it; I'll just leave that to your imagination.

Shortly after returning to work, I was stuck on the morning shift in the west yard. This was my first time doing the yard other than a short training session that really didn't amount to much. Once roll call was completed, the east yard officer (I think his name was Gord) and I reported to the main gate to pick up our radios, punch clocks, and flashlights. After we had received our equipment, I told Gord this was my first time in the yard. He suggested we both go to the west yard so he could do the first trip with me. Once we settled down in the yard shack, Gord told me the duties on this post were simple, and in his opinion, the most difficult part was staying awake. He told me we had to do a tour at least once an hour. "And don't forget to carry those damn punch clocks."

So here were several more points I had to add to what seemed like the thousands of things I had already planted in my little head. The problem was that every little thing was tremendously important.

I was also beginning to get the impression that locking inmates into their cells didn't guarantee they were going to stay there. I had been told this or something similar several times during the induction course and also by numerous staff at the Bay. The overriding consideration seemed to be that you just never knew what was going to happen. Believe me, this kind of knowledge certainly doesn't make an officer feel very comfortable. Especially when you are out in that large, dark yard and you know that no one, at least no one in a uniform, is behind you. The only backup a yard officer has is the four officers posted to the towers. And a tower really wouldn't be much help unless you happened to be close when you started screaming! Also, after hearing some of the staff talking, I wouldn't want to bet my life they would be alert.

Noises and shadows take on a whole new significance in a situation like this. However, thankfully, in all the years I did yard patrols, I never did bump into an inmate, and as far as I know, I never stopped an escape or even caused an inmate to change an escape plan. However, as I've said, you just never know.

While we were walking around, Gord returned to the subject of punch clocks by saying, "The keepers always check that damned dial at the end of the shift to make sure we stayed awake and did our rounds. Also, when you come to a corner, make sure you stay wide, and then if there's someone waiting, you'll at least have a chance to run like hell." He also reminded me of the episode in Two Block and said to make damned sure I glanced at all the windows to watch for any missing or bent bars. I still recall him saying, "If one or more inmates ever do get out of their cells and make it into the yard, the yard officer is the only guy between them and the wall. And if they've done that much planning and gone through that much work, they know they are in deep shit, and one way or another, they sure as hell don't want you in their road."

Once we completed the first walk, Gord went to his yard shack, and I went back to my side of the yard and settled in until it was time for the next walk. As I mentioned, one of the dozens of things I was told was to stagger patrols. I always used this advice no matter what post I was on or what rank I happened to be at the time. Of course, one thing about this type of work is that if you have done your job properly, you very seldom find out if you've stopped an escape, beating, or something similar. You always hope you have, but once again, who knows?

One thing I noticed when working the yard was that it was a lot quieter than the cell blocks. Eventually, I found out one of the major dangers of this particular post was skunks. Yep, that's right, skunks—the four-legged variety. There were several that made their homes inside the walls. So, believe me, not only did we use our flashlights to check barriers, we also used them to watch for skunks. I found out the best thing to do when you spotted a skunk, unless you had actually stepped on the little guy, was to stand still, and they usually just gave you a nasty look and ambled off and went about their business. Unless you were unlucky, all you got was that dirty look. This was another reason, and a major one, to make damn sure we took wide turns around the corners.

Speaking of skunks, I have to take a little sidetrack here. South of the main control were two wing doors allowing access to each yard. These doors were controlled electronically by the officer in the main control area. During the summer, but only on the morning shift and if it was hot, they were left open in the hope a breeze would blow through. One morning I was in the main control with both wing doors open, and one of our resident skunks strolled in through the east door. I have to admit, I was a little excited. Part of me wanted to shut both doors and urge the skunk down the strip to the cell blocks. But my good side was hoping it would ease out the other door and go about its business. My good side won out, and I just let the powers that be make the decision. The skunk looked around a couple of times, and I swear to God he looked right at me with a disdainful stare, and then he just ambled out to the west yard. I have always wondered what would have taken place if he had scooted down the strip to the cell blocks.

I just loathed the towers; they were absolutely the most boring posts in any institution. But luckily for me, several of the guys at the Bay wanted to work only mornings or towers. Most of these officers were older and had several years experience and were just fed up with inmates. I also think in some cases they were equally fed up with management.

For me, tower duty really was a horrible job. If you were posted to one and it had been unmanned during the previous shift, you had to report to the main control to draw a rifle, revolver, ammunition, radio, and keys. Then you and the other officers had to lug all this gear out to the mobile. Finally, once you reached your tower, everything had to be carried up several flights of stairs. Once our gear was sorted out and we had checked in over the radio, our job was to sit there and make sure no inmates climbed over the wall. But most importantly, as I mentioned earlier, if an officer in the yard ever got into trouble, he only had the towers for protection. I think that was the reason more than any other that I almost never fell asleep.

During one morning shift shortly after the induction course, I was posted to the northwest tower. After a couple of hours, I looked over to the east and noticed it was starting to get light; suddenly, the next thing I knew, there it was—bright daylight! That was the first and, I think, the only time I ever dozed off even for a few minutes. Finally, after what seemed like a day or two, my relief showed up, and I beat it home to bed. And wouldn't you know, the first thing Sheila said when I crawled out of bed that afternoon was that there had been an escape from Frontenac Institution, which is an institution adjacent to CBI's south wall, during the night.

Immediately, my mind snapped back to that little snooze I had taken, and visions of that inmate walking away right outside my tower flooded into my mind. I'll tell you, my stomach dropped down to around my knees and stayed there. I spent most of that day waiting and just knowing I was going to be called in to explain to the warden how an inmate could just up and walk away right under my nose. I could just visualize him saying, "Why, you weren't asleep, were you?" while all the time he would know damn well I had been. Of course, that phone call never did come. Frontenac Institution was a minimum farm camp, and the living unit was in the southeast corner of Collin's Bay. I was in the northwest tower, and that's as far from Frontenac as you can get, and I knew that. But when you're new at something that is so completely foreign to anything you've ever known, the mind sometimes just doesn't do what you tell it to.

It was not unusual for inmates to take off from Frontenac, but when they did, they usually just walked out over the back field. Also, quite often they would go out on a pass, go to a bar, have a few drinks, and forget to come back. Sometimes, though, while out on a pass they would go to a liquor store, buy a bottle, and bring it back. Things could be tough in the federal system.

Frontenac Institution and tower duty gave me my first really frightening experience involving a rifle; thank God I had some experience by that time. I mentioned earlier that Frontenac was a farm camp with no wall, no fence, and basically no perimeter security of any kind. If an inmate wanted to leave, he usually just walked away. Some of these inmates liked to drink, and as I mentioned, it was relatively easy to bring booze in from the street. This saved inmates from the necessity of making home brew, and believe it or not, once in a while a few even got drunk. When this happened, Frontenac requested assistance from the keeper at the Bay, and he sent whatever staff he could spare to bring the drunks back to be segregated. Once an event like this started, we could only hope nothing serious happened, because there were never enough staff at the best of times, and sending a few to another institution left us that much shorter. And in this business, things were not always as they seemed.

This particular event took place on the night shift, and I was in the southeast tower, which overlooked Frontenac's main building. I received a phone call informing me that the keeper was sending staff to FI because of a few drunks causing problems. I was also told to stand out on the parapet in case the situation deteriorated. There went my stomach again! You would think I'd have gotten used to this crap, but I never did.

There were two main considerations to think about in this situation. The first thing was that we had orders to always carry the rifle when going out on the parapet. The second consideration was that we'd been advised to be extremely careful any time we used force on a minimum-security inmate. However, this was a situation where staff might require protection, and in my mind, that had to be the overriding consideration. So the van came, my rifle and I went out onto the parapet, and I just hoped to hell nothing would happen.

The van stopped, four officers climbed out, and into the building they went. A couple looked up at me and waved, and I knew they were making sure I was aware of the potential trouble. Four guys are not very many when it comes to drunks. And in addition to that, FI only had a few staff on shift, so there really wouldn't be much help in that area. I stood outside with my fingers crossed, and within a few minutes, I could hear angry voices that seemed to be getting more agitated, and then the banging started. Right about then the radio squawked, and I was told a bunch of cons were coming outside. And sure enough, the four officers and ten or twelve inmates came pouring out of the building!

The inmates were screaming, threatening, and seemed to be getting more pissed by the minute. In fact, with all the milling around, it was becoming difficult to see the officers, and that scared the hell out of me. Just about then, one of the guys looked up at me, and even though it was fairly dark, I could tell he figured everything was going to hell in a hand basket and *fast*. And that did it for me. I stepped to the railing, put the rifle up my shoulder, worked the bolt, and slammed a round into the chamber! I wanted to make damned sure the inmates could see a rifle pointed in their direction. And they did, because all movement instantly froze, and all eyes swung up toward me. As I had hoped, everyone heard the round being hammered into the chamber, and it caused the inmates to hesitate and take another thought about what they were screwing around with. The staff took this opportunity to put the cuffs on two inmates, shove them into the van, and take off for the institution. I just stood on the parapet and let the inmates curse and threaten just about everyone I had ever known, including my whole extended family. You could say they were slightly unhappy. Me, I just stood there and thanked whoever's up there looking after me that I didn't have to fire a round off. Not even a warning shot.

Once everything settled down, I had to clear the rifle. You can't run around with a round up the spout, you know. So I stepped back inside the tower, removed the magazine, very very carefully worked the bolt—and wouldn't you know, the damned round flew out onto the floor somewhere. That's when I learned that a little .303 round can disappear into the dark very easily. It still feels like I was on my hands and knees using that old, dim flashlight for twenty minutes or so attempting to find that round and at the same time trying to figure out how I could explain a missing round to the keeper. I could just imagine the consequences of losing a live round. However, in reality, I likely found it in a minute or two.

After a half-hour or so, I received a phone call from the keeper, and lo and behold, he told me I had acted properly and thanked me. That was an immense relief, because I wasn't sure if I had. He also said he was sending an early relief so I could head in and fill out the ever-present report before going home. At the Bay, it was very seldom that management ever admitted someone had reacted properly to an incident, so that conversation was really something. That was another thing about this job. It was unique; there was no yardstick for me to compare decisions or potential decisions to. Even after I'd gained several years of experience, a decision that worked in one instance could backfire in a similar situation the next time. You just never knew, and in this line of work, many decisions had the potential to have major consequences. It was very easy on the one hand to be complimented and have people say, "Great job, Vern. You did well," but then on the other hand have people look at you and you know they were thinking, *Jesus Christ, Thibedeau, where the hell was your mind when you did that?* As I said, you just never knew.

A few weeks after the tower episode, I was working nights in One Block, and I had my first of many physical confrontations with an inmate. It was after the 2000 hours count when an officer came into the block and told us to watch for inmate Sturgis coming back from the kitchen. During those days, inmates were allowed into the kitchen to just sit around and talk during recreational hours. I was told that when I saw him coming I was to signal the staff in Two Block and we were to grab him and force him into segregation. Naturally, up until we grabbed the con, everything had to be very casual so we wouldn't tip him off. Apparently, the keeper had received a tip that the inmate had gone to the kitchen to buy drugs, and even at the Bay, that's illegal. My partner was told to stay close to our barrier and not do any patrols in the block until someone came in for backup.

A few minutes later, I spotted the con approaching from the kitchen area, and very nonchalantly, I gave the staff in Two Block a nod. Once the inmate was more or less even with me, I eased over toward him, crowded him a little, and informed him he was going to Two Block. At the same time the other staff hurried out to give me a hand. The inmate threw me a stricken look and immediately tightened up, and I thought, *Oh boy, here we go.* But once he glanced around and saw the extra staff, he shrugged his shoulder and let us hustle him into Two Block.

Once we were in segregation, I spotted the keeper and the two staff assigned to segregation waiting for us. The keeper informed Sturgis we knew he was carrying and to open his hands. Sturgis opened his left hand but wouldn't open his right hand, so we had to open it for him. And that was not an easy job—not if you didn't want to break a finger. I was holding his right arm, the other staff was crowded around to make sure he didn't hit anyone, and the keeper kept trying to force his right hand open. After several minutes of pushing, pulling, and grunting, I got fed up fucking around and suggested we put him down on the floor so I could stand on his arm. Well, based on the looks I received from both the staff and the inmate, you'd think I had suggested stringing him up on a meat hook or something. But my suggestion must have startled him, because he opened his hand, and lo and behold, he had a whole twenty dollars in it! *Jesus H. Christ*, I thought, *big score.*

I went back to my block while the other staff strip-searched Sturgis and placed him into seg. I don't remember the outcome, but Sturgis would have been charged with possession of contraband and would have lost the twenty dollars. A bigger problem for Sturgis than going to the institutional court (the court at CBI was very lenient) was that he probably owed someone the twenty dollars we'd scooped from him. Usually, when we found drugs or money on an inmate, he was just a runner, not the owner. As a rule, the runner was just doing it to get some dope or to pay off a debt. His problem would really start when he lost the contraband and had to come good for it one way or another. That's why, quite often, we found inmates beaten up or much worse and why some ran into protective custody. This particular inmate seemed to be a survivor though. I know I had several run-ins with him, and he was still up to his old tricks when I transferred to Millhaven several years later.

So there ended another eventful shift, and no one was injured. What more could one ask for?

Chapter 6

Inmate suicide. My first grievance.

As my first summer approached, I kept learning more about the correctional service and found myself becoming much more comfortable in this weird environment. Not that I didn't get tensed up anymore; I just had a better idea of when I had reason to tighten up. One thing that was making life a lot more pleasant, though, was finally having my family in Kingston.

But once July and August rolled around, the most difficult thing to contend with was the heat. Once all that cement, stone, and steel heated up, it stayed sweaty hot. Heat, humidity, and little or no air movement does not make for happy staff or smiling cons. Add to the heat all the overtime most us were working, and it was not a happy environment. There were so many guys working overtime on each shift that at times the keeper didn't even know who was on straight time and who was on overtime. I saw keepers come down with overtime forms to be signed and have to be told it was the guy's regular shift.

About half-way through the summer, my wife insisted I take a whole long weekend off and not work any overtime. That gave me three whole wonderful days at home, and it was great. On my first day back to work, I walked down the strip and felt like I could float. God damn, it was a great feeling. However, it only took a couple of hours before I had that dragged-out feeling back. One thing the rest did do was force me to realize Sheila was right. I still worked overtime—after all, we did like to eat—but I cut back and felt a lot better for it.

Around the middle of August, I was working nights in One Block when an inmate came staggering in. Luckily other staff had noticed him and came in with him. Once again, I was facing off with a con that was one hell of a lot bigger than me. Unfortunately, this was not unusual; I'm about five-foot- eight and a hundred and twenty-five pounds soaking wet—I wasn't hired for my size. I kept trying to talk the inmate down, knowing it was an exercise in futility but that I still had to go through the motions. Unfortunately, he just became more worked up, started pacing back and forth, and then suddenly spun around and took a clumsy swing, and that was the end of our talking. We piled on him, and in very short order the four of us and the con were rolling around on the cement floor in the dust and dirt and listening to the other cons screaming at us. Eventually, with much sweating, swearing, and puffing, we managed to get him onto his back. Each of us had a limb, and I ended up trying to control his right arm by holding the damn thing down with both hands and my knees. So there I was with all my weight on that one arm, and he just lifted me right up off the floor. My first thought was, *Holy Christ, I'm going to be dead shortly!* Thankfully, about then extra staff charged in with handcuffs, and we managed to get them on the guy. Once we had him secured, the other guys dragged him off to segregation while my partner and I tried to get our breath back, our shirts tucked in, and ourselves cleaned up a little. I never did find out what precipitated the incident or what the outcome was for the inmate. It was just one incident of the many that I was going to be involved in.

Shortly after that little episode, I bought some weights, took them home, and started working out.

Once I had been involved in a few situations like this, I realized that usually inmates were careful not to get too carried away with the physical end of these confrontations. I got the impression they didn't really want to seriously injure us, although I imagine they were more worried about consequences to themselves than they were about our well-being. You will note that I said *usually.* Believe me, that was not always the case. But as a rule, staff could sense the difference, and we reacted accordingly.

Eventually I began to wonder about the mentality of some women who hooked up with inmates. I think I've mentioned that at the completion of visiting hours, inmates were counted out of V&C and sent to the cell block area before the visitors were allowed to leave. A couple of staff were always placed between V&C and the entrance to ensure no inmates managed to get mixed in with the visitors, and one week end I got stuck with the job. Out strolled the visitors. I noticed one young mother chomping on gum with a child of around three or so. They walked out of V&C, and as they were passing in front of me, I heard her say to her off-spring, "See that man over there? He's the bugger keeping daddy in here and not letting him come home." And then to make matters a thousand times worse, the kid ran over to me, put his arms around my leg, and said, "Please let my daddy come home; I miss him."

Christ, I just about passed out; in fact, one of the guys told me I turned white. But what could I say? I guess it just shows how some people think. I could only imagine how that child was going to grow up and what he was going to think of peace officers. Over time, I learned just to shrug my shoulders at idiot things like that and think, *Well, it's job security for people working in the justice system.* One night the mobile officer told me he was driving past the front entrance and saw a mother hold her child up so he could take a crap against the wall. Well, what can you do? Job security is great.

For years, when I got home from a shift at the pen, I honestly believed I should act like I was just coming home from a day at a normal job. I'm not really sure why I felt I had to put on that façade. The inmates' right to privacy was always stressed to us, and we weren't supposed to have conversations about what went on inside the prisons. So all in all, I didn't have many in-depth conversations with my wife about the job. This wasn't due to any macho feelings on my part; being macho was the last thing on my mind. I honestly believed it would be easier for Sheila if she didn't know all the crap I was going through or what I was involved in. It took me a long time to realize this actually made everything a lot more difficult for her. The old saying about the unknown being worse than the known turned out to be true. I just didn't give my wife nearly enough credit for her inner strength, and I've apologized to Sheila several times about this. I can only imagine what she must have thought when I came home smelling of smoke from fighting a fire or stuck my head in the door and told her I wasn't hurt even though my uniform was a mess. I'm not saying we never spoke about what went on at work; I just never mentioned a lot of the crap. I thought, *Well, why should I? It's better to try and forget about it.* I can attest to the fact that that doesn't work. A person is able to internalize situations for just so long, and then, one way or another, it's going to bite him on the ass. But I'm getting ahead of myself.

A couple of months after my family moved down, I reported for roll call on the night shift and was given an envelope by the keeper along with the comment, "You're on your way back to the college."

I went over to a corner and sat down on a sofa to read my letter. But before I could open it up, the guy I was sitting with said to me, "Did you hear about what went on in Four Block this morning?"

Earl had even less time in the service than I did, and I could tell something was eating at him. He was extremely agitated, kept jerking around, and he looked tired as hell. Usually, when coming on shift, we sat around the tables talking or watched the euchre players. We certainly didn't sit on a sofa by ourselves, and whenever one of us did, it was noticed, and I saw the keeper glance our way every once in awhile. Earl stared at me and said he had worked overtime in Four Block that morning and around two or so had done a patrol on the top range. It had been a usual shift, and other than being tired from doing a double, things were just chugging along. He told me that about half-way down the range, he had stopped at a cell to look in and felt something on the floor. Earl said it felt kind of sticky, and when he looked down, he saw that he was standing in a pool of blood. He took a closer look into the cell and saw that the inmate had slashed his wrists. Earl, in a quivering voice, said, "He did a good job!" In other words, he was telling me the inmate had accomplished what he set out to do—he was dead. With his voice still quivering, Earl said things really had hit the fan then. He remembered running to the office and phoning for help (we were under very strict orders never to open a cell on the morning shift if we were by ourselves) and within seconds, several staff members had come charging in. The rest of the shift had been a blur. But he did recall medical people, the police, and of course the coroner coming in, and naturally he had had to fill out a report. Earl said things had moved along pretty quickly and he had almost made it home at the usual time. And that was a good thing, because he had had to come back in and work his regular night shift. Once he finished his story, he was kind of quiet, and I thought he was done, so I started to open up my envelope. Then all of a sudden, in a loud, heavily stressed and still shaking voice, he said, "Jesus H. Christ Vern, I had to wash the blood off my boots before I could even get into my car to go home! What kind of fucking asshole job have we got here, anyway?"

Earl startled me so badly I jumped and damn near slid off the sofa. I didn't really know what to say. So I told him it sounded like he did everything he could have. I said, "I know we're going to be seeing things a fuck of a lot worse, and if a con wants to top himself, there really isn't anything we can do to stop him." I don't know if it helped him or not, but I'd be willing to bet he wished he hadn't worked that overtime shift.

Once I made it down to the block, I opened the envelope and found out I was on my way back to the staff college to finish my induction course. *Well, at least this time I have a home to go to each night, so what the hell.* I was familiar enough with the system that I wasn't concerned about it. When I got home, I told Sheila about going back to the college, and she certainly didn't seem to mind at all. I imagine she was thinking I was out of the pen for five weeks, and during that time I would be strictly day shift and no overtime—hey, life was great.

One evening just before the course ended, I bumped into a guy from the Bay, and we sat around and chatted for a while. Eventually he asked if I had heard the rumour about the officer smoking dope while working in Four Block and even selling some to the inmates. I didn't know the guy we were talking about very well, because he was on another squad and we very seldom worked together. As soon I was back at the institution, I learned the guy had left. No one really knew anything other than that he had stopped showing up for work. So maybe this rumour had some fact to it; however, we never did learn if he was charged with anything. Believe me, there were a lot of incidents of which we never heard the end results. I guess being at the bottom of the totem pole, we just didn't need to know.

During my career with the penitentiary service, now known as Correctional Service of Canada, I worked in five major institutions, and I worked in one of those twice. Of all the institutions, Collin's Bay was unique (I'm being polite here). All pens have their own identities, but CBI had one unto itself. Eventually, at the Bay, I became so disillusioned with the job that I came very close to resigning. I think it was a combination of things. It was not so much because of the incidents but mostly because the majority of the staff attempted to do a fair and honest job, but we had the distinct impression that management didn't really want us doing that. In fact, I felt they seemed to actually prevent us from making inmates adhere to the rules.

One time I charged an inmate for an infraction and then, naturally, I had to listen to him rant and rave and tell me it was garbage and the charge didn't mean a fucking thing, and of course there were also the usual comments directed at my family. I guess he knew more than I did, because he went in front of the inmate disciplinary board, was found guilty, and received a punishment that was nothing but a joke. Of course, then I had to put up with him grinning at me and saying, "I told you so, you asshole." And they wonder why staff got pissed off after running into things like that. It did get to you over time.

At that time, management personnel chaired the board, and I was so incensed over the decision I submitted a grievance, the first of only about three during my career. The warden passed it on to RHQ, and they sent it up to Ottawa. As you can imagine, all this took an enormous amount of time. and when the results finally came down, it basically said we were both right. So once again, dick all solved.

The inmate disciplinary board became so useless that inmates just laughed at us and it. Eventually, it was so ineffectual and frustrating that most of the staff got together and decided not to write any offence reports. Our decision didn't pertain to serious incidents, but even so it took a lot of discussion and certainly was unofficial. But we decided to give it a try. At the time, we didn't think it could get any worse, but we were wrong. It didn't take the inmates long to catch on to what we were doing (or I should say not doing), and they sure made use of it. Naturally they loved the idea, and I still think management fell in love with it also. I do know they didn't kick up a fuss about us not charging inmates. With much grumbling, a pissed-off staff finally had to give up. It seemed like we were losing even more authority over the inmates, and that was just defeating our purpose. Well, it had been worth a try.

Another run-in I had with management was a major disappointment. This episode involved a keeper who was very strict with both staff and inmates. He had been promoted and transferred from Kingston Penitentiary, and even though very abrupt and grumpy, he did have the respect of most staff members; he certainly had my respect. During this unfortunate incident I was posted to the strip barrier on the day shift. At this post, we were under strict orders not to allow any inmates through the barrier without a written pass, with absolutely no exceptions. They also had to be dressed in work clothing, which meant green pants and a green shirt with their institutional number on the front. Staff in the main control had to be able to differentiate between inmates and visitors, and this was an extremely busy area. Our job, naturally, was to keep all inmates inside the institution; we certainly didn't want them to get mixed in with visitors and walk out the Door. If that ever happened, there was no doubt who would be blamed.

Some time during the morning, an inmate sauntered up for an interview wearing a leisure shirt. I told him he'd have to go back and get dressed properly. Well, you would have thought it was the end of the world. He just blew up at me; I guess he had that red hair for a reason. He ranted, raved, and—among other unkind things—said that he was going to have my fucking job. He also informed me he was going to go in to see the keeper and have this fucking rule straightened out. The keeper's office, the seven's office, and the assistant warden of security's office were all in one area, and that's where the con headed. This time I wasn't concerned, because it was a strict rule and I also knew this particular keeper was on duty. To be honest, I was kind of happy, thinking, *Well, I've won this one, and if the little prick keeps it up, he may just end up in the hole.*

You can imagine my chagrin when the inmate and the keeper came out to the strip and the keeper waved the inmate through. I couldn't believe it. I would have expected this if it had been some other keeper, especially one I can think of, because he used to call the cons by their first names and treat them like friends. I even saw him walk down the strip more than once with his arm over the shoulder of one. But once again, here I was, putting up with an inmate grinning at me and making snide remarks. To say the least, I was extremely frustrated over this particular episode. As a matter of fact, I was quivering and really felt like smashing someone. I also knew God damned well that if I had allowed him into the area dressed the way he was, I would have been in serious trouble if management had seen him or if, God forbid, he had escaped. But I must admit a small part of me thought it would be justice served if he did get out. God, I would have given anything to write a report about something like that!

Several years later, after I had become a keeper, I often thought back about that incident and wondered if it was actually the seven or the assistant warden who had told the keeper to allow the inmate through. I know once I attained that rank, I ran into similar situations several times. And it's not as though a keeper could go running to the staff and say, "Oh, I'm so sorry guys, but that wasn't my decision; it was the damned management that made me do it." At least, I could never have done that. After all, supervisors were part of management, unionized or not. At least in my eyes we were. It's strange some of the things a person remembers years later.

One time, while I was still at the Bay, I was being given my personal evaluation by an acting keeper, and the evaluation was a good one. But at the end, he said there was one thing he hadn't put into the report that he wanted to mention. He told me I should be careful of my facial expressions, because sometimes people could tell what I was really thinking. I was a little surprised by this and told him I didn't realize the inmates could tell what I thought about them.

And then he replied, "Oh no, Vern—not the inmates. Management can tell what you think of some of their decisions."

Well, what could I say? I must admit he was right; I thought some if not most of their decisions were idiotic. But this was definitely a very rough time for me. When I started this job, I thought most or all of the problems would be with inmates. But at the Bay, it was management that I had the most difficult time dealing with and that more than once almost caused me to resign. I guess that's what made it so rough. I expected problems with inmates and learned to ignore threats and confrontations and all kinds of crap. I thought, *Hey, they're cons; they don't like it here, and they don't like you for keeping them here.* But when management seemed to stick up for the inmates over the staff and appeared to want a quiet institution no matter what the cost, it began to eat at me.

Eventually it got so bad that I demanded to go on the tower squad even though I hated tower duty. That was another major mistake on my part! I only lasted a couple weeks and then had to go, hat in hand, to ask to get back inside. I must admit they were good about it, and I was back inside in very short order.

I mentioned earlier that goodies like jam, butter, and bread were delivered to the ranges every evening. One evening the stuff was delivered, but in the place of butter, we had to issue margarine because of a butter shortage. The reason was explained to the inmates, and they were assured it was for one night only. Well, you can bet there was a reaction to that earth-shattering announcement. Immediately the hollering, screaming, and banging on bars started. The end result was that the kitchen staff jumped into a vehicle, sped off to another institution, and borrowed some butter. Heaven forbid that inmates should have to use margarine in place of butter. The thing is, though, there were no repercussions!

Several years later, an edict came down from on high (Ottawa) stating that institutions had to cut back on their budgets. One of the first things to go was butter! Back to the old margarine.

Chapter 7

Inmate disturbance. Staff walk-out.
Mounties in the blocks.

I had now been working for the penitentiary service for several months, and I wasn't classed as a new officer any longer. Several staff had been hired, and management had managed to fill a number of the vacant positions. Unfortunately, several positions still remained vacant, and a few staff members, for one reason or another, had left. Hell, a few even had been fired. You can imagine what that procedure would entail. Christ, working for the federal government in a unionized position and still getting fired! In fact, I was such an old hand by now I even had new staff members assigned to work in the blocks with me for training. Yep, I was a real pro.

One afternoon after my rest days, I reported for the night shift. As soon as I walked into the lounge I knew something wasn't right, and once I spotted the night shift keeper, the seven, and the assistant warden, there went the old stomach again! The wheels stood around talking among themselves, so the officers coming in just sat there staring at each other and wondering what the hell was going on. The keeper told us not to head down to our posts, because there was going to be a preshift briefing. That bit of information caused some intense discussions among us, because we weren't used to having preshift briefings. As I mentioned, information sharing was not a strong point at Collin's Bay, and usually the keeper or his three came up, took the roll call, and that was it. So when something like this happened it really set us off. In some ways we were as bad as the cons.

Once the full shift had reported, everyone gathered around to listen and hoped it wasn't going to be too drastic. The assistant warden, who did most of the talking, told us the problem was between the whites and the blacks, and so far, the few injured had been black. This really wasn't good, especially for the blacks; they were certainly outnumbered. He told us this had started the day before but now seemed to be escalating, and four or five black inmates had requested segregation. As soon as he told us about inmates requesting protection, we knew this was serious. Inmates sure as hell don't request segregation without some major inducements, and of course that also left fewer blacks in the population to protect each other. "About all we can do," he said, "is keep our eyes open and try and get some information from the inmates."

He talked a bit longer but said nothing really important except that he was going to try and have an extra officer on the shift. I immediately thought, *Holy crap, if the Bay is going to spring for an extra officer, it must be serious.* Just before we headed down, we were asked if we had any questions. One of the guys said we would really like to know if any staff had been injured.

"No, no staff injured. I should have mentioned that at the start, sorry," was the stiff reply.

This upset most of us. We hadn't really thought an officer had been injured, or it would have been mentioned right away—or we would have liked to think it would have. It was just the thought that none of them even had bothered to bring up that little point. This helped reinforce my belief that in the grand scheme of things we weren't really very important. I had no way of knowing at the time, of course, but in four or five months, management was going to drive that point home emphatically to both my wife and to me!

Down we went inside. I was assigned to Three Block, and

most of the inmates living there worked in the kitchen. Naturally, this caused more inmate movement during the day than in the other blocks.

As soon as I stepped onto the strip, I could tell things were not normal, and when I reached Three Block, it really jumped out at me. It was like someone was shouting, "Big trouble, big trouble!" through a megaphone. Inmates were tensely standing around in little groups, talking in low voices, and they didn't look happy. As usual, my partner and I got a very careful onceover when we walked into the block. So there we were. And there I was, with five or six months in the service and a partner who had even less experience. I can only imagine how this must have made the inmates feel—probably not very secure.

At least the day shift was happy as hell to see us. Christ, they were almost dancing when they saw us coming in, and they did look a little frazzled. They told us that so far not much had happened in this block, but the other blocks had had to get a few inmates into protection and stop several fights. They figured we would likely have problems in our block during the evening because of the high number of black inmates, and I tended to agree. Usually when we had problems the day shift wasn't too bad, because the inmates were all over the place. However, at the end of the work day, they all came back inside, and that gave us something like six hundred or so convicts and only around thirty of us good guys.

Management was serious about the extra officer; one ended up working with us, and that was extremely unusual. Also, the strip boss stopped in several times to chat and have coffee. Remember, Three Block was sort of a meeting place and most importantly held the coffee urn.

Relatively speaking, our night wasn't bad. The institution still adhered to the normal routine—counts, jug up, yard, and gym. We completed our regular duties and also made sure one officer stayed at the strip barrier while the other two worked the ranges together. We also did several extra range patrols and made sure we took a look into every cell. By the end of the night, we felt like we had walked several miles—and maybe we had. But at least we didn't find anyone injured or dead.

That was another thing I noticed on my first extra walk—no cat calls! Not that night. The inmates just watched us and never said a word. I could almost believe they appreciated the extra patrols. On top of that, they were just standing or sitting around in small groups and quietly talking, at least until we got close, and then they just clammed up and stared at us. The silence was deafening; this was when I found out exactly what that phrase meant.

It didn't take very long into the shift for our shirts to get soaked with sweat; Christ, those cell blocks were hot! But it wasn't just the temperature; the three of us were a bundle of nerves, waiting and expecting something to break out at any time. And if we felt like that, I can imagine how the inmates must have felt. In situations like this, I found I not only worried about myself or another staff member being injured but also about not reacting properly. There was the distinct possibility that a poor decision could cause a situation to escalate. This anxiety hounded me until the day I retired. And in addition to the danger, I really didn't want to make a fool of myself.

I tried talking to a few inmates I knew. Most of us had a few cons we could chat with and at times gain a little information from, but not that night. We got the message loud and clear that they just didn't want to be seen speaking with staff.

About half-way through the shift, two black inmates from the upper range came down to the office and told me they had better get into segregation. Luckily, just then the strip boss came in, and he phoned segregation to inform them we were on our way with two inmates. As we were leaving with the inmates, I told the guys to get up and lock their cells before their personal effects disappeared.

The strip boss and I got the inmates into segregation without incident, except for the usual screaming about fucking cowards running to the hole and asking why they didn't stay and fight like men, and of course all comments were liberally sprinkled with the *n* word. It didn't take me long to find out that in situations like this, all blacks suddenly became "niggers" to the other inmates. There were also dire warnings screamed at them: "We're going to cut your fucking nuts out when we get our hands on you assholes!" You can take my word that it was one tense walk. Thankfully, the staff had the seg barrier open by the time we arrived, and we just hustled right in. The inmates didn't give us any problems and were quite willing to submit to the strip search and get into their new cells; they were two scared, shaking inmates.

That was about the only thing that could have been deemed even close to exciting during the shift. Mind you, we were constantly on edge and expecting it to hit the fan at any time. We were positive someone would be badly beaten up at the very least. But other than everyone being extremely tense, the high temperature, the sticky clamminess, and the strange quiet, the shift was not too bad. All the counts came in correctly, no one had to be rushed to the hospital, and all staff went home at the end of the shift. Even the eleven o'clock count was good. All in all, a good shift.

At the end of the shift and just before the keeper informed us the count was in, he said he had to hire one more guy. He gave us the "look" and asked if anyone could come in for the day shift. I waited, hoping someone would volunteer, but no one did. I hesitated as long as I could and then told him I'd come in, and he looked a little relieved. Now all I had to do was explain to Sheila that I had to go back in the morning and work a double. I knew she wouldn't be happy; hell, I wasn't either. And Sheila was not happy. At the end of a night shift, I didn't get home until at least eleven forty or so, and God knew what time I would get to sleep, especially when it had been a rough shift like this one. And then

I had to be back in for roll call by 0645 hours at the latest—not a lot of sleep. I also imagine I was just a tad cranky for a couple of days after a double shift like that.

The next morning we had another preshift briefing and found out there were only four black inmates who hadn't asked for protection. The keeper said a decision would be made about them before work-up. He told us there was a distinct possibility the inmates would be scooped for their own good. If this happened, it would affect me, because once again I was in Three Block, and three of the blacks lived there. I must admit, I was praying they would be locked up. Hopefully, that would forestall any potential problems, and it would certainly make our lives safer and easier. The other black inmate lived in Four Block. Staff members had been trying to get him to go into seg, but he insisted he was okay. He said he was a Canadian black, and the problem concerned the blacks from Jamaica and the States.

As soon as I made it down to Three Block, I could tell everything was about the same as the previous night. Inmates stood around talking in low voices, staring at us and wondering what we were going to do—and added to all this was the ever—present God damned heat. In Three Block, inmates got out of their cells earlier than in the other blocks because of working in the kitchen. That was one of the perks—less lockup time. However, that also meant I had them all over the place while inmates in the other blocks were still locked up. And I guess that was a perk for the staff in the other blocks.

Around 0730 hours, we received a phone call telling us that several officers were on their way down to lock up the three blacks. I learned later that someone had received word that these three inmates were going to be shanked! Within a few minutes, several staff came in, and we stomped up to the upper range to collect the three inmates. As soon as they heard us coming, they came out of their cells with their little bags of goodies and were all set to go. I honestly think they were glad to see us. Being locked up in this manner meant they could be heroes and could tell their buddies the fucking pigs had forced them into the hole. You can bet they would say something like, "Yeah, those goddamn pigs just came and scooped us up. There were too many of the bastards to fight, and we knew the pricks had a can of mace with them!" They would have been correct about the mace; we did have a can handy, but it was as much for their protection as it was for ours. Once the three inmates were gone and we had their cells locked up, the block felt almost normal again. Almost.

Around 1030 hours, the phone rang; as soon as I picked it up, a voice yelled, "Get out on the strip! A con's been stabbed—may need help!" I ran for the barrier with my old stomach tightening up again and yelled for my partner to lock it behind me. Just as I made it out of the block, I spotted a couple of officers helping a groaning black inmate shuffle out of the school area. One officer had blood splattered on the front of his shirt, but luckily it didn't seem to be his. It only took a glance to tell the inmate had been stabbed on the left side somewhere around the armpit; his shirt was torn open, and his side and chest area were covered with blood. I found out later he had been stabbed with a pencil.

A pencil used as a weapon! I would end up seeing weapons made out of just about anything. I once found newspapers rolled up so tightly they were as good as our nightsticks. Oh yes, anything could be a weapon.

The rest of the day shift sailed along without any problems—that is, except for the God damned heat. I made it to One Block on time for my regular night shift and enviously watched the day shift head out. Naturally, before they got away, I had to face the usual good-natured comments about working all this overtime and being money-hungry.

Early in the evening, just after my partner had left for the mess, I heard a commotion coming from Two Block and the strip.

I could hear staff tearing around hollering about a fire and to get extra help to clear the inmates out! I left the office running and headed for the strip barrier. The first thing I saw was the smoke and then three or four staff members racing into the block. *Oh God, more problems.* It only took a few seconds for the overtime staff in the mess to rush out and head for the block. And sure enough, I spotted my partner tearing up the strip. He threw a quick look in my direction to make sure I was okay before heading into Two Block; he even gave me a little wave.

Since I was on my own in the block, all I could do was keep the barrier locked and make sure no inmates got out. The problem was that as soon as they heard the hollering, they all came storming off the ranges to see what the excitement was about. After much cajoling, threatening, and explaining that it was just a small fire in Two Block, I got them to retreat back to their ranges and managed to get the range barriers locked. I'm still amazed that I managed to get that accomplished. From then on, all I could do was hang around the barrier watching the guys run up and down the stairs in Two Block acting excited and making a lot of noise. All this just about drove me nuts.

I kept thinking I should be over there giving them a hand, but at the same time I knew it could very well be a diversion for something else. It was a common practice for inmates to start a fire or a fight to get us out of the way while they went about the real business of cutting bars, beating someone up, or God knew what else. As much for something to do as anything else, I made several trips to the range barriers. I wanted to keep checking the ranges at least as well as I could with the barriers locked, and all the time I was hoping nothing unusual was happening. Several inmates were hanging around each barrier, and I gave them a running commentary on what I could see going on across the strip. The inmates all thought I was doing it to be nice, and you can bet I didn't tell them any differently.

An hour or so later, my partner made it back to One Block and told me the inmates had torched the wooden wall on the upper landing next to SIS. I had never understood why that wall was there in the first place. Well, I didn't have to wonder any longer—it was pretty well gone!

One good thing about not having to fight that fire was that I didn't smell like my partner when he got back, and I'll bet he didn't appreciate me asking him to stand downwind. Not that there was any wind; in fact, the fire just made things that much hotter. The rest of the shift was normal, or at least what passed for normal in a prison. It seemed like the fire had burned up most of the tension, and the inmates were back to being their old noisy selves. And we were back to being pigs again.

When the last count was in and we were walking out, I had a chance to chat with the staff from segregation. They told me that when the noise had first started and they smelled the smoke, they had almost wet their pants! They didn't know what was going on, and then to top it off, the black inmates—and there were a lot of them in there—got it into their heads that the population was coming in to get them. Don expanded on his story as we walked out by saying, "The inmates were so fucking scared they were shaking, and honest-to-God, you could see the whites of their eyes. You know, I never believed that old saying, but by Christ, it's true, and who the hell can blame them for being scared? Christ, until someone had enough fucking brains to phone and let us know what the hell was going on, we were as scared, or maybe more scared, than the cons. Jesus Christ, you'd think someone would've had enough fucking brains to give us a phone call."

Work continued to float along, and a few more months slipped past. The service kept hiring more staff, and most of them stayed; however, a few did quit. And of course there were a few idiots we prayed would quit but didn't.

One of these characters managed to earn the nickname of

"the Marshall" or "the Sheriff" or something similar. He appeared to believe that because he was a sworn peace officer, and a federal one at that, he just had to bark and the inmates would jump—wrong. But it did cause problems for any of us working with him. Worse than that, rumours started circulating about him doing some kind of policing on the street. Thankfully for us, he eventually stopped showing up for his shifts. We figured he had been fired or someone had kicked the shit out him, but it didn't take us long to find out what had really happened. Apparently the idiot had bought himself a flashing red light for the dash of his car and had been pulling vehicles over in front of the institution for speeding. And then to top that off, the fool was wearing his uniform. We were told he would pull a car over, give them hell for speeding, and then threaten them with a ticket if he caught them again. This of course was nonsense; Christ, we didn't have any tickets to give out except for raffle tickets, for God's sake. I don't know how long this had been going on, but it came to a screeching halt when he pulled over a keeper from Kingston Penitentiary! I imagine that's when he stopped coming to work. Correctional staff had enough of a bad name in the Kingston area, and we certainly didn't need jerks like him pulling stunts like that.

As time rolled on, there was more and more talk among the staff about being pissed off with the job. This was not just at the Bay but widespread, and it seemed to get worse each week. Correctional staff were unionized at the time with the PSAC. I never was a strong union person at the best of times, but to me the PSAC didn't seem like a bad one. At least they weren't radical; in fact, some staff accused them of being in bed with management. Things went from bad to worse, and eventually the staff voted to walk out even though it was illegal. We didn't really expect to get fired—that almost took an act of God—but officers on probation were doing some sweating. There is a huge difference between thinking you know something and being damned positive about it. But eventually, we did walk out.

The walk-out was planned as responsibly as possible. Management was told about it and informed that it was for twenty-four hours, and in addition, each institution was given a phone number. It had been decided that every institution would have several staff on standby, and if there was a serious problem, they could phone the number and staff would respond. Ottawa was even given sufficient notice so they could get the armed forces and the Royal Canadian Mounted Police on site. The commissioner decided to use the army on the perimeter and the Mounties inside. That was really about all the Mounties could handle. There weren't nearly enough to do the perimeter and the inside. I wasn't at work when they came in to take over, but I was told they were not happy campers, especially when they were informed they couldn't carry side arms inside. A couple of our guys said they actually felt kind of bad about leaving them in there. I guess they looked a little bewildered even though the keepers stayed to help them out. On top of that, cons do not like police of any kind. They don't really care if they're federal, provincial, or municipal; as far as inmates are concerned, we're all just fucking pigs.

This walk-out was a big thing; nothing like it had ever been done before. The union even organized a march through town. I know I was worried; I didn't really think I was going to be fired or anything like that, but you never knew. We knew any decision like that would be made in Ottawa, and to the "suits", we figured we were nothing more than numbers. If I remember correctly, we all received written reprimands, but since there were so many reprimands, they didn't really mean a hell of a lot. So it ended up not being so bad after all, but to be honest, I don't remember the walk-out solving any of our problems either. But it did let management know we could get our backs up once we were pissed off enough!

I was due to go back to work the following morning, and I must admit I was looking forward to relieving the Mounties.

I headed down into the block after roll call, and the Mounties looked at me and said we must be crazy to work in a place like this. One officer stared at me and said, "I don't know how much money you guys earn, but whatever the hell it is, it should be a lot more."

I didn't bother to tell him we likely earned about half what he made. I guess I didn't want to be embarrassed, but it was no exaggeration.

In fact, I didn't start to make a decent salary until around 1975. That was when my buddy (I'm being facetious again) Pierre Elliot Trudeau put wage and price controls into effect across the country. When that was implemented, we ended up with one of the largest wage increases the pen service had ever received. It's kind of a sad statement that we required wage and price controls to get a decent wage increase. Damn, ain't that a great commentary!

Chapter 8

Coworker doing time. I am seriously injured.

Finally late fall came, and the weather started to change. It became much cooler; in fact, some mornings were damned cold. Already I could tell that the humidity, which caused the summers to be so uncomfortably hot, was going to make the winters feel much colder as well.

Work was humming along; naturally there were the usual problems with inmates and disagreements with management, but nothing really serious. I suppose, though, the word *serious* depends on a person's point of view. A few inmates, for one reason or another, ended up at Kingston Pen as protection cases; a few were transferred to higher security, usually to Millhaven Institution; and some were seriously injured in fights or attacks. I'm sure for those guys those events seemed serious.

One of the posts that I filled quite often was nights and mornings in the main control. This was an interesting post, although like most posts it could become extremely boring. But it was also an important post. It controlled the last impediment between the convicted and the public, so even if we were bored, we had to be very cautious. I know I didn't want to explain why I had allowed some inmate to go running out the Door. This area also contained the base radio for the institution and several firearms. But, as I stated earlier, it took almost an act of war before any of these horrible items would ever be issued to the staff at Collin's Bay.

About the only interesting thing on this post, apart from the skunk episode, was listening to the radio calls of other institutions. Most calls were routine, but every once in a while they could be exciting. Sometimes I would hear their control telling staff extra help was on the way in or the coroner and the police were coming or other odds and ends. One night, I was listening to radio calls from Millhaven Institution while they were having major problems. Naturally, I didn't know what the call signs referred to, and not being clairvoyant, I didn't realize I would be well versed with them within a few years. On this particular night, Millhaven staff were radioing back and forth about inmates refusing to go in and suddenly about not being able to see due to the smoke. One officer got on the radio, stated his position, and reported that he could see smoke pouring out, and then after a second or two he came back on and said, "Whoops, there's the flame; it's coming out of the window about half-way down K!" I must admit it sounded exciting, and I bet the staff was a little late getting home that night.

One morning shortly before Christmas, I reported for work and found out I was on newcomer orientation. I picked up my list of inmates and proceeded to One Block. I started down the first range, came to a cell, looked in, saw the inmate, took about two more steps, and came to an abrupt halt. *Jesus H. Christ*, I thought, *that's Mac!* He was a former coworker. He had operated a bulldozer, and I had operated a loader, and at times, we had both worked on the same job site. I didn't know what the hell to do, so I basically did nothing. I had told each inmate to meet me in the vestibule of One Block after breakfast. I wanted to make sure Mac realized I had recognized him and let it go at that. We went through the usual tour during the morning, and I answered the usual questions. At the end of the day I told the inmates I would pick them up the next morning at the same time and headed up front to find someone with a hell of a lot more authority than I had. I didn't know what had to be done, but I remembered instructors stressing that we had to be very careful if family or friends ever showed up as inmates. Hell, for all I knew, Mac would have to be transferred.

The first ranking officer I found was the seven, and we headed into his office. Once I explained my problem, he asked a few questions and then said he didn't see any difficulty. But he did stress that if anything unusual happened, I was to make sure I told someone.

Mac and I had a few quiet conversations when no one was around, but that was about it. But spotting him sitting in a cell sure was a shock to my system.

One morning about a month later, the weather was so damned cold the car wouldn't even start. In fact, that particular January day was the coldest day we had all winter. It's still planted in my mind that whoever's up there looking after correctional officers was trying to tell me to stay home; I should've listened!

Once roll call was completed, I headed for Two Block. About the only thing going on was the inmate disciplinary board, and that really wasn't unusual. It was held once a week, and we always had extra staff standing around in case of problems—you just never knew.

I recall watching the courtroom door open and the keeper we called Manix waving to us that the inmate coming out was going to disassociation. And he was a huge one. I remember the con stepping out and me looking towards the range to see if the barrier was open. The next thing I vaguely remember was being dragged across the floor toward segregation!

A couple of days later, I was told that the inmate came out of the courtroom, looked around, saw me, let out a scream, took two lunging steps and whacked me on the jaw. Apparently my glasses flew up to the ceiling, I headed to the floor, and my head literally bounced when it hit the cement. Verne, who was working in seg, had been watching, and when he saw me hit the floor, he stormed out, grabbed me by the shirt collar, and dragged me inside and locked the barrier. Two Block went straight into mayhem. Luckily, there were several extra staff members present, and it didn't take long for several more to get there. Fortunately, the other inmates just stood around screaming about the fucking pigs beating up their buddy even though in fact, for the first while, the staff got the worst of it. Eventually they wrestled him into segregation and locked him up.

The next thing I knew, I was up in our on-site hospital, but I had no clue how I got there. And then suddenly I was standing in front of the main control by myself with blood all over my shirt and someone in the control asking me where I was going.

I distinctly remember replying, "I don't really know; where am I now?" I really didn't have a clue where I was. And I never did discover how I made it down those stairs on my own.

Somehow I ended up at Hotel Dieu Hospital lying on a stretcher with a doctor asking for my phone number. I managed the first digit, but that was it. The next thing I knew, I looked toward the door and saw Sheila rushing in. She looked a little disheveled and awfully scared! I'm not sure of the time span, but it must have been a while later, because she had to get a sitter and a ride to the hospital. I don't recall saying it, but Sheila said the first thing out of my mouth was, "Oh, what are you doing here?" Not too nice of me, especially when she was almost out of her mind with worry—and with good reason. Sheila told me later she had been doing whatever wives do when their loving husbands are at work when the phone rang. She answered it, and she swears to this day that the person on the other end said she was from the Hotel Dieu Hospital and then asked, "Did you have a husband named Vern who worked at Collin's Bay?" Notice the past tense; Sheila did, and she just about passed out! Our daughter Cheryl was standing beside her, so Sheila turned her back, but not quite fast enough. Cheryl, to this day, remembers her mother staggering and suddenly turning white. Thank God Cheryl was young at the time and didn't realize the implications of that phone call.

An officer we called Murphy was in the room and told me that he had driven me down. He also said he had phoned Sheila, but the hospital had beaten him to it. Murphy said he thought it would be a good idea to phone, because he wasn't sure if anyone from the institution had bothered. Apparently he had about as much faith in the Bay management as I did. Sheila, to this day, is still thankful that he phoned her.

And you know, not a damned soul from the Bay ever did call my wife. That says a lot for the ever-important next-of-kin forms. And to make matters worse, almost exactly one year later, I was involved in another incident. That time, a neighbour heard it on the radio, names and everything. God, people can be stupid—or at least uncaring—and to be honest, I'm not sure which I would prefer.

The doctor sewed up the inside of my mouth, and I assume they x-rayed my head. I know it took a hell of a hit; those cement floors were hard. But eventually we made it home. I don't have a clue how, but we did.

I ended up taking two weeks off work. The doctor wanted me to take more time, but two weeks without overtime was long enough.

Any time there was a serious incident involving staff, there was always subtle encouragement from management not to get the police involved but to handle it within the institution. This is not to say inmates were not charged by outside agencies when it was appropriate, and I want to stress that there was never any attempt that I was aware of to conceal any incident from the authorities. But at the time, there was a real abhorrence to any type of publicity, and I guess the Bay can't be faulted for this. Reporters were constantly writing articles in the local paper about prisons, staff, and mistreated inmates. One particular reporter's favourite pastimes was writing editorials about the staff and the system, and believe me, they were all negative. And lo and behold, I was told that her husband was doing time. Imagine that.

The first person to contact me on my return was a union official. We had the usual discussion—glad you're back, hope everything's okay, we sure want to keep good staff, etc. Remember, it wasn't only management that never bothered to phone; the union never had the time either. What he really wanted was my assurance that I would have assault charges laid against the inmate with the Crown. His concern, and it was an honest one, was that if it appeared inmates could assault staff with little or no consequences, the assaults wouldn't stop. The Bay at that time was full of mostly young, macho inmates, and naturally there was a fairly high use of home brew and drugs; unfortunately, glue sniffing was also very popular back then. This was not a good combination inside a penitentiary. So the union did have an honest concern. I had assumed any decisions would have been made by then, so I just told him I would have to think about the whole issue for a time and I'd let him know.

Shortly after the start of the shift, the keeper we called Manix came down to talk to me. Manix said he wanted to chat about the assault and whether I wanted to lay charges or have the inmate disciplinary board handle it. He was very up front about my options. He made sure I realized it was strictly my decision and said if the inmate was charged by the police, it would definitely go to court. Once I testified, if he was convicted, he might receive two to six months, which would be added to the end of his sentence. The bad part was the inmate still had a length of time to serve and wouldn't see the consequence of his action for several years. On the other hand, if he was institutionally charged, he would receive a minimum of thirty days in disassociation, which was an immediate consequence, and he would be transferred to Millhaven Institution and likely into the special handling unit.

The SHU was a very high security unit and was reserved for inmates who committed a serious offence while still serving a sentence. This included escape or a serious escape attempt, an assault against another person with or without a weapon, and a number of other breaches. The one stipulation was that the offence had to be serious.

Manix told me that in his opinion this was the best way to go. He said he thought this would give the inmates the biggest jolt. But he stressed that it was entirely up to me.

I ended up opting for the IDB. I don't know if it was the best decision, but I think it was. I do know the inmate was still at MI when I transferred there, and whenever he saw me, he just looked away, and I don't think he ever spoke a word to me. In fact, I don't think he ever gave anyone a problem; maybe it did pay to go to the IDB after all. I did find out that this incident cost him his stereo system. During his transfer to MI, the staff unloaded his effects from the van, and the three tried to hand him the stereo. Even though inmates have cuffs and leg irons on, normal practice is for them to help carry their stuff. This jerk told the officer it was his fucking job to carry it and to fucking well do it. He was told once more to hold out his arms, and the idiot gave the same reply. Well, that was the end of the stereo; it ended up on the ground in pieces under number one tower at Millhaven.

So that ended my first day back at work. It was just a regular day except for a very sore head and a few comments along the lines of, "Hey, glad you're back," or "Hey, how's the head? It looks a little funny!" Correctional staff have a bit of a black sense of humour.

Chapter 9

Two sex offenders. My first cell extraction.

So I was back at work and heading into my second summer, and once in a while I even went and played some poker and had a few drinks after a night shift. In addition to getting to know the staff, both their good and bad points, I was becoming familiar with the inmates. One thing I learned was that we had two sex offenders at the Bay. There may have been more, but I was only aware of these two. I can't fathom how they managed to survive in the Bay. I'm sure most of the inmates must have known what these two were in for; if the staff knew, you could bet the inmates did as well. One of the inmates even had a preferred job. He lived in Three Block and was assigned to the radio room. I never tried to find out what his particular offence was, and I didn't really want to know. Besides, in those days it was stressed that line staff had no need to know. Basically, we were told it was none of our business and to treat all inmates equally—as if that was really possible. However, I was going to run into this particular inmate again at two institutions, and he was going to cause me one pile of paperwork. I was told the other inmate, whom I will call Roberts, had raped a nurse with a bottle. This idiot didn't have enough brains to stay quiet and acted just like any other inmate. He did become involved with a religious group that came in one evening every week, though. A naive person could almost think Roberts was trying to make amends for what he had done. But even forgetting his crime, he was the type of jerk you just didn't want to be around.

The Bay, like every other prison, had several social groups that came to the institution during the evenings and weekends. Several of the outsiders who came in were young, giggling, impressionable girls. We knew they had to be at least eighteen years of age, because that was the law, but sometimes we wondered. I imagine some of these girls even thought they were saving the inmates from a life of crime. And I think a few wanted to believe they were living dangerously—and they were. I've often wondered if their parents knew what was going on. But then, maybe some of the parents were as naive as their kids. Most of us just shuddered at what could happen when these jerks got out on the street and tried to hook up with these girls—scary thought for the girls and the parents.

Eventually rumours started to fly around about Roberts and a married woman. This woman had been coming in with her husband with this particular group for some time. Apparently, Roberts always made sure he was sitting as close as possible to the lady, and each week hubby seemed to be sitting a little farther away. After a few months or so, we noticed that this lady was coming to the group wearing civilian clothing rather than her uniform. *Well, well,* we all thought; *now it starts.* It wasn't difficult to see what was happening. In due course, she stopped coming altogether, and a short time later she started coming into V&C to visit Roberts as a regular visitor. Oh well, what can one say? Sadly, I was going to see love triangles like that quite often.

Another post I often ended up working was Three Block. This was one of the better blocks to work. The one problem, though, was the temperature in that damned office. There was one large window, and it faced the west, and when anyone was sitting at the desk, the window was directly behind him. So from around 1500 hours or so, the sun would happily shine in for several hours. I can remember sitting at that damned desk writing in the logbook and trying to hold my head back from the pages to prevent the sweat from rolling off onto the page and making a hell of a mess. And the pen kept slipping because my hand was wet. Such damn fun!

One night I was working in Three Block when an inmate came tearing into the office and yelled that an inmate was flipping out in his cell on the upper range. I headed for the stairs and yelled at my partner to phone for help. Before I even reached the range, the screaming made me hesitate and consider waiting for backup. At least between the screaming and the pounding in my chest, I forgot about the heat. I reached the head of the range, took a quick look around, and saw several inmates just standing around and not doing a damned thing except stare at me. But at least they weren't trying to stop me from getting onto the range. This told me that either the inmate had been truthful and the con was flipping out or that he had been attacked and the attack was over. You just never knew what in hell you were stepping into. The thought even crossed my mind that the cons were setting me up, and I mentally kicked myself for not waiting for backup. I wanted to get to the cell as fast as possible, but I also realized I was still on my own, and that was never a good thing. Thankfully, I heard steps pounding up the stairs before I even made it to the cell. And by the sounds emanating from that cell, I knew I would need all the extra staff I could get!

My first thought when I looked into the cell was *Holy God; I've never seen anything like this*, and even in my short time in the service, I'd seen quite a bit. The cell was torn apart—water from the toilet was all over the floor, pictures were shredded and thrown around, the bed was upside-down, and even the mattress was torn apart. One of my first thoughts when I saw that bed with the metal legs sticking up was that we'd better be careful; they were dangerous. On the other hand, seeing all four legs told me he hadn't broken one off to use as a weapon! The inmate was crouched in the corner, soaking wet, with just his pants on. He was still screaming and had a terrified look on his face. When he saw me, I wouldn't have thought it possible, but his screaming got louder and he looked even more terrified. *Christ*, I thought, *he looks like an animal staring into the pit of hell.* Thankfully other staff arrived right about then, because I didn't have a clue what to do; really, there was bugger all I could have done by myself anyway.

One of the officers that showed up was the keeper, which took a load off my shoulders. As the senior officer in the block, the cell block and all of its problems had been my responsibility, but now, with the keeper present, it was all his. Thank God for small mercies. He took one look into the cell and said, "Holy Christ, this'll be fun, God damn fucking drugs anyway. We've got to get him to the hole and have the nurse check him out."

The keeper stood in the doorway and tried to talk to the inmate, but that just made things worse. The con remained crouched in his corner in a pool of water, soaking wet with his teeth bared and screaming at us to leave him alone and to stop grabbing at him. I didn't know what the hell the inmate was thinking, because we weren't even close to him; hell, we hadn't even decided what to do yet. Finally, the keeper decided he'd had enough bullshit and pointed to me and two other officers and said, "Enough of this shit, get in there and put him down!"

So with adrenaline surging, we squeezed into the cell and rushed him. At the same time, we were very careful of those damned bed legs; no one wanted to break a back on one of those. Another positive thing in this mess was that we could see his hands, and we were fairly sure he didn't have any weapons. However, having said that, you could never be sure, so one of the first priorities was to always get control of the hands. We managed to overwhelm him by sheer weight of numbers and force him down onto the floor. Once down, we got him turned over onto his stomach and succeeded, after a lot of struggling, screaming, and arm bending, at getting the cuffs on. Once this was accomplished, it was a relatively simple matter for the staff to drag him off to the hole and have the nurse come down to check him out. The remainder of us locked his cell and then stood around panting, puffing, and trying to get ourselves more or less back to normal. Once we finished gasping for air, we tucked our shirttails in, straightened our uniforms, and brushed most of the water, sweat, and dirt off ourselves and eventually managed to look more or less presentable. That was my first cell extraction, and the one thing I learned was that they are never ever any fun.

About a week later, that same inmate came into Three Block office and apologized to me for acting out! He said that had been his first time trying drugs and swore to God it would be his last.

Prior to that incident, my biggest concerns at work had been the heat and the boredom. Now here I was once again, hoping Sheila would be asleep when I got home. I didn't like sticking my head in the door and telling her I was okay; it was just a dirty uniform. But this just went to show that you never knew what could happen on this job. And to be honest, one of the things I liked about it was the idea of never being sure what you might be doing in the next few minutes; I liked the potential for excitement.

So there I was, back at the desk filling out my report, changing the count board down one inmate, being bored, and complaining about being too damned hot.

When I first joined the service, it was carefully explained to me that sometimes when an inmate was sentenced to disassociation he was put on a diet. My immediate thought: *Oh, bread and water; that will smarten him up.* Ha, you'd think I would have known better. The diet was a complete meal but no dessert or coffee. However, within a year or so, even this diet was cancelled; apparently it was judged too cruel and inhumane. Hey, life is tough in prison. During working hours, though, they did lose their mattresses. The idea of this I assume was that they'd have to stay awake and contemplate their evil deeds. But all kidding aside, any time inmates ended up being sentenced to dissociation, especially at the Bay, we knew whatever they had done was fairly serious.

One day I was assigned to segregation for the night shift. Before starting down the range to check the inmates, I took a look at the names and spotted a familiar one. It wasn't a common name, and I was hoping it really was the person I was thinking of; in fact, I was almost praying. And it was! This guy was from my hometown and had been, of all things, a lawyer. A friend of mine, who was a city police officer, had had a run-in with this asshole, and my buddy had come out on the losing end. I had also been told this guy used to hang around trying to pick up high school girls. And oh boy, here he was in the hole. Sometimes things just make your day, and seeing him looking up at me from his cell was one of those days!

A few days later, I was chatting with Jim. At the time, Jim was working Four Block, and he mentioned that he and his partner were a bit concerned because things were a little tense and the inmates appeared restless. He told me he'd mentioned it to the higher-ups and had been told nothing could really be done and just to watch for anything unusual. Actually, this time management was correct; there really was nothing that could have been done. If something did happen, staff just had to cope with it and hope it wasn't serious, and if someone was injured, hopefully it wouldn't be a staff member. As they say, it was part of the job.

It's sad statement, but this type of situation was common in our line of work. We often knew when something was about to happen, but there just wasn't a damn thing that could be done about it. We couldn't lock inmates up or lock down a cell block or the institution or hire extra staff on overtime because we *felt* something was wrong. About all we could really do was try and protect each other and make sure our backs were covered. Later during the same shift I heard that there had been an incident in the block and an inmate had been put into the hole. Apparently, Jim and his partner kept a close watch on inmates entering and leaving the block, because they caught one coming in with an iron bar hidden in his pant leg.

A few days after this episode, Jim and I were discussing it again, and he couldn't remember if anyone had gone running for protection over it or not. One thing he did know, though, was that no one had ever come to him and said, "Thanks, boss, for saving my ass; I really appreciate it."

But that's par for the course, I guess.

Chapter 10

I'm abducted. Two police officers and one civilian shot.

Another January, exactly one year to the month since I had been punched out, and the day started out as normal as any other. I reported for duty at around 0640 hours, little knowing that I wouldn't be off duty again for twenty-four hours! I was assigned to escort duty, so I headed down to find out what was on for the day. The first and only escort was to the Armed Forces Hospital at 1400; that meant we would be leaving around 1300 hours.

I found Arnie, who would be our boss, and together we located Ron, our other escort officer, and arranged to meet as soon as we finished lunch. During the morning, Arnie discovered that we were taking several inmates out, and we discussed how we were going to handle it. Arnie and I weren't sure if we should use restraint equipment and eventually decided it would be awkward putting the stuff on and off so many inmates. At that time, post orders were not specific regarding the use of restraint equipment or the ratio of staff to inmates on escorts. Shortly after this escort, though, post orders for the Bay, and I think other institutions, became much more specific. I'm not aware if Arnie checked with a keeper or not, but we ended up not using the equipment; in fact, we didn't even take any with us.

We decided Arnie would search the inmates going on the escort at A&D and I'd stand in the strip and watch them come out. From this position, I'd be able to see them until they reached Ron, who was waiting at the south end of the main control, and then

Ron could eye them until they were in the van. The idea was that once they were searched, we didn't want another inmate passing anything to them. And right or wrong, that's how we did it.

Once the inmates were searched and we had them in the van, the three of us climbed in. Arnie stayed up beside the driver, Ron sat behind the driver, and I sat in the rear where I could watch both staff and inmates. We pulled out of the sally port, and my mind shot back one year: *God, this is as cold as the day I got thumped.* A few of the inmates wore only their green jackets and were already shaking. And wouldn't you know it, shortly after pulling out of the institution, the God damned heater quit. But with only twenty minutes or so to the hospital, we figured we might as well keep going—big mistake. If only we had turned around, maybe three people wouldn't have been shot!

God, it was cold; before we were even on the other side of Kingston, the windows were iced up. While we were driving through Kingston, I noticed two inmates who were sitting in the seat across from the sliding side door acting a little strange. They were just too busy whispering and looking around. Several minutes before we were due to turn onto Highway 15, Pasqua stepped over to the sliding door, scraped frost off a section of the window, looked outside, and then sat down again. And then they were into the whispering again. A few minutes later they had another whispered conversation, and Pasqua got up and took another look out the window. I could feel my stomach start the old tightening up, and I knew, just knew, something was going to happen. But I never even came close to guessing the way things were going to explode! I would've bet the two inmates were going to wait until we slowed down for the left turn and then leap out. I figured there'd be a vehicle waiting to pick them up. I knew in my heart of hearts this was going to happen. The problem was I couldn't get the attention of the guys up front, and I didn't really want to yell at them, because I could always be wrong, and I didn't want to make a fool of myself.

Suddenly, Hein, the younger of the two, leaped up, pointed his arm toward Arnie, and BANG! I knew it was a starter's pistol, and the son of a bitch wasn't going to pull that crap on me. I had had my right leg braced to jump the two of them, and I was all set to take that leap.

As soon as he fired, he spun around and pointed that pistol at me, and that's when I realized it had ejected an empty casing. I knew starting pistols don't eject casings. In the same split second, I remembered seeing a small hole in the windshield that hadn't been there earlier. At the same time I looked into that barrel, and suddenly it looked ominously huge and my mind screamed, *Christ almighty, I'm going to be dead—that's no fucking starter's pistol!* I was just letting my leg relax when he screamed, "Sit the fuck down or you're a dead man!" Believe me, I sat. I still didn't know if he had shot Arnie or not; thankfully, he hadn't. But he had fired close enough to cause him to have powder burns on his cheek.

So there we were: a driver, three correctional officers, and six or seven convicts, one of which had a handgun, and we didn't know what else or who else might have been involved. And none of the inmates even had restraint equipment on—not that it would have helped. It didn't take a lot of brain work to figure out that we were in a hell of a lot of trouble.

For the next few seconds, which seemed like several minutes, I watched the inmates. I wasn't sure if something else was going to happen or if any of the other cons were involved. At the same time, I tried to watch the traffic. I still expected a car to pull up and one or more inmates to leap out of the van and jump into it. You could say I was a little concerned; actually I was scared witless. If any inmates did jump into another vehicle, they would have to keep us quiet somehow so they could get away. I just couldn't visualize escapees jumping into a car and merrily waving good-bye as they drove off. They would realize that all we had to do once they were gone was step out and wave someone down. And I've never said inmates were that dumb. Maybe impulsive, macho, greedy, and some full of hate, but not usually that dumb.

These thoughts only took a split second to process, but as soon as Hein started waving that pistol around and screaming at the driver to keep going straight up the highway, I knew there was no vehicle coming—at least not yet. And that, I thought, was good for us, at least for now.

He ordered the driver to keep going and Arnie to stay in the seat beside the driver. He ordered Ron to stay behind the driver and for me to get my ass up beside Ron. He also advised me to be very very careful and not do anything stupid. Hein stated in no uncertain terms that he had a lot of time left to do and there was no fucking way he was going back in. I can assure you I was very careful moving up to the front! But at the same time, I was starting to get very pissed off, and I really wanted to make a grab for that handgun and wrap it around his head.

I think I could have managed it, because he wasn't much bigger than me, but I still didn't know if he was the only con involved. I also knew if I did grab it and someone jumped on my back or anyone got shot, there would be hell to pay. And the way things seemed to work, there would be a lot more hell raised if it was an inmate who was injured or killed. So I just eased up to the front of the van and plopped down beside Ron. As soon as I sat down, the son of a bitch put the gun up to my head and in a very quiet but deadly voice said, "Don't do any screwing around, Thibedeau, or somebody will be fucked, and it sure as hell won't be me!"

Once I cooled down a little, I thought, *Jesus Christ, less than two years in the service and I'm fucked again!* I tried to recall how much life insurance I had and desperately wished I had boosted it up. I knew there was a very good chance I wouldn't be seeing my family again, but then I started to get mad, really pissed off. And that's not a good thing to do when someone has a gun pointed at your head. I told myself that over and over again, but I still got more pissed by the minute.

We headed up Highway 2, and when Hein told the driver to turn, we turned. I'd never been in this area and didn't have a clue where we were heading; in fact, I was lost. Once we'd been traveling for a while and things had settled down a little, Hein made the inmates move to the back of the van and ordered them to keep their mouths shut. Hein even sent his buddy Pasqua to the back. He told the inmates he wasn't out to do them any harm and once we stopped they could either stay or fuck off; he didn't give a shit one way or the other.

Shortly after things calmed down, Ron started to fidget around, and I figured he either had to go to the can or wanted a smoke, and I was hoping it was the latter. And sure enough, he finally told Hein he was going to have a smoke. Ron definitely wasn't the only one who wanted one, but there was no way in hell I was going to ask some inmate if I could have a cigarette—not in this world. So I managed without one, at least for a while, and that's when it struck me. Hein was a smoker, and he had to bum one from Ron; ergo, the pistol must have been hidden inside his tobacco pouch.

So here we are, cruising along on a highway, and me not even knowing where we were. Before we reached the end of our journey, we spotted two or three police cruisers, and I couldn't fathom how they didn't notice us or have a roadblock set up. And wouldn't you know, we found out later someone in the institution had given the police the wrong plate number—can you imagine? Although, with the crap that hit the fan in Ottawa, maybe it was better they didn't have our license number. Who knows?

That van was cold. I think that was the coldest I've ever been in my life. Eventually, a couple of the inmates had to piss. Their sympathetic buddy Hein told them it wasn't his problem and they could piss on the floor if they wanted. I almost felt sorry for them; I imagine they were almost as scared as we were. Within a short time, my lack of a cigarette was driving me crazy, but I was still determined there was no way in hell I was going to ask a convict if I could have a smoke. So I reached very slowly into my shirt pocket and eased my cigarettes out, and that was about the best smoke I've ever had. A couple of days later I found out that smoke came close to costing me my life. Pasqua and I were chatting, and he said when I had reached inside my parka, Hein had jerked the gun up to the back of my head. Pasqua swore he had seen Hein's trigger finger whiten from the pressure he was exerting on the trigger! Apparently, even though we were almost never armed on escorts and never armed around inmates, Hein wasn't absolutely convinced we didn't have any weapons.

We'd been driving for a couple of hours when Hein told the driver to pull over as soon as we rounded the next curve. I thought, *Christ, this is it!* I had visions of us being forced over a snow bank and shot. The only other option was leaving us on the road, but he had to know that then the alert would be out within a few minutes. I decided we had to jump Hein while we were getting out. I was positive I'd be able to send a signal of some kind, and hopefully we could work together. There was no doubt in my mind this was our best and maybe only chance.

Luckily, it didn't come to that. As soon as we were around the curve, we spotted a hydro truck and a crew of workers. That was a beautiful sight. As soon as Hein saw that hydro truck, he freaked out, jumping around and hollering, "Keep going, keep going, don't stop, keep fucking going!" And believe me, that's exactly what we did.

Eventually I saw a big old sign, and it told me we were almost in Ottawa, and the closer we got to the city, the more agitated Hein became. He started prancing up and down the aisle and waving that frigging gun around and making comments about how he would rather die than go back inside. He really didn't care much for Collin's Bay, but then I didn't either. Hein started telling the driver how to drive by yelling at him to slow the fuck up, be careful how he turned, for Christ's sake speed up, and other similar orders. I think he was worried the driver was trying to catch someone's attention. At any rate, if he was, it didn't work. Finally, Hein guided us into the parking lot of a large mall and made us park at the far end well away from the traffic. The driver shut the van down, and we just sat there basically doing nothing. And believe me, sitting there didn't help us to warm up, but at least I knew that for better or worse, we had reached our destination.

Hein started his pacing again and at the same time kept staring out the windows. So here we were, right back where we had started; how was he going to get away without us raising the alarm? That was the million-dollar question for us.

Several minutes dragged by, and he sort of mumbled to himself, "Ha, there's the fucker."

I didn't see anything, but traffic was a little heavy, so I could have missed a particular vehicle. But I also thought he might have just said that for our benefit and maybe, just maybe, no one was picking him up and he was actually on his own.

Suddenly, he seemed to reach a decision. Hein looked at us, pointed the gun in our direction, and ordered us to hold our hands behind our backs so Pasqua could tie us up. And then, in no uncertain terms, he told us we had better not give him a hard time or things would end a hell of a lot differently. Hein completed his instructions by saying, "All I want is to be left alone and to get the fuck out of here."

That sounded fine with me; I just hoped to hell he was being truthful. After all, inmates are not really known for their honesty, and it would have been a lot easier and safer for him to just shoot us. And he did stress many times that he wasn't going back inside.

Pasqua hustled around taping our hands and, believe it or not, the idiots used electrical tape. Some thinking that was. I was the last one taped up and naturally couldn't do anything, because Hein was standing there with that damned pistol. As soon as Pasqua finished with me, Hein sent him to the back and told him to sit on his ass. Hein glanced at the cons sitting in the back and with a little bit of hesitation informed them that once he was gone he didn't give a crap what they did; they could stay or fuck off. But he stressed that if anyone got out of the van before he was gone, he would shoot. I, for one, tended to believe him. He was just a tad tense, to say the least, and he was getting tenser all the time. But by then I was beginning to think this just might work out all right—at least for us!

As soon as he finished his little speech, he started looking around outside, and I started working on that stupid tape. He slid the side door of the van open, and with a glance at us, he stepped outside. He was just standing there with his back to the door and his hands in his parka pockets, but I knew the pistol was in his right pocket, and I assumed his hand was clutching it.

Within a minute or so, my hands were free, and I thought I just might be able to jump him while he was standing there looking around. It was also in my mind that if I had my hands free, at least one of the other guys likely did too. While I was processing this bit information and trying to think of the best course of action, I noticed several civilians coming and going, and in addition, there were several kids running around. I was positive I could tackle him, but if he did manage to get a shot off and someone was hit, especially a child, I knew I would have to live with that. I was also concerned that one of the inmates might warn him, and then for sure someone would be hurt. I didn't realize it at the time, but three people were going to get shot anyway, so maybe I should have jumped him! This is just one of those things you never know. But even to this day, it's on my mind, and I can't help but wonder if I should have taken the chance and tackled him.

In short order Hein was gone, and we were alive. Arnie and I tore into a store, borrowed a phone, and contacted the police. Believe me, they were swarming the area in very short order. Eventually, we were escorted to the police station, and the other inmates were locked up; not one of them took off. We ended up staying at the station, because there was nowhere else to go, and besides, we were still responsible for the other cons. And the police had coffee and washrooms, both of which we needed desperately! The station also had phones, so Arnie contacted the institution, and then we phoned our families and let them know we were alive and hopefully would be home in a short time

It didn't take us very long to start feeling uncomfortable in that station. None of us had ever spent much time in a police station, but we were getting the distinct impression we weren't very welcome. And then word started flying around that Hein had shot a police officer! I still remember that news smacking me like a ton of bricks. We were told the officer was badly injured but would likely survive; he'd been shot in the chest, and Hein had taken his side arm.

Once this news flashed around—and believe me, it didn't take long—we knew we weren't welcome. On one level, I could understand their feelings. After all, we were responsible for this asshole, and he did get away. But on the other hand, we were all peace officers doing a job, and the guy that got away was the criminal—not us—and at least in our minds, we had done the best we could with what we had. I didn't realize just how bad the feelings were toward us until the lead detective came in, climbed up on a chair, and bellowed that he had something to say. Everyone froze and turned to stare at him, and he said, "You're all acting like a bunch of assholes. I'd like to see any one of you get into a van with a bunch of cons that are not chained up and doing God only knows how many years and then doing it without your fucking guns. There's not one of you that has the guts to do that, and these guys do it every day, so stop acting like a bunch of heroes; there's not a damn one of you that would do that job!"

We didn't know what to do, so we just sat there with our jaws hanging down. Once he was finished, he climbed down off the chair, said he was glad to meet us and he'd be back shortly to have a coffee—and he was. I wish I'd had the presence of mind to thank him; Christ, I could've given him a hug!

Things improved somewhat after that, although we still weren't welcomed with open arms. Anyway, about all we could do was sit around, drink coffee, and watch everything roll along. And then word came down that another officer had been shot by Hein! We were told the doctors figured he would be okay, and I thought, *God, please let that be true*. Hein also had shot a civilian in the arm.

Well, there was no doubt in my mind that after all this Hein had been correct when he said he wasn't going back inside. I really didn't think the police would have any choice but to shoot him. And if we had been told he had been shot, I really don't think it would have hurt anyone's feelings. After hearing all this news, though, I kept feeling lower and lower. I guess being wiped out didn't help any. It was around nine or ten by then, and we'd been going since six thirty or so. It's a slight understatement to say we were beat. And there we were, still in Ottawa.

Somewhere around eleven thirty or so, we were told they had Hein. And he was alive. I was a little surprised by this, because we had made sure the police were aware of his statement about not being taken alive. Apparently, when they caught up to him, he did what most of these heroes do—he threw his gun down and put his hands up. So much for his, "I'm not going back to do any more time; I'll be dead first!" I guess prison didn't seem like such a bad choice after all. Mind you, I was also told there were several people watching out their windows when the police caught up to him.

We eventually made it back to the Bay, and surprising even myself, I was glad to see the place, but we still couldn't just jump into our cars and go home. The inmates had to be put into segregation, and naturally, we had to retell our story several times. The assistant warden even showed up, said he was glad we were okay, and told us we could take the rest of the day off. Christ, wasn't that wonderful of him! We had started the day around six thirty in the morning, it was now a little after six the following morning, and now here was our boss telling us we could take the day off. *God, isn't he just wonderful?* That was enough for me, though; home I went. Sheila was rather happy to see me—almost as happy as I was to see her.

And believe it or not, but during this whole episode, no one from the service came to the house or even phoned to inform Sheila I was missing! So much for their precious next-of-kin forms. I've often wondered what would have happened if I hadn't made it home.

In fact, Sheila had been going about her normal day when our neighbour rushed over to ask if there was anything she could do to help. I guess Sheila gave her a blank stare. because the neighbour mentioned the escort, and Sheila replied by saying, "Escort, what escort? What are you talking about?" And that's how she found out!

Our names, including the fact that we were missing, had been released to the media, so naturally it was all over the radio and television. It was just chance that Sheila wasn't listening to the radio that day. Her memory's just a little hazy about the timing, but she's pretty sure it was shortly after the neighbour showed up that I phoned her to let her know I was okay, and that would have been somewhere around five in the afternoon. She also thinks someone from the institution may have phoned shortly after I hung up, but she isn't sure. Another lucky thing in our favour was that the kids weren't home, so they didn't know anything about it. No official ever did contact my wife during or after these two episodes, and I still can't understand why Sheila didn't insist we pack up and get the hell out of that craziness.

When I finally made it home, I had a couple of drinks while I tried to explain everything to Sheila. Luckily for me, I didn't stay up very long, because Sheila woke me up around ten to tell me a provincial police officer was on the phone and had to talk to me. Well, I'll tell you that impressed the hell out of me. Two or three hours of sleep after something like that is not really enough. We didn't have much of a chat; he said they had to write up their reports and needed us at the Bay. Well, so much for a day off. We all met in the lounge and immediately made a run for the coffee machine. To be honest, I didn't really mind having to get up and go in, because I hadn't been sleeping all that well anyway.

That ended another exciting day, and luckily, I got to say I was another day closer to retirement.

The next morning at 0640 hours or so, like a good little soldier, I reported for duty. And wouldn't you know, I was on escort. In fact, my next few shifts were on escort. Silly me—I just took it for granted they would have given me another post. But, they didn't, and there was no way on God's green earth I was going to ask to be changed. I don't remember if I went out on one or not (it was too long ago) but I was very uneasy on escorts for several years after this little episode.

I was told the institution found out we were missing when the Armed Forces Hospital contacted our hospital to find out why the inmates hadn't made it for their appointments. I guess it really hit the fan. Several staff, on their own time and with their own weapons, ended up driving around checking the alleys. I was told they really expected to find us somewhere either tied up or dead. I'm very happy to say they were wrong about that.

Arnie and I never did discuss that escort, but I wish we had. As far as my career goes, I don't think it had any repercussions, and I always hoped Arnie's career was okay. I do know it didn't take long for the post orders governing escorts to be rewritten. Also, I always believed Pasqua, at least to some extent, was involved with Hein. Maybe he didn't take part physically, but I know damn well he was aware that it was going to happen.

So about twenty-one months on the job, and I already had experienced two major incidents that could have ended very differently. I couldn't help thinking it might not be a very good omen of things to come.

One of the burning questions everyone had on their minds was where in hell the con got his hands on that damned gun. That question was never satisfactorily answered, at least not as far as the line staff was concerned. About a week or so after the escort, a rumour started to circulate that an officer had brought it in. Apparently he was in dire need of money and was well paid to smuggle it inside. Also, we heard that when the police confronted him, he broke down and started to cry. I can't say this is true, but I can say he suddenly stopped reporting for work, and as far as I know, no one ever saw him again. If he was the one, his father ended up working for me when I transferred to Kingston Pen as a supervisor. That was just a tad awkward.

There's another little aside to this. A month or so before the escort, there had been a complete search of the institution when an inmate reported seeing a .38-caliber revolver in a cell and another inmate either breaking it down or putting it back together. At the same time, there was supposed to be a .45-caliber and an unspecified caliber hidden within the institution.

We never did find a firearm, but we always wondered if maybe Hein's twenty-five automatic was the unspecified caliber. You never could tell what was fact and what was fiction. I'm fairly certain the powers that be knew, but they worked hard never to tell us anything, or at least anything they didn't absolutely have to— there is that old saying, "knowledge is power," and they certainly didn't want us to have any.

Chapter 11

One block office fire-bombed.
Promoted and transferred to MI.

Several months had passed since the escort. Sheila and the kids were enjoying the area, which meant there was no doubt we would be staying.

One day I walked into Three Block to get a coffee and Don was sitting there. Don was a CX 3 and was liked by almost everyone. He was one of the older officers (he even rode a horse on perimeter patrol). On this particular day he was in his favorite position, which was sitting in a chair in front of the desk with the chair tilted back against the wall. He asked for a cigarette, and once he got it fired up, he said, "Vern, you're a hell of a nice guy, but I have to tell you, you should get out of this business while you can. I've been here for over thirty years, and you've had more nasty things happen to you in your two years than I have in my thirty-some!"

What he said about my experiences was true, but I must admit I'm glad I didn't take his advice.

A few weeks later, I was parking my car to start the morning shift, and one of the guys from the night shift hustled over and asked if I had heard about the excitement.

"Not a word," I replied, "Just coming on."

"Well," he exclaimed, just bursting with news, "we had some action on our shift. John was on mobile, and he's lucky he wasn't fucking shot!" Apparently John was sitting in the vehicle near the front of the institution and some goof jumped in beside him. The problem was that the stranger had a pistol and, in no uncertain terms, ordered John to hand over his revolver or he'd be dead.

The guy telling me this said he didn't know how John managed it, but he started to fumble around as if he was trying to get his revolver out, but instead he pushed his door open and bailed. He hit the ground rolling and at the same time drew his revolver. By then the stranger was behind the wheel and took off with the tires squealing. John told the keeper he couldn't get a shot off because the mobile was almost at the highway, and he was scared he might hit a passing car. Not firing was probably a very wise decision; between adrenaline pumping, panting and puffing, and a sore shoulder, he wouldn't have hit the car anyway. And even if he had, one or two rounds from a .38 revolver wasn't about to stop a car no matter what they show in the movies. All in all, John was lucky—just a sore shoulder. He could very easily have ended up much worse.

One afternoon I came in for a night shift in One Block and was told we had a new inmate whose brain was a little fried by drugs. I made sure I took a look at him on my first trip down the range, and sure enough, there he was. His cell had almost nothing in it, and he was just lying on a mattress staring at the ceiling. Christ, he was young. I don't think he could have been more than twenty-one or so, and he was thin as a rail. I have to say here that he was a walking advertisement for staying off dope. I couldn't help wondering if he should even be in a prison; hell, there were times we even had to tell him to go and eat. This guy was still at the Bay when I transferred out and then, for whatever reason, ended up in Millhaven. I can't imagine the transfer was due to bad behaviour; he never even so much as swore at us. In fact, other than staring at the ceiling all the time, he was rather pleasant.

I reported for duty on the evening shift one afternoon and was told the cons had torched the One Block office. *Aw, great,* I thought, *that's where I'm working.* I headed up to the lounge and played a game of euchre, but I couldn't keep my mind on the game, so I scooted down to see what had happened. And yep, the office had been torched; there was no doubt about that. The walls had been burned, the count board was no more, and even some of the floor tiles were blackened and warped. In short, it was a smelly mess. Luckily, no one had been in there when it went up. The day shift told me they were in the office, heard a scream for help, and took off down the range. About half-way down they heard a loud thump from the office area and figured they'd been set up. They whipped around and headed back, and as soon they rounded the corner they knew the office had been torched, because even with all the smoke, they could see the flames dancing around inside!

We chatted about it for a while and agreed that whoever threw the damn cocktail likely waited until they had left the office; anyway, that was our line of thinking. I know we certainly hoped the inmates had caused the commotion to get the staff out of the office; at least that would have shown they weren't out to do us in. That would have been a hell of way to get injured—or dead.

We were sure the inmates just wanted to let us know they could get us if they wanted to, but we already knew that; they didn't have to torch the damned office! It took a long time before we didn't feel nervous in that little cubbyhole; in fact, it wasn't used nearly as often as it had been before.

Thankfully, most shifts weren't like that. I always thought excitement was good, but there were limits. As a rule, though, shifts were pretty boring.

One afternoon on a weekend, three of us were sitting in the east yard shack watching inmates bouncing around in the exercise yard. As usual, we were trying to kill time, and we were discussing what we would do if someone escaped from the exercise yard. We had just started chatting about this when the CX 3 in charge of the area walked in and joined the conversation. So we asked him what should be done if we saw an inmate disappear over the wall.

"That's pretty simple," he told us. "Remember, just because you saw one go over doesn't mean one or more didn't get over first. You would have to get on the radio to alert the posts and then ask the keeper for permission to send the cons in for a count. Nothing to it."

This made sense to me and was more or less what I had been thinking. But very shortly, this conversation and the results of a selection board were going to have me shaking my head.

On another day I was working in Two Block, and my partner headed up to Three Block to get us some coffee. He was back in a few minutes with the coffee, and I could tell something was up. "Holy shit," he said. "The cops came in with a warrant to search Rocco's cell!" This inmate worked in the kitchen and was one of our quieter inmates. At least he didn't cause us any problems—not that we knew about, anyway. But we all knew he was high up in one of the crime families; in fact, rumour had it that he was the son of a crime boss. I do know he certainly received a lot of respect from the other inmates. The police (I'm not sure if they were federal, provincial, or municipal) came in with a warrant, and one of our guys asked why they had bothered with a warrant. The police were told that if they wanted to search the cell, we could have just taken them down and helped them do their thing. They replied that if they did luck in, they didn't want to chance some lawyer getting the search thrown out. In the end it didn't matter though, because nothing was found; I guess you can't win them all. A few years later, like most inmates, he was released. Some time after his release, I think in 83, he was found shot to death on some railway tracks. The video didn't show the body, but it showed the blood, lots of it. I guess it was actually safer for Domenic when he was locked up.

Like at most workplaces, a few of the staff at the Bay seemed to be able to ignore several of our rules with little repercussion; an officer named Jerry was one of them. Jerry was an okay officer, and even with our disagreements regarding work habits, we worked fairly well together. Suddenly, we all noticed that Jerry had started wearing his hat, tie, and tunic. In fact, he was reasonably well turned out, especially compared to the way he used to come in. This had been going on for a couple of months when we heard there was going to be an institutional competition for senior correctional officer positions. Shortly before the competition, a rumour started to circulate that we couldn't trust Jerry. The word was that he was spending more time up front talking with keepers and management than he did working his post. I never really paid much attention to stuff like this. I always did my job, and if someone didn't like how I did it, they could let me know. Also, you never knew if these rumours were true or not, and I wasn't going to fault someone unless I was sure of what I was talking about.

Sure enough, a poster for a senior correctional officer came out.

A few of the staff asked if I was going to write it. At the time I didn't have any plans to give it a shot, because I didn't think three-and-a-half years or so in the service was long enough. However, after some encouragement from a couple of officers I respected, and even though I really wasn't all that sure I wanted the job, I submitted my application. I had also been told it would be a good experience even if I didn't make the list.

In due time, I received a letter stating that I had been accepted and giving me a date for the written examination. On the specified date, several other staff members and I reported to the testing room, and I must admit I was excited. I completed the written portion, and it didn't seem to be all that difficult. But once again, who knew?

I passed the written exam, and eventually, I nervously presented myself in front of the board for the oral section of the competition. It was almost like the hiring board, only this time I knew what I was doing. And once I was finished, I was positive I had done well; I just had that old up feeling.

I only remember one question, and lo and behold, it referred to our discussion in the yard shack a while back. The question was, "You are in charge of the exercise yard and an officer reports that he's positive he spotted an inmate climbing over the wall. Tell us what steps you would take."

Basically, my answer was just as we'd discussed: contact staff and the keeper by radio, tell them what was reported, and suggest to the keeper that we should send the inmates in for a count—a text book answer. All in all, at the completion of that board, I felt pretty good about my answers.

A couple of weeks later I walked into the house and Sheila handed me an envelope from the penitentiary service and said, "I'll bet this is what you have been waiting for."

Well, there it was: the next step up in my career. I think my fingers were actually shaking while I was opening it up. And there was my career, exactly where it had been before I wrote that stupid competition! It didn't matter how many times I read that memo; I couldn't find my name on it anywhere except to say I had not been successful. I have to admit I felt bad; actually, I felt like a failure. I do know I was wishing I hadn't written the damned thing.

Luckily, I was off for a couple of days before I had to go in and face everyone. Jerry passed, and if I remember correctly, he was just about at the top of the list. A few days after the list came out, Jerry and I were talking about the competition, and I asked him how he had answered the question about being in the yard. "Simple." He grinned with confidence. "I told them I'd get over and lock the pedestrian gate and then phone the keeper to tell him what I had been told."

I couldn't believe that was his answer. I really began to wonder how on earth he had made the list when he had messed up a simple question like that. Then I started to think that maybe the guys were right and possibly management did owe him something, and then you had to wonder what that debt could be. You did tend to get paranoid in this business, and I was to find later that stranger things than this could happen.

A lot of talk started going around about that competition. Once the talk started, I began to pay a little more attention. It didn't take long for me to notice that Leon, who had been the keeper on the board, was really upset about the thing. He wouldn't even talk about it, not that he would have been allowed to say much anyway. But whenever the competition was mentioned, he'd get red in the face and simply walk away. That shouted to us that something was wrong. Eventually, I was quite happy I had failed it, because I ended up successfully writing a regional competition and transferring out of that damned place.

A few months later, I came in to work, and the first thing I was told was that we'd had an escape! Sure enough, an inmate had run to the yard fence, used it to climb onto the south wall, jumped down, and had last been seen raising dust as he headed south. I was surprised he hadn't broken a leg when he jumped down, because it was quite a drop. I was also told the officer in the southwest tower had never fired a shot, and several officers were saying he didn't have the guts to get it off.

I knew the officer and I had a lot of respect for him (he was the one who had dragged me into segregation when I was punched out), and I knew damned well Verne would have fired if he had had a chance; there was not one iota of doubt in my mind. We had a chat about it a couple of days later, and he was still upset—actually, pissed off would be the proper term. He told me he didn't see the con until he was almost on top of the wall, and when he tried to ram a round up the spout of the rifle, it jammed on him. We were still using the old .303 Enfields, and I wasn't surprised that it had jammed. He told me the keepers had the round, and you could see the scoring on it. I tried to reassure him, because anyone with a brain knew he would have fired if he'd had a chance. But this ate at him for some time. In fact, he ended up transferring to MI, and the Bay lost another good officer.

I'm not sure if the inmate was ever recaptured; it was just too long ago. Occasionally an inmate got out and disappeared forever. Or at least, we never heard about him again.

One day—luckily, I wasn't at work—staff completed a count and came up one short. They recounted and were still short. Well, it hit the fan! The police had to be notified, the institution had to be searched, staff had to find out where he had last been seen, and all kinds of other jobs had to be completed. Believe me, a missing inmate is a lot of work. This escape took place during the summer, and there was a lot of construction going on; in fact, there were even a couple of backhoes digging trenches to run new pipe.

A month or two went by, and word started to circulate that the escapee had had a run-in with some heavies and came out on the short end of the stick. The rumour mill stated he'd been killed and dumped in one of the trenches, and the longer the inmate was gone, the more persistent the rumour became. Finally, word came down from on high that they were going to bring in a backhoe and dig the trenches back up to look for the body. Luckily, a few weeks before the backhoe was due in, the police contacted the pen service and told us they had captured him.

I've always had the feeling the inmates had a great laugh over that one. Just imagine the cost to do that digging. After it was all said and done, we never did find out how he escaped, but several of us thought he must have gone out through the sally port in a vehicle. And I still believe it was the inmates who started the rumour.

By now I had been at the Bay for over three years, and except for the keeper and the CX 3s, I was usually the most senior officer on duty. Believe me, I didn't have enough time in the service for that to give me a good feeling—not in this business. Around this time, someone had a great inspiration! Instead of hiring mature staff to work with the cons, they would hire younger guys just out of university or college. I guess they were thinking that if staff members had more education, they would have more of a chance of rehabilitating the inmates.

So we started to get younger guys just out of school. Several had never even worked at a permanent job, let alone worked in a place like this. A few of the inmates even looked at us and gave their heads a shake. One young guy actually came in to work wearing his rain coat hanging over his shoulders like a movie star. If memory serves me correctly, for some strange reason, we thought he was trying to copy Pierre Elliot Trudeau. Hell, he even looked a little like him. I have to give him credit, though; no matter what was said to him, he stuck it out—at least until one night in Three Block.

On that particular night "Pierre" (naturally, we nick-named him after Trudeau) seemed to be doing okay. He was having a few problems relating to the gritty demeanor of the inmates, but it was a tough job to land in right out of school. But I thought, *What the hell, he's young and he's learning.* Later on in the evening, Pierre and I were standing next to the main barrier when an inmate came down from the upper range. As he went past, he leaned toward me and whispered, "You'd better get upstairs fast. Injury—need the nurse."

There went my stomach again. When an inmate tipped an officer off to something like this, it was usually extremely serious. I didn't want to waste time, so I quietly said to Pierre, "Phone the keeper, tell him we need some help, then phone the nurse and tell her to get down here now!"

I'd just started running for the stairs when this guy yelled, "Jeez, Vern, shouldn't we phone the nurse first?"

So much for keeping things quiet, I thought. I must admit I lost my temper and hollered back, "Just do what the fuck you're told and then get your ass upstairs."

Up I go and sure enough, in the middle of the range, an

inmate was on the floor and not moving. And of course there was blood all over the place; I couldn't even tell if he had been stabbed or beaten, and he sure wasn't in any condition to tell me. I glanced around and noted the inmates were all staying clear, in fact, the range was ominously quiet. Because they were just standing and staring, I assumed, and vehemently hoped, that everything was over. Once again, I was on my own. And there were times when an officer didn't want to step into the middle of situations—at least not when he was on his own!

As soon as I reached the inmate, I squatted down to check his breathing, and just about then I sensed movement behind me. Just before spinning around, I realized it was my partner and not an inmate, and I think my adrenaline rush dropped about 50 percent. I told him to get to a cell and grab some towels. The next thing I knew, I heard a thud and saw my partner hit the floor! My first thought was, *Oh Christ, he's down, a con got him and I'm next!* My adrenaline level shot right up again. I spun around, but there wasn't a con near us! *What the hell?* I didn't know what was going on. Just then an officer and a nurse ran onto the range, and I realized that my partner had passed out. At the same time it flashed through my mind that having him pass out was far better for me than having an inmate put him down. Immediately, my hands stopped shaking and my stomach more or less settled down again. Wasn't that something to be happy about?

The nurse took a couple of minutes to check the inmate over and said she thought he would be okay and then proceeded to work on my partner. It appeared he was in worse shape than the inmate. The inmate ended up in our hospital for a while (it's amazing how tough some inmates are) and the next day went into segregation for protection. That's usually the better part of valor on an inmate's part. I don't think my partner was badly injured, but it was his last shift. He resigned shortly after that little episode, and I think that was better for him and for us.

It was around this time a friend of mine transferred to Millhaven, and I wasn't happy to see him go. In the long run, though, it ended up being better for me that he did transfer. When I was promoted and transferred to MI, I'm sure he helped pave my way.

Eventually, there was another competition for senior correctional officers, and this one was regional. Naturally I submitted my name, and I heard that my friend Jack, who had transferred to MI, had also submitted his name. He was quite a guy. His memory was next to photographic and was something you had to see to believe.

At any rate, I applied and was accepted and eventually placed on the list. Once the list came out, it was a matter of waiting to see if any appeals were submitted, and wouldn't you know, this one was thrown out. I'll tell you that didn't make me happy. In fact, I think I told Sheila they could stick their competitions; they were a waste of time, and I was done with them. I'm pretty sure she knew I was just blowing off steam (I was likely a tad bitter by this time). But just the same, it was really disheartening.

Things at the Bay just kept ticking along, and one day I reported for duty in One Block as usual. Another boring day shift—at least, for a while it was boring.

My partner and I were down at the end of the range for some reason, and suddenly there was a tooth-rattling thud! We couldn't tell where it had come from other than somewhere around the front of the cell block. We both took off running, and I was thinking the office had been fire-bombed again. Nope. All the smoke and dust was rolling out of 1-B. My next thought was that an inmate had tossed a bomb into a cell to get someone, and if that was the case, I wasn't eager to witness the results. I knew it had to be a hell of a bomb to make that much noise and smoke.

We didn't have to call for any assistance; by the time we tore into the vestibule, staff was pouring in from the strip, and several of us took off down 1-B. By the time we had made it part way down the range, the smoke was clearing out, and that told us there probably was no fire—that was always good news. Once the smoke cleared enough, we started checking the cells. In one of the empty cells we found bits of copper wire and some other material that had been burned and thrown around. Thank God they'd used an empty cell! I guess it was just another we-can-get-you-if-we-want kind of thing or possibly a warning to an inmate. Who knew? I don't recall if anyone went running into segregation or not, but if it was a warning to an inmate, that would have been the smartest thing to do. It was a little scary what inmates were able to come up with.

That made two homemade bombs and I don't remember how many fires, and that was all within four years or so. And I don't remember ever having any contact with fire officials or being questioned about fires or bombs—strange. I know things changed before I retired, but looking back at it from today's point of view, you would have thought officials would have been in the Bay almost constantly questioning us about fires, bombings, assaults, and God knows what else.

Eventually another regional competition was held; once again I submitted my name, and once again it was accepted. Again, I got home and Sheila handed me that old envelope. I was really nervous when I opened this one up, but once again, there was my name in black and white; I couldn't believe it. I was as high on this list as I had been on the last list! And once again, Jack's name was right there, either just behind or just ahead of mine.

And this one wasn't thrown out. Eventually, word dribbled down that I would be offered a position at Millhaven. I definitely wanted out of Collin's Bay, but the thought of MI made me nervous. There were a lot of stories about how rough the place was. And I don't mean just cons; the staff didn't have a very good reputation either. But once again, this was just what I had heard; I hadn't worked there, so what the hell did I know about the place?

Millhaven Institution opened up under extremely adverse conditions. Kingston Penitentiary had a riot and a hostage situation in 1971. During this episode, several sex offenders were tortured, and two died. Also at least one officer was held by the inmates, but thankfully he wasn't killed. On the other hand, I don't know what he may have had to endure during that hellish period. Once staff regained control with the help of the army, they had to ship a number of inmates out. They certainly had to put them someplace, so whether MI was ready or not, that's where they were shipped!

In the meantime, life at the Bay kept rolling along with its ups and downs, and eventually I was told I would be receiving my transfer papers for Millhaven Institution as a senior correctional officer. It was also hinted quite strongly that I didn't have to accept the transfer. I was told I could turn it down and stay at the Bay. I imagine I might have given the guy a bit of an incredulous stare; I really didn't know if I should laugh or cry—he was actually serious! Sure enough, two days later, and after five years, my papers were waiting for me; I only had one more week left at the Bay.

When I walked out of the Bay on my last day, I had no idea if I would ever go through those doors again. And to be honest, I couldn't have cared less if I ever did. Well, I ended up going back several times for court, but at least it wasn't to work there, and my leaving the Bay was anything but dramatic except in my own mind.

At any rate, I left the Bay as a correctional officer, and in two days, for better or worse, I was going to enter Millhaven as a *senior* correctional officer. I should mention here that the term CX originally designated a pay grade, but it had evolved into a rank designation.

I can still recall driving home after that last shift at Collin's Bay. I was so happy I felt like singing; even the weather was great. I could only hope it was a sign of things to come. During the drive, I couldn't help reflecting on my five years at the Bay and on some of the things that had happened to me. It was strange, but one of the episodes that kept popping into my mind was a relatively unimportant memory regarding a cell fire and firefighting equipment.

I was working the night shift in One Block when someone screamed, "Fire! There's a fire in 2-B!" I instructed my partner to stay in our block and I took off on the run for Two Block. I made in through the main barrier just in time to see an officer grab the fire hose from the fire cabinet and run for the range. He was holding the nozzle, and as he ran, the hose unwound from the cabinet and dragged behind him. So, there you go. This guy was going like a bat out of hell with a hose, and I was looking around to see what was going on, and suddenly, there was no more hose! The officer was still about twenty feet from the range, and all he had was about fifteen feet of hose behind him—suddenly there was no more. It just stopped. I have to admit, after things settled down, it was a little comical, but at the time it was serious. I hollered at him, and because of the noise, when he looked at me, I just pointed to the hose or lack of hose. He looked back, stopped dead, and I swear his mouth dropped open. I ran over to the cabinet to grab the fire extinguisher (these held water and a hand pump—not the best) and yelled at him to get to another fire cabinet. He finally made it with a hose from segregation, but luckily, by then we didn't need it. I had made it down the range and used the extinguisher. Someone else had grabbed a pail and filled it with water from the shower a few times, and that was it. It was not really a bad fire as fires go, and we had already known no one was in the cell. There was the usual smoke, and the inmate lost his belongings, but no one was injured, and that's always the main thing.

Once things settled down, we checked the hose, and sure enough, it had been cut. We figured it was just some inmate being a wise-ass. Like I said, most of them weren't known for their brains. But I'll tell you, that shook things up a bit and caused every fire cabinet to be checked. And that was a good thing. I forget how many hoses had been cut, but in addition, some of the extinguishers had had the water dumped out and replaced with home brew! Staff also found some other contraband and a few weapons.

So all in all, that particular cell fire was a good thing. I don't remember whose job it was to check the equipment, but it certainly hadn't been done, and I imagine someone heard about it. Eventually, all the cabinets had plexiglass doors and locks installed, and believe me, that took a lot of effort. A fire inspector came in several times to check out our problem. He couldn't understand why fire equipment would be purposely damaged. Eventually he relented, and the cabinets were secured. But we had to carry another key on each ring. This one was painted red so we couldn't mistake it. But all in all, it was an interesting experience and taught me a lot.

I was going to run into a similar episode at KP during one of several hostage situations. This was also kind of comical but certainly not until the incident was over. And the consequences could have been much more serious!

On the drive my mind drifted to another episode; this one still pops into my mind every once in a while.

I pulled into a parking spot on an exceptionally cold winter morning, and as I was closing the car door, lo and behold, there was the assistant warden of security. He threw a look at me and yelled, "Come on, there's been an escape!" And he took off for the entrance with me in pursuit. On our way down to the blocks, he said he didn't know much yet other than that the escape had taken place in Four Block, and he wanted me to stay with him for the time being. I couldn't help wondering how in hell something like this could happen during the morning shift. We headed straight down the strip, and you could tell this was not going to be a regular day in the pen. There were staff all over the place, and no one looked very happy. We reached Four Block and headed for the top range. By now there must have been five or six of us, including the very unhappy keeper who had been in charge of the morning shift. Although I didn't know it at the time, I was eventually going to be in the same position, so I can appreciate just how he felt.

The door was wide open and as soon as you looked in you could see one of the cement bars was missing from the window. That certainly left little doubt about how he had made it out. But that still left two yard officers wandering around outside and the wall to get over. And to get over that wall was no mean feat. Once we were outside, I saw a couple of officers standing next to the wall waving us over, and that's where we headed. Strangely, it didn't even feel cold any longer. Once we made it to the wall, one of the officers reached up, grabbed a piece of conduit pipe that ran down from the top, pulled it out a couple of inches, and bitterly exclaimed, "This is how the fucker got over! All he had to do was yank the pipe out from the two clamps, climb up, and hope he didn't break his fucking leg when he jumped."

While we were discussing all this, I glanced over at the southeast tower, which I could see just fine, and thought, *Thank God I wasn't up there; how's he going to explain this?* The escaped inmate was captured within hours. He had crossed the highway and broken into a store and was found hiding under a trailer. He had stolen a firearm and ammo, and when a police officer checked under the trailer, he looked directly into the barrel of that gun, but it just went *click!* The story is that the con stole the wrong ammunition. And knowing that inmate, there is no doubt in my mind he was willing to shoot an officer; police or correctional. I would also bet the officer's first job after that episode was to change his pants. We were also told the inmate had known where the yard officers were, because he'd managed, or someone had managed for him, to convert his AM/FM radio to pick up our radio signals. I don't know if this is true or not, but I've learned inmates can be absolutely ingenious when they want to be. There is no doubt, though, that the yard officers were damned lucky they didn't bump into the inmate when he was heading for the wall!

I was told later the inmate should not have been able to scale the wall in that manner, because there had been at least three reports submitted asking to have that pipe removed. The two staff who told me this were very upset and said words to the effect that just like everything else at the Bay, the fucking reports were ignored. And then I understood why that officer had sounded so bitter. Just imagine if the police officer had been killed!

I was going to run into this particular inmate again when I transferred to Millhaven. However, as far as I know he wasn't any problem—at least not until he escaped again. He was sure a determined little cuss.

Chapter 12

First couple of months as a CX 4 at MI.

Monday morning finally rolled around, and off to Millhaven I went. I turned off Bath Road and headed toward the institution. On my way in, I passed an administration building and its parking lot, not knowing that in the future a correctional officer was going to commit suicide there, and a little further along I spotted a cluster of buildings that laid claim to the name Bath Institution. I passed Bath, cruised around a curve, and there it was—the famous Millhaven Institution, also known as the Mill or the Haven.

The first thing that couldn't be missed was a very high double fence with coils of razor wire attached to the top. Razor wire is very nasty stuff, much more deadly than barbed wire. If you ever have the urge to climb over razor wire, my best advice is—don't.

The next thing to jump out at me was the three towers. And I knew there was a fourth on the other side guarding the sally port. They were certainly strange looking compared to the Bay. They were much larger and looked like overgrown mushrooms with large windows.

As I headed toward the front tower, I spotted a small building with a sign that said it was the ID building. The sign also stated in no uncertain terms, "All persons must enter before being allowed into the main institution." So that's where I nervously headed, wondering how well I would survive this next step in my career.

I entered the building, spotted an officer behind a large counter, and informed him I was being transferred in. He took a look at me and said to follow the sidewalk in through the fence and report to the CX 8 taking roll call. I left the building and headed toward that big mother of a fence. Just before I reached it, the gate started to slide open, and I realized the tower officer was controlling it. Once the outside gate slammed shut, the inside gate started to slide open, and I stepped through. And suddenly, there I was— inside Millhaven Institution! I headed toward a set of glass doors, trying to act like I did it every day. And then I was in! No barrier had to slide open, and not even a door had to be unlocked; it was almost like entering a large store or mall—just pull the handle and in you go.

The first person I saw was standing in front of a control center with a clipboard in his hand. I gave him my name, and he said he'd be with me in a few minutes. I retreated to a corner and just tried to stay out of the way. A few more staff came in and gave me the eye. The CX 8 checked their names off, and away they went, I assumed to their posts. After a few minutes, the eight told someone in the control that he was heading back to the office, gave me a bit of a wave to follow, and off we went.

Inside his office, he looked at me and said he realized I was supposed to receive seven days of training, but he wanted to cut it short. He explained further that, as usual, they were short staffed. I didn't argue, but I made sure he realized I had never been inside the Mill and that I was a brand new CX 4. He acknowledged all that and assured me I wouldn't be put into a bad position. And that was the end of that. He used the phone to contact someone and asked to have an officer sent up to his office. While we were waiting, he told me there was another new CX 4 transferring in from KP and asked if I had seen him. I was just telling him that I hadn't noticed anyone when an officer came into the office. Ron, the eight, asked him if he'd show me around until he left with the escort.

Tom replied by saying, "Sure, but I don't think it's fair,

because this is the guy that's taking my place as a four."

Well, I thought, *isn't this just fucking ducky*. I couldn't think of a worse way to start in a new institution! I felt like crap.

Once we left the office, Tom looked at me grimly and said, "Look, Vern, don't take my spouting off personally. We've heard good things about you, but I'm pissed because I didn't make the list, and most of us think the fucking thing was just political."

Other than that little episode (and I give Tom a lot of credit for being up front with me), things went along just fine. As we made our way along the hallway from the eight's office, Tom told me I would likely find the inmates at the Haven much the same as at the Bay. Once we reached the control, which Tom said was called T control, we turned right, went through a barrier, and headed into the bowels of the Haven. When we reached the end of the corridor, the barrier opened, and Tom told me we were in N area and that all inmate movement at Millhaven started here.

I looked around this large circular area and noticed what must have been eight or nine barriers. At that moment I realized N area served the same purpose at Millhaven that the strip did at the Bay. Several barriers led into the living units, a couple to the hospital and gym area, and a couple more to the shops. The barrier heading to the hospital and gym also had a sign saying the ECA was in that direction. Because I didn't have a clue what the hell ECA stood for, I had to ask Tom for an explanation.

"Oh," he said with a grin, "that's the environmental control area, which is a fancy name for the hole."

"Well, thank you," I replied with a laugh. "That does sound much better."

There was a large control in the middle of this area, and naturally it was called N control. Tom told me there were several shotguns secured in the control and that the control officer carried a sidearm at all times. He continued his explanations by saying, "The staff in N control operate all the barriers in this area and are responsible for all inmate movement, both coming and going. As you can imagine, we're extremely careful any time someone's going in or out of the control. If the cons ever got in there with all those weapons, it would be game over!"

As we strolled around N area, Tom told me the living units had a similar setup and that they controlled the range barriers and the cell doors. And for security reasons, staff gained entry to the unit controls and the armory through N control.

"Christ, you weren't pulling my leg when you said N control was one of the most important posts in the institution, were you?"

"Yep, no matter where an inmate's going in here, he goes through this area. That's why there's a CX 4 in charge of the place with two CX 2s on the floor plus the one in the control. And that's also why, for all major movement, unit staff lock the offices and come out to N area to help."

N area even had a scanner similar to those found at airports, and Tom told me every inmate coming and going had to go through it. The four in charge of this area was also responsible for the timing of all movement. He was the one who started and ended work-up, yard-up and every other *up* we had. This was similar to the Bay; in fact, most routines in all institutions, except the SHU, were basically similar. And like in every other institution, the CX 4 wanted to be sure everything started properly. If you got the inmates out late for work, management was pissed off at you. If you were late getting them out for recreation, you can imagine who was pissed off at you. And inmates certainly were more vocal about it than management ever thought of being.

Tom said he thought he had an hour or so before going out on his escort, so he decided we should go into A unit and grab a cup of coffee. I must admit that sounded good to me. Just before we reached the barrier there was another magical opening, and Tom gave a little wave toward N control.

He explained that A and J units were laid out very similarly to each other. E Unit was basically the same, but because it was the Special Handling Unit (SHU) it operated with a much different routine and had a few more barriers.

I didn't realize it, of course, but during this stint at MI, I would be posted to A unit and then to the SHU, spending about a year and a half in each unit before my transfer to Joyceville.

Once through A unit's barrier, I heard voices behind a metal wall, and Tom told me it was the unit servery and a few inmates were likely working inside. He said their food was prepared at Bath, brought into MI in heated carts, and wheeled into the servery area. Once the count was in, the inmates picked up their meal through the food slots and they had a choice of eating in their cells or going to a common room.

On the left side of the corridor was an area separated by a partition made of heavy wire. Tom explained that the unit staff stood behind the wire and observed inmates picking up their food. He stressed that the inmates, no matter where they were, were watched almost constantly.

Just as Tom finished explaining all this to me, we reached the end of the corridor, and I followed him through a barrier into the servery. He said hi to an inmate worker, went to a coffee machine, and poured a couple of cups of coffee. We took our coffee and headed out of the servery and before we were into the unit, I spotted another barrier. I mentioned to Tom that I had already seen more barriers than the Bay had in the whole fucking jail. Tom kind of laughed and told me this one was controlled by the unit control, and the stairs just ahead of us led up to the control.

The control had the usual steel plating, lots of glass, and the ever-present gun ports. I had no doubt the staff in there had received phone calls and been told who I was. And I imagined they were wondering what kind of boss I would be. I must admit, I was wondering too. This would be my first job as a boss and boy, what an environment to start in.

We walked around the control and entered the unit office, and I noticed it held the usual desk, cabinet, and count board. I was thinking that so far, except for the physical difference and a hell of a lot more security, everything was basically the same as at the Bay. An officer was sitting at the desk, and while introducing us, Tom told me Mac was the CX 4 in charge of the unit.

Mac gave me a hi, and after introductions, he proceeded to explain a little about the unit. He told me each unit had a four in charge, with two officers on the floor and two in the control. *Jesus*, I thought, *that's three more than the Bay has in their blocks!* He also informed me that each unit had five ranges and each range had fifty cells, which gave a total of two hundred and fifty cons. We sat around chatting and I met the other staff when they came into the office.

Tom explained some of the routines of the institution while we finished our coffee. The more he spoke, the more I realized MI was more aware of security than the Bay ever thought of being. However, in defense of the Bay, it was a medium-security institution, and this place was a maximum. But it was much more than just the classification. Staff at the Haven seemed to be aware of the procedures, and there was no way they were going to circumvent them. And I had the impression the keepers or the fours would jump all over them if they did. Christ, I had only been here for one morning, and I could *feel* the different culture already. It was one hell of a good feeling!

One thing the Haven had was control points—lots of them. When inmates left their units to go anywhere, first they had to go through N area and the scanner and then through another electric barrier. Once they reached the end of any corridor, there was another electric barrier controlled by an armed officer at another control point. And in addition to all the barriers, they were locked in their units to eat. Like I said, lots of control, and I thought, *God, I'm going to like working here.*

Tom also told me that when there was major movement, the inmates moved in small groups, usually only fifteen to twenty-five at a time. And there were always plenty of staff around to supervise. After a short time, Tom left for his escort, so I stayed in A unit to see how it operated once the inmates were out of the unit. I chatted with Mac, walked around the ranges with the staff, and just generally got the feel of the place.

The cells were similar to Four Block at the Bay with the usual small window in each door. I took a look into a couple of them and recalled that we had had an inmate get out of Four Block. And that same inmate was now here and was going to take off again. He really didn't like being locked up. These cell doors didn't have any locks on them, though; they were controlled from the unit control. The mechanism, chains, gears, and whatnot were inset into the wall above the cells and protected by thick steel plates. Once again, this didn't mean the inmates couldn't get those panels off. I don't know how they managed it, but I've seen those steel plates pried off and bent all to hell during disturbances!

Also, just like in Four Block, the cell doors slid open along the wall, which enabled the control officers to see all the way to the far end of the range. It was definitely a nice feeling to be down on the range and know an armed officer could see you at all times. Thankfully, though, at MI during the evenings and weekends, the inmates that remained in the unit were either locked in their cells or in a common room. And as usual, the front of each range had a range barrier that was operated by the unit control.

Eventually it was time for the inmates to come back from the shops, so Mac said he was going to lock up the office and we'd all go out to N area. I don't mind saying there were a lot of staff, certainly more than I ever saw at the Bay for any kind of major movement. The inmates started back from the shops, and they all went through the scanner. Every once in a while, the scanner would beep, and every time it went off, the inmate was taken aside and given a hand frisk. During that one major movement, I saw more inmates frisked than I ever saw get frisked in a week at the Bay. Things were just getting better and better for me!

I noticed the officer in N control was constantly on the radio, and one of the staff explained he was talking with U control. He said the two controls worked in conjunction to keep the groups of inmates fairly small. The inmates kept coming, and I really can't explain how much of a relief it was to see them in such small groups. The staff stood around talking, but at the same time they were watching everything. I had already spotted a few inmates I recognized from the Bay, and then, shockingly, I spotted the son of a bitch who had decked me in Two Block! It wasn't very difficult to pick him out; he was head and shoulders above most of the inmates in his group. I suddenly felt that old feeling in the pit of my stomach again. He saw me seconds after I recognized him, and from the way he stiffened, I could tell he knew who I was. He slid his eyes down to my rank insignia and then looked away. I couldn't help but wonder if his stomach felt like mine, and I hoped it did. One of the CX 4s spotted the interaction and asked me if I had a history with him.

"I sure do; he's the son of a bitch that cold-cocked me at the Bay."

"Well, don't let it get to you; it's not very likely he'll do anything in here."

I agreed and said, "He does seem like a different asshole. That loud mouth he used at the Bay isn't going off."

"Yep, as far as I know, he's never caused any problems since he got out of the hole."

"Well, I hope he keeps it up. He's a mean son of a bitch and tough as hell."

I'm not sure how long he stayed at MI, but he never so much as looked at me in all the time I was there. As I mentioned, he was a different con.

Once the inmates were back from the shops, A control phoned to let us know they were locked up, so we headed into the unit to do the count. The floor staff went straight for the ranges, and when they were finished counting, they brought their counts to the office and Mac added them up. When he was satisfied that the numbers were correct, he filled out the count form, looked up at me, and said, "Come on, we'll head up to the keeper's office."

We entered the office, handed over the counts, and the keeper compared them with his count sheet and told us it was good. And with that news, Mac said we were heading for lunch.

The first thing that struck me when we entered the mess was that I didn't see any cons. In answer to my question, Mac said, "Christ, no. You won't see any cons working up here."

The other thing I noticed was that the staff, uniformed or not, seemed to be friendlier with each other than what I was used to. Everything just seemed much more relaxed. Well, once again I said to myself, *Things are looking better and better all the time.* Staff even worked under a different schedule, and I liked it. We worked seven shifts on and two off and then seven shifts on and four off. Boy, it was a good schedule.

It now seems prophetic that Mac was worried about inmates working in the mess. Like most correctional staff, except in the SHU, he drank the coffee from the unit servery. Mac got along well with most inmates, which ended up being a good thing for him. Sometime around my transfer into the SHU, I reported for duty, and one of the guys asked if I had heard about Mac. Well, I hadn't heard anything, but the day before, an inmate had sidled up to Mac and quietly told him to not put milk into his coffee. The inmate said one of the cons was out to get him and had doctored the milk. The milk was checked; it had been poisoned, and everything hit the fan! I don't recall everything that happened, but I do know I immediately stopped taking milk in my coffee. It could just as well have been me, and would an inmate have tipped me off? Who knows? I do know I really wouldn't want to bet my life on it.

All in all, my first day was exciting, and once I got home, I sure had a lot to tell Sheila.

I settled down at Millhaven with a lot less inner turmoil than I had at the Bay. But on the other hand, I must admit I had a lot more experience by now, so I suppose it was a combination of everything. I do know that when I was still at the Bay, every time I bumped into someone that had transferred to Millhaven, the first thing out of their mouths was to get out of that nuthouse and transfer over to the Haven.

I can honestly say I never had any regrets about transferring. I know I was much happier at Millhaven. Some of the confrontations may have been more serious and have the potential to result in more harm to staff or inmates. But there seemed to be a sense of the staff—all the staff, uniformed or no— pulling together. I never regretted my transfer out of the Bay.

Chapter 13

Two staff at CBI murdered. I'm transferred into the SHU.

I had been at Millhaven Institution for a few months now and was, at least as far as I knew, fitting right in. One day when I arrived at work, I parked the car and started for the ID building. As far as I knew, it was just going to be another day, and most such days so far had been pretty good. Of course, I had no idea about the horrific news I was about to hear. So I just bounced along and entered the ID building, said a quick, "Hi, how you doing?" and was about to keep right on trucking when the officer hollered at me to hold up for a minute. I stopped, knowing immediately that this wasn't a good sign, turned, and headed back toward him. Just before I reached him, he asked me if I had heard what had happened at the Bay. With a sinking feeling I told him I hadn't heard a thing.

"Jesus Christ, they had two staff killed in there!"

My stomach gave a sudden lurch and hit bottom. He explained that it had happened in the kitchen and that one of the dead was a senior correctional officer and the other was a food steward. My knees literally went weak, and I had to grab the counter!

I remember saying, "Who, for chrissakes? Have you got the names?"

He did, and when he gave them to me, it was like being hit in the chest with a fist!

Jesus Christ, I knew both guys! The food steward I knew by sight and to say hi to, but the officer I knew socially. Sheila and I had met him and his family and had been to their home. I can't really put into words how I felt, but the word *shattered* comes close. I asked if he'd heard what happened, and he told me there was no word yet other than that it was a kitchen inmate and that he had used a knife. I vaguely remember thanking the officer, and I headed inside with my mind swirling and knowing full well my mind wouldn't be on the job.

Just before I reached the CX 8 doing the roll call, I realized that I had better phone Sheila before she heard it on the radio; she didn't need to hear any more bad news in that manner. Unfortunately, she was at work, and I knew I wouldn't be able to contact her.

Later that night, while Sheila and I were talking about it, she told me Frank's wife had received a phone call and had left with the store manager. At any rate, because Sheila worked with Frank's wife, she knew about it before I did. I still wonder to this day who it was at the Bay who made the phone call to Frank's wife. Hopefully management had learned something from my incidents. I would like to think so.

I was right; it wasn't a good day. Even the inmates were quiet. I guess they realized it wouldn't be a good time to screw with us. To make matters worse for me, staff kept asking how something like this could happen. Because of the security at MI, the staff, unless they had worked in a medium, couldn't understand the lack of security. I even had one officer ask me why in hell they hadn't shot the bastard before it happened. If that had been possible, there would have been a lot less heartache! During the day, news about the incident kept coming in, but just in dribs and drabs. Eventually, we had most of the information.

I never did hear what precipitated the incident, but the inmate grabbed a butcher knife and just about decapitated the food steward and then took Frank hostage. I was told the inmate was walking behind Frank with the knife when Frank tried to

143

spin around and do a kick. It didn't work, and he was stabbed in the chest. Apparently, when he tried to spin around, he slipped on the floor. I really don't think he would have tried a kick if he thought there was a chance of the situation ending peacefully. He was a Brit and had served in a British commando unit. But that had been some time ago, and a person can lose his physical edge. However, you never forget the training, and I'm sure he would have thought it through.

The staff member who had introduced Sheila and me to Frank and his family was on duty and in the area when the incident took place. In fact, he was one of the officers who carried Frank to the institutional hospital. He told me they didn't even come close to making it there before Frank died. He said they had just started carrying him when they heard him take that last breath (take it from me, that's a horrible sound). I guess there was nothing anyone could have done.

Several months later, I was asked to go into the SHU to work, and wouldn't you know, the son of a bitch that killed Frank and Maurice was in there. For some reason, I hadn't even heard that he had been transferred there. But he was, and I just had to deal with it.

Several years later, when I was a supervisor at KP, an officer I had worked with at the Bay told me that during the incident, before Frank was killed, he had asked a keeper for a firearm and had been refused. This officer, and he was a good one, told me he was practically in tears begging for one, but oh no, not at the great fucking Bay! He said he couldn't really say it would have made a difference, but it certainly couldn't have made things any worse.

That was a horrible day, one of my worst at MI. Eventually, though, the day was over, and I could go home. That wasn't a lot of fun either, but at least I was home with my wife, and that helped us both.

One thing about the Kingston area, at least back then, was that a good portion of the population didn't think too highly of correctional officers. And our favourite reporter at the daily newspaper was still writing her articles and appeared to have a large following. Of course, the area had a high number of families who had family members doing time. This, of course, led to a relatively high percentage of John Howard employees and the usual number of people who believed everything they read in newspapers. To say the least, we were not highly thought of by a large segment of the population. A large portion of citizens seemed to think we couldn't wait to get to work so we could lay a beating on the cons.

I am not sure where these people got their information, but according to them, we certainly were a bunch of cruel bastards. It does seem strange, because almost every time there was a physical confrontation between staff and inmates, it seemed to be the staff who received the worst of the injuries.

I can still see the picture that accompanied one article. It was in the editorial section, and above the editorial was a large picture of a pig's head staring out from the page. Sitting on the pig's head was a correctional officer's hat. I couldn't believe it. How could any editorial board allow something like that? At any rate, I just put it down to free speech and remembered that my dad had died in the Second World War so people would be allowed to state their thoughts freely. I must admit, though, that the pig was kind of cute. But it did hurt, especially when every once in a while one of my kids would come home and ask why they couldn't play with someone because of where Daddy worked. It even affected Sheila and me at times. One year we went to a Christmas party that Sheila's employer held, and we were having a great time. We were at a large table with three or four other couples when the subject of everyone's employment popped up. We were having such an enjoyable time, Sheila and I didn't think anything of it. But when I told them where I was employed, one guy jumped up and said words to the effect that there was no way in hell he was sitting at a table with someone like me and stormed off with his wife in tow. I've always wondered if he worked for the John Howard Society. At any rate, it certainly did put a damper on the evening for us. But they were the only ones to leave the table, and that was appreciated.

I was at the Haven for several months before anything of any consequence happened to me. But before that incident, I was in charge of N area one night, and we were just sitting at the desk talking and generally killing time. Shortly before the inmates were due back, N control notified me that an inmate was coming back early from a group because he wasn't feeling well. He came through the barrier, through the scanner, and headed toward J unit. The control officer was just reaching for the switch to open J unit barrier when it struck me that something was wrong. I signaled the officer to hold it and told the CX 2s to follow me. The inmate was standing there waiting for the barrier to open, and when he saw us approaching, he started to act very uneasy. I told him to get up against the wall for a frisk, and he shot me a "look" before turning to the wall. I started to frisk him and as soon as I ran my hands around his crotch area, I could feel something that shouldn't have been there. I couldn't tell if it was a weapon or drugs, but I wasn't about to take a chance. I grabbed his hands and told the staff we were going to take him to the office for a strip search.

Once we reached the office, I told him not to make things any worse and to get his clothes off. He started to jerk his clothing off to make sure we'd know he was pissed, but when it came to his underwear, he began stalling. He finally took them off when I told him he either had to take them off or we'd do it for him. Eventually, they were off, and we found two hundred dollars rolled up into a cylinder. Once I had the money, I could tell he was on the verge of tears, but he still had to put on the show and act tough. He wouldn't give me any information or tell me where the money came from, and he just kept repeating in an extremely stressed out voice, "Jesus Christ, that's not mine; I don't know how the fuck it got there!"

At any rate, off to the hole he went, and I think I was actually doing him a favour, because I'm sure he was a lot safer in there than in the general population. It was a large amount of money to have inside, and I tended to believe him when he said it wasn't his. However, I couldn't really believe him when he told me he didn't know how in hell the money got into his crotch. But it sure did belong to someone, so I imagine he was suddenly in a very tough spot.

Once everything was back to normal and we were sitting around waiting for the next changeover, one of the guys asked what had tipped me off that the inmate was carrying. I had to tell him I honestly didn't know. I said he seemed normal until just before he made it to the J unit barrier and then something just didn't seem right. But I honest to God can't explain what set me off.

"Well, I guess that's why you're the CX 4," was all he said.

I must admit, I felt pretty damn good about it, and I didn't doubt most of the staff would hear about it eventually. Most shifts were like that: generally quiet, but almost always something would happen. You just hoped to hell it would be something small and not turn into anything physical, at least not on your shift.

It was fairly common to have to deal with inmates who had had too much booze. Yep, they made homemade brew! A big part of the job was searching for it. Brew was one hell of a troublemaker. It was a booze situation that forced me to think about how easy it was to make an error and momentarily forget your training. When this happened and you were lucky, there were no repercussions and you got to put it down as a lesson reinforced. One such episode happened to me in A unit one evening.

Staff had completed a range patrol after the cells were locked and reported seeing two extra inmates in a cell. Because that added up to three or possibly more inmates, I phoned N area for extra staff to help us check it out. In they came, and the six of us trooped up to the cell. I stopped at the unit control to tell them what was going on and to open the cell when I gave them a wave. We arrived at the cell, and I took a quick look and spotted three inmates passing a cup around. That was a pretty sure sign of brew. I waved at the control, and as soon as the cell door was wide enough, I slid in. I hustled all the way into the cell to make room for the other staff and at the same time took note of what was going on. It was certainly brew; I could smell it, and there was no doubt they had been drinking for a while. I informed all three of them that they would be getting locked up and that I didn't want any problems.

But stupidly, when I had rushed into the cell to make room for the other staff, I had put my back to an open cabinet. That was a definite no-no at least until you had looked inside. So there I was, standing in a cell watching three inmates, knowing they had been drinking and were half in the bag, and I asked myself, *What in hell am I doing in here?*

Suddenly, one of the staff screamed, "Don't you move a fucking muscle, you son of a bitch!"

I jerked around to see what he was yelling about and saw him staring behind me at the cabinet. I swear to God my heart stopped beating and I almost wet myself! Sure enough, there was an inmate standing in the closet staring at me. I'm happy to say that as soon as I spun around, he put his hands out to show us they were empty—no weapon! Thankfully, he had just slipped in to try and hide from us. But that just shows how easy it was to screw up. I knew better than to turn my back to an area before checking it out, especially in a situation that could have turned very ugly in seconds. He could just as easily have had a shank, and the whole situation could have ended very differently.

And this was one of the problems I ran into quite often after I was promoted. I'd been told on several occasions that I was to supervise, and if I was in the middle of a wrestling match I couldn't supervise crap. That advice was correct, but I just couldn't seem to help it.

But we did have larger problems, and during one evening shift, I was in charge of A unit, and it wasn't a quiet night. The inmates had decided they weren't going into their cells for the count, and they were very emphatic about it. Luckily, it was only one range, but that still added up to about fifty inmates—a lot more of them than us. We talked to the range rep but couldn't make any headway, and the situation dragged on until the next day. Naturally, I was late making it home and had to go back in early, and sure enough, the cons were still going at it.

Just about every time a situation like this got going, the inmates tied blankets up at the front of the range so staff couldn't see what was going on. And the noise level was absolutely horrendous. Staff, unless they were standing around N area, had to scream at each other to be heard. These situations were tough for everyone. Staff couldn't see down the range, the hollering and screaming bounced off the walls, and then management, with input from the staff, had to decide if they should use gas or some type of force to get onto the range.

If the decision was to use force and there were injuries, especially to an inmate, there was hell to pay! When this happened, officials from HQ swooped in to carry out their investigations, and believe me, they second-guessed every decision made by everyone. The only thing worse was trying to talk the problem out and then at its conclusion find out an inmate had been beaten up, raped, or worse during the negotiations. Then there really was hell to pay! It was kind of a lose-lose situation.

I'm not saying institutional staff shouldn't have tried to negotiate these problems. I've learned that talking is always better than fighting, and if at all possible, that was always the first step. It was a matter of timing—how long did you talk?

If you did talk and talk and talk and the problem was solved and the inmates finally went back into their cells and no one was injured, the warden—and it was usually the warden's decision—was a hero. If you talked and talked and talked and finally got onto the range to find that an inmate had been seriously injured, someone was an asshole and should have known enough to send in the IERT to save the inmate.

In any case, injuries or not, it was an expensive proposition. Naturally, there was all kinds of overtime, but there was also property damage; it's unbelievable what humans can do to cement and steel, or to each other. I mentioned above seeing the steel panels that protected the cell gears ripped off the walls and bent almost double. It's just unimaginable what can be destroyed. Every time I saw something like that, I just shuddered and thanked the good Lord I had never been grabbed before one of these incidents. When I said inmates could get pissed off, I was not kidding. I can't recall the cost of some of these episodes, but I certainly remember being shocked at the amount. Of course it was the taxpayers who paid for the damage, and that also used to piss me off, because I'm also a taxpayer. And every time I looked at an overtime cheque and saw how much tax had been deducted, I realized just how much of a taxpayer I was.

I think this disturbance went on until the following evening, or possibly the next day. Luckily, it didn't take force to settle it. This time it was talk and talk and talk and thankfully, as far as we know, there weren't any injuries. Eventually, we emptied another range in the unit, and the inmates finally agreed to move to the empty range. They even agreed to allow us to frisk them as they moved through the common room—nice of them.

But boy, the damage! Like I said, a person had to see it to believe it!

I eventually met the new four who had transferred in from KP. It was about two days after I arrived at Millhaven, and Nelson told me he had had to finish up some work at KP before he could leave. We didn't work together, because there was usually only one CX 4 in an area and he was assigned to another unit; we did, however, get along. In fact, we later ended up working together at KP and again at Bath Institution. I know Nelson wasn't happy at the Haven. In fact, after having a couple of run-ins with staff, he transferred back to KP.

I thank the stars that everything worked well for me at Millhaven with both staff and management; I think I even had the respect of some of the cons. In fact, after I had been at the Haven for a couple of years, one of the guys came up to me and asked me if I remembered a particular inmate. I certainly did remember him. We had had several run-ins, mostly because he had been on the inmate committee and had been rather vocal about it. Anyway, Mike saw the inmate at A&D just before he was transferred out, and the inmate asked Mike if he knew me.

When Mike said yes, the inmate said to Mike, "That fucking Thibedeau is a strict son of a bitch, but at least he's honest and fair about it."

I have to admit this made me feel pretty good.

I spent a total of three years at Millhaven, and the first one-and-a-half years were in A unit. I was doing a damned good job and was relatively happy there. And then David, the keeper in charge of the SHU, asked if I would be interested in working for him. Well, it was decision time again. I didn't know what to tell him, so I said I would have to talk it over with my wife, which was true. There was no way I was going to make a move like that without discussing it with Sheila.

I certainly had a lot of thinking to do on my way home that day.

Chapter 14

Armed in a hospital.

Driving home, I reviewed what I knew about the SHU. It was actually a unit in MI but was operated under a completely different set of orders and with a much stricter routine. Inmates were sent there for committing serious crimes while still under sentence, and this included everything from murder to escape or a serious attempt at an escape. But I did like the idea of the higher security. Also, by demonstrating good behaviour, the inmates could earn their way back to a regular institution, starting at a maximum and working down. So there was some incentive for good behaviour. On the other hand, a few of the inmates didn't give a crap about demonstrating good behaviour.

When I got home and told Sheila I had been asked to go into the SHU, she just sort of looked at me with that 'look'. She knew a bit about the SHU and emphatically informed me that she couldn't understand why anyone would want to work in a place like that.

Once Sheila had a better grasp of the security procedures and the number of staff on a shift, she was much more receptive to the idea of me working there. I also told her that David had mentioned that working in the SHU would likely help my chances in the service if I wanted to go any higher.

The staff in E unit were really busy, at least during the day shift. Luckily, the night shift was much slower. But regardless of the shift, it was always security and safety first. Staff and inmates knew they had to wait until staff were available, and this included official visitors, and it didn't matter if it was someone from RHQ or higher—safety first! Like I said, it was a good place to work. It didn't take me very long to get the hang of the place; I seemed to fit right in. And I was only in there for a couple of weeks before I ended up on the floor in a wrestling match.

An inmate was being escorted somewhere and insisted on talking to the person in charge of the shift. Well, that was me. When staff members informed me of the problem, I strolled out of the office and around the corner to see what was going on. I guess I couldn't solve it, because we ended up rolling around on the floor. It only lasted a few seconds, because staff just piled on him, and off to ECA he went. I was getting up off the floor and trying to catch my breath when I looked up, and sure enough, there was the keeper staring down at me.

"For Christ's sake, Vern, what in the hell are you doing down there?"

Well, into his office we headed with me following and still trying to get my breath and tuck my shirt in. Before I could explain, he told me my job wasn't to fight the cons; I was being paid to supervise. I thought, *Boy oh boy, sometimes a person just can't win.*

Maybe not very often, but sometimes there were humorous or even idiotic situations in these places. I'll let you decide under which heading this incident should be listed.

I was working days in the unit when one of the guys came in and told me there was someone from RHQ who wanted to interview one of the cons regarding a grievance that had been submitted. Naturally, my first thought was that the inmate felt he had been mistreated and wanted the drastic wrong rectified. The officer, with one of those wise-ass grins, continued, "Vern, you have to go out in the corridor and have a chat with this guy. You never know; maybe you can get it straightened out."

Normally, an officer would come in to let me know what was going on and then escort the visitor to the interview area. After that he would collect the inmate and lock him into the interview room. So this was an odd statement, and I knew something was up, especially when I spotted that silly grin.

Out I went to talk to this guy to find out just what was so interesting. I must admit he had the grace to look embarrassed. He told me the inmate had submitted a grievance about the Rice Crispy cereal. Apparently, the inmate was given the cereal for breakfast at one time or another, and it didn't snap, crackle, and pop as advertised, and therefore he had complained that it was stale! Once I picked my jaw up off the floor, I had to ask if he was serious—he was. He said the inmate had laid the grievance, a keeper from MI had interviewed him and basically, in the written reply, had said this was nuts and he had better things to do. Naturally, the inmate didn't accept that answer, so it was bounced up to RHQ, and he had to come in and interview the con. I couldn't believe it. I want to add a little note here: I swear to God this is true; it actually did happen.

One thing to note is that an inmate could be denied the use of grievance procedures if he continued to submit frivolous complaints. However, this almost took an act of God. In my twenty-six years, I can only remember this happening to one inmate, and that was Clifford Olson.

One morning I had to go to Collin's Bay for one reason or another, and as usual, my first stop was at Three Block for a coffee. I went in, said hi to the guys, poured a coffee, and got all set to shoot the shit for a while. However, one of them immediately said, "Hey, Vern, did you hear about Alex?"

I knew Alex really well. When I was at the Bay, we had often worked together. He drank a little too much but never let it interfere with his job—at least he hadn't up till then. Now I was about to find out he had allowed booze to affect his job in a big way.

"Nope," I replied. "I haven't run into him since I left this place."

"Well, he took a con out on a resocialization escort and ended up drinking with him in a bar!"

"Holy Christ, what in hell was he thinking?"

"Oh, that's just the start of it. They were in there drinking and ran out of money, and the con told Alex to hold on for a few minutes and he'd be right back. The con went across the street, robbed a fucking bank, and then came back to the bar to have a few more drinks. They were still there when the cops found them!"

Jesus, I thought, *what can anyone say to that—nothing.*

I really felt bad about this situation, but Alex had made his bed, and I guess he had to lie in it. I also imagine it cost him his job.

During my time at Millhaven, there was one situation I missed. And to this day I still thank whoever is up there looking after correctional officers for having missed it. I certainly picked a good time to take my annual leave and head up north with my family for a visit.

I was told this incident started out as a normal disturbance in one of the units. God, what a way to live—calling a disturbance normal. Anyway, the inmates were out on the range and refusing to go back into their cells. As usual, the yelling and banging started, and it continued for some time. But in short order things went horribly wrong, and an inmate ended up being stabbed and slashed several times. The officer telling me about it said the two guys in the control still hadn't returned to work. I managed to speak to one of them a couple of weeks later. He tried coming back but within a short time was off again. As far as I know, his partner never did come back.

During our conversation, he told me they saw several inmates grab the victim and hang on to him. At the time, they figured the inmates were just screwing around, but while he was being held a couple of inmates pulled out shanks and started stabbing and slashing the guy. He said there was not one fucking thing they could do. There were dozens of inmates milling around, and there was no way to get a shot off! Near the end of our conversation, he started becoming very agitated and told me the inmates hadn't even tried to hide what they were doing. After it was over, two or three of them dragged the inmate to the stairs and yelled at the control that they were finished with the asshole and we could have the fucker back. "Then," he said, "they just threw him down the stairs like a sack of fucking dirt! That's what got to us. Here's this con who is one of their own, and Jesus Christ, Vern, they just threw him away like a bag of shit. Can you imagine what the bastards would do to one of us?"

I certainly didn't blame these guys for being off work. I always hoped they never had to come back in. Sometimes a person can take just so much before he reaches his limit, and then that's it; the game's over.

Things could turn very, very nasty extremely quickly in these places. A warden in Quebec was out shoveling his driveway one day when someone drove by and shot him. And worse than that, while I was at KP, I had to take several officers to Quebec for the funeral of three correctional officers killed in a riot. Every officer working in these places always had this in the back of their minds. You just never knew what could evolve from even a simple argument. This tended to keep a person on a bit of an edge, and then you had to go home, turn yourself off, and be normal again. It could be tough at times.

One time I was on some kind of training, and a few of us got talking with some OPP officers. One sergeant put it quite succinctly. "When we're working, about 75 percent of the time we're trying to help normal people. Christ, you guys go in and deal with assholes for 100 percent of your shift; I honestly don't know how in hell you do it."

There were times I couldn't understand how or why we did it either. It certainly wasn't to get rich.

Time just sped along in the SHU. There were the normal ups and downs, but if you were going to work in a penitentiary, this certainly wasn't a bad place to do it. One day I headed into the unit to start a shift after being away for several days. The first words out of the four's mouth were, "Did you hear the big news about the coke?"

"What, you guys found more dope while I was off?"

"No, no, nothing as simple as that."

And then he filled me in on what had happened. I'd never heard anything like it, and I still haven't to this day.

The staff were carrying out random cell searches when one of the officers spotted a case of coke. He told me later he had looked at the case for a few seconds and then decided to pick up each can to give it a little shake. Everything felt normal until he was about half-way through the case and one can felt a little heavier. He said he almost opened it but instead decided to take the whole case down to the office and show the CX 4.

The four very carefully opened the can and gently tipped it over. Instead of pop, out came a few drops of something that looked and smelled like oil. He immediately called up front, and down came the 'wheels', and away went the case of coke.

We were told everything was sent away for testing and eventually word dribbled back to us that it was oil in the can. Also in the can was a short coil of what appeared to be thick dental floss imbedded with some kind of diamond chips. The can must have been doctored at the factory before it was sealed. And the floss with the chips was used for cutting specialized material. It certainly would have cut through the bars and fences we used to help keep the inmates inside.

Somehow, someone had arranged for that material to be

put into an empty can at a factory and for that same can to make its way to Millhaven's inmate canteen and then somehow into the hands of a specific inmate. I never did hear any more about it, but it makes a person think about what can be accomplished with connections, great effort, and no doubt a good sum of money; in fact, it's scary.

One evening on a day off, I received a phone call asking if I would work overtime the next day. Once I told the eight I could, he informed me it was to watch an inmate at Hotel Dieu Hospital, and he gave me the room number. As soon as he hung up, I started thinking this was a little strange; CX 4s didn't normally work at the hospital. I also had the distinct impression the CX 8 was leaving something unsaid, but then I thought, *Aw, I'm probably being paranoid.* I was wrong.

The next morning I parked at the hospital, and as soon as I entered the place, something didn't "feel" right. Whatever was setting me off caused the hairs on the back of my neck to stand up. I found the room, and unsure what to do, I knocked. Someone asked who it was, and once I identified myself, the voice said, "Christ, I'm glad you're here, Vern; come on in."

As soon as I entered, I saw the four I was going to relieve. He had a shoulder holster and a revolver on. Then I spotted someone standing off to the side in a corner, and he was also armed. *Well,* I thought, *at least the inmate shackled to the bed is unarmed, and that's something positive!*

Terry, the four, asked me if I had been briefed. Short answer—no. He said he wasn't surprised, because they had been trying to keep everything quiet. He waved toward the bed and said the con was from the SHU and had injured his eyes. Terry informed me the institution had been warned by an informant in the States that the inmate was going to injure himself to get into the hospital. And then while he was here, his girlfriend, along with a couple of male friends, was coming up to break him out, and they were bringing weapons with them. Once again Terry waved toward the inmate. "Lucky for us, Vern, they screwed up on two counts. One, someone mouthed off so we were tipped, and two, the jerk helping this idiot fucked up, and he's really going to be blind. You may have noticed there's police all over the place, and they're also watching the highway. With any luck they'll get them before they even make it to Kingston."

Terry introduced me to the police officer, handed me the holster and revolver, and said, "I'm outta here. Good luck!" And he was gone like a shot.

Christ, I thought, *won't this be great, a shootout at Hotel Dieu Hospital! Good God, there are people all over the place, including kids.* Needless to say, the police officer and I were both just a little nervous. We both realized if they made it through everyone and got to us, we were in big trouble. I even told the con not to be too comfortable, because there was no way in hell he was walking out with his girlfriend. That earned me a look—my first "look" from a blind inmate!

Thankfully, a few hours later, the police pulled the car over on the 401 and arrested the three armed occupants. To say the least, it was lucky they caught them on the highway. Just imagine if they had reached the hospital with all that firepower. It could have turned into a bloody mess!

The inmate remained in the hospital for some time, and we were told his eyes really had been badly damaged. Apparently, because of the screw up, he was blind, and nothing could be done for him. I must admit I don't recall anyone feeling all that broken up about it. In fact, we had some doubts that he really was blind, so we ran a few tests without any doctors being involved. The escort bringing him back from the hospital ran the first test. They were walking him down to the unit and attempted to walk him into a closed barrier. Well, it just couldn't be done. He certainly wasn't blind, at least not completely. So much for this "the poor guy's blind; can't see a damned thing." He could certainly see well enough to try something else. I must admit, I tried to walk him into a post to verify what I'd been told, and he had no problem seeing that thing either; so there you go.

On my way in to work one afternoon, the eight who was taking roll call asked me to hold up for a minute because he had to talk to me. Once he cleared a couple of guys, he looked at me and asked if I knew about the stabbing.

"Nope, I haven't spoken to anyone yet. What's up?"

"They were feeding lunch and one of the food stewards was stabbed! A con broke a broom handle and jammed the splintered end into him. He's downtown, and we haven't heard anything back yet, but it's serious as hell, and he might not pull through. The con is in the hole, and we have no idea why he did it. But you're going to have to watch things down there; the guys are really hot, and it could blow pretty fast."

This inmate was fairly large, at least six feet tall, but he was young, and to be honest, not overly intelligent—just one of the many followers we had doing time. He certainly couldn't have been too bright to do something like this. There was no way he could get away with it, and the young lad he attacked hadn't even been on the job long enough to piss anyone off. We found out later he had been told to do it, but he had been instructed to get the head steward, not the young fellow that he stabbed. I don't know if the powers that be ever found out who ordered the hit, but I know I couldn't stand to look at the puke. And that was not good, because it was the SHU staff who had to look after him. We were told later the food steward was going to live, but wouldn't be able to return to work. Now here I was with this useless piece of shit in the unit in addition to the asshole who had killed the two officers at the Bay. It certainly didn't make things any easier for us.

The day after the stabbing, this jerk's mother came in to visit him. I guess everyone has a mother. Anyway, the warden authorized a visit, and this really pissed everyone off. We knew he didn't have a choice; you certainly couldn't circumvent an inmate's rights or his chance at rehabilitation. But believe me, that still didn't help our feelings any.

Because he was an SHU inmate, it was up to us to escort him to V&C. Management must have been a little concerned about the inmate's health, because I was told to take an officer and escort him up and back down when he was finished. I imagine they were thinking he might bump into a wall or something, and I must admit that was a distinct possibility.

We got him up and back without incident, but it was difficult. My stomach kept churning when I looked at him, and I'm sure he knew exactly what I was wishing for. But he was very careful; in fact, he didn't so much as speak. Maybe he had more brains than I thought.

Later during the week, I was told that the deputy warden wanted me to go up and see him. So up I went, wondering what was going on. We chatted about the usual things for a while, and then he mentioned he hadn't had any complaints about me, so everything must be good. And then out of the blue he asked if I would be willing to take an acting keeper's position for a couple of months. He said Mike was going to be on leave, and they wanted me to fill in for him.

I didn't know Mike very well. I'd never been in his squad or worked very many shifts around him. Also, being in the SHU, I was kind of isolated from the rest of the institution. But I was concerned about his paperwork. Keepers did a lot of it, and Mike didn't appear to be a paperwork kind of guy, and I could envision it being a month or more behind. I think the deputy must have read my mind, because he kind of laughed and said, "You don't have to worry about Mike's bookkeeping. His books are just about the best of them all."

Taking the keeper's position wasn't a huge change of duties

for me. A keeper at the Haven wasn't in charge of the shift; he acted as the 2 I/C, and that was kind of neat. It meant I didn't have a lot of the responsibility (the CX 8 had that) and better yet, I wasn't tied down to one area, and that was a break. I could just wander around and try to act important. To be honest, it wasn't really as simple as that, but I did get a good start on learning a keeper's job.

I'm not going to dwell on the time I spent acting, because nothing momentous happened. But coming in for that first shift with three stripes on my shoulders was something. It was a great feeling; me in the exalted position of keeper! As I mentioned, I wasn't in charge of the institution unless the eight had to leave, was injured, or became ill, and you can bet I wasn't wishing for that. But all in all, it was an interesting two months.

I had been back in E unit for a couple of weeks or so; it had been relatively quiet, and I must admit we had sort of become a little relaxed—maybe too relaxed. One afternoon, I was coming in to start the night shift and headed down into the unit. I bounced into the office and saw the four I was relieving sitting at the desk with his back to me, writing. I should have known better; he tended to be just a tad high strung. Actually, he was damned hyper. Anyway, I bounced into the office, headed toward him, and said, "Hey, how ya doing?"

I'm forever thankful I was looking at him when I spoke, because he hadn't heard me come in, and unbeknownst to me, his shift had had a bit of an incident. Just as I opened my big mouth, I noticed something shiny in his left hand, and he leaped up, the chair went flying, and he spun around with his left arm flung out! Luckily for me, I jerked back and sucked my gut in at the same time. I'm also very thankful my stomach was a little smaller than it is now. His left hand was holding a shiv, and I swear to God, it came so close to my stomach, I thought he'd cut my shirt. I was positive it had to be just my shirt, because I didn't feel any pain. I looked down and took note that neither I nor my shirt was cut, so I guess it wasn't quite that close after all. But if I hadn't jumped back—? And another lucky thing was that no one else was in the office to witness the incident. He apologized, and we never spoke of it again. But both of us were really shaken up!

Once we settled down and caught our breath, he told me one of the inmates had come out of his cell with a shank and tried to "stick" an officer. There was a wrestling match, but eventually staff got the weapon and muscled him into ECA. And once again, except for some shot nerves, no one was injured. So we came out ahead and everyone went home at the end of the shift.

Shortly after this incident, that particular CX 4 transferred out of the CX group and started driving for the service. I think it was a very wise decision for him and for us.

One sunny morning, I was headed into ECA for a day shift. It was a good day, at least up until the afternoon. Somewhere around two o'clock, I received a phone call that we were getting an inmate admitted and he wasn't happy—not that they are ever very jolly coming into this place. I was also told three guys were bringing him down, and since there were three of us, I thought, *Well, no problem.* Within a few minutes I saw them coming down the corridor, and there didn't seem to be any problem. The inmate was walking normally, and the staff, as usual, just followed along. The inmate was strip searched and given a clean pair of coveralls (we could still use coveralls at the time), and we headed for the range to tuck him into a cell. When we headed for the range, two of the officers said they had to get back to their posts, and I thought, *Sure, why not?* The inmate was quiet, and that still left four of us, so I told them to take off. We made it down the range and headed for a cell. Just as we made it to the cell door, the inmate turned to me and said, "There is no fucking way in hell I'm going in there, Thibedeau!" I thought, *Oh, oh. I should've kept those two guys.*

I tried reasoning, explaining that it was almost meal time and there was even clean bedding and so on. But no way was he going to change his mind, so I gave the staff the nod, and they started wrestling. The con managed to get his arms and feet up on each side of the doorway, and there was just no way they could force him in. So there we were, once again trying to get an inmate to do something he didn't want to do and trying our damnedest not to injure him.

The staff grunted and groaned while trying to pry his arms off the doorjamb and shove him into the cell, and I was standing several feet back trying to supervise and not get physically involved exactly as I had been told to. At the same time, I was thinking of all the paperwork this asshole was causing me and the work that still had to be done, and I was getting extremely pissed. Finally I'd had enough. One of the guys told me later he spotted my look and knew something was going to blow. I let out a bellow, took a run at everyone standing in the doorway, and smashed into the whole damn pack of them. An officer and the con both went flying into the cell, and the inmate landed on his ass with the officer on top. I stood there and stared down at the con, suggesting very strongly that he'd better stay the fuck down or I was coming in and would personally put him down! I guess he figured he'd pushed us far enough, because that's right where he stayed.

Dave, the officer who ended up in the cell, came out, looked at me, and with that deep laugh we all recognized, said something like, "Boy, wasn't that something?"

Dave and I became good friends. He'd been at Millhaven since it opened, and I really don't think there was a staff member who had a harsh thought about him. He'd been with the original heavies but had seen the change coming, and like most of the staff, he had changed with it. In fact, he ended up a keeper. Several years later, he told me with that great laugh of his that I had cracked one of his ribs that day when I took a run at them in the hole. Dave ended up with back problems and sadly passed away at a relatively young age. I still remember that laugh of his, and quite often incidents we were involved in together jump into my mind.

A program for youths at risk had been operating at MI for some time. I don't know how or when it started, but the inmate committee was deeply involved with the program, and the staff were in favor of it, at least for a while. A group of youngsters would come into the institution, be shown around by some inmates, and then go into the gym. A few of the tougher looking cons would come in and start screaming at them and telling them all kinds of dire things that could happen in these places. Unfortunately, everything they were told was true. Usually during their tours they would go to the ECA, and if everything was quiet, we would lock them into a cell for a short time. The overall idea was to scare them into smartening up. Eventually word started circulating that it wasn't working all that well and the powers that be were planning to cancel it.

In fact, I was chatting with one of the officers in the ID building shortly after a group of these kids had left. He just shook his head and said, "They don't seem very scared to me. In fact; one of the little fuckers told his buddy he can't wait to get in here, and his buddy said, 'yeah, me too.'"

A few weeks after we had this discussion, I was working in the ECA, and the buzzer went off. I went to the door, and it was one of the inmate committee members with a couple of these kids. The con yelled through the door, "We're coming in; I'm going to show these kids the hole!"

Well, I thought, *someone must have made this stupid asshole the warden and forgot to tell me about it.* I have to admit I didn't get along with this particular inmate very well; we just couldn't see eye to eye. I always believed in the idea of an inmate committee, but sometimes a jerk would get elected who firmly believed he ran everything, and that was all there was to it. This guy was one of the jerks. As soon as he informed me he was coming in, he made my mind up for me. I simply informed him in no uncertain terms that he wasn't coming in and to get the hell away from the door. He kept insisting and I guess I lost it a little bit, because I told him the only fucking way he was coming in was to go into a cell!

The poor kids weren't sure what was going on. I could tell they didn't really know if this was real or just put on for their benefit. I advised them to go back to the control and wait for someone to come and get them, and that's when they realized this was not a show. I could see the S control officer watching us, and I signaled him to phone for extra staff. Just as he was reaching for the phone, the inmate looked around and saw the same thing I did. I guess he thought he had pushed things far enough, because he took off with the kids in tow.

That was the last time the program ever came to the ECA; in fact; it was cancelled shortly after that episode. I don't know if my report was part of the decision, and to be honest, I don't really care. However, I do fervently hope the program helped straighten out a few of the kids. Even if it kept one of them out of prison, it should be classed as a success.

A few months after I finished my acting assignment, I was called up to the deputy's office for a meeting with him and David, my boss in the SHU. Once I was sitting down, the deputy started the meeting by looking at me and saying, "Vern, we've received a phone call from the police regarding a threat against you, and this time we're taking it seriously."

I don't really remember where the information originated other than that it was from an outside informant somewhere. *Christ,* I thought, *here we go again.*

"And that's it; no more info. All the police could get was that an inmate's going to try to get you; we have no names and no method."

If inmates really wanted to get an officer, it was relatively easy. Fortunately, I was in the SHU, and security was exceptionally tight. But that didn't mean it couldn't be done. It would have been simple for an inmate to wait for me to open a cell door and then step forward to "stick" me. The con would certainly have gone to court and been sentenced, but several of them were doing life anyway, and in Canada, you could only be sentenced to life once! An inmate who accomplished something like this would likely have had his parole held up for a few years, but that was about it, especially if his future behaviour was adequate. And on top of that, he would have been a hero to most of the other inmates.

The deputy told me the institution was willing to transfer me to another unit or even to another institution, but I had to make that decision. He added that any of the institutions would have been glad to have me. It was nice to know I could transfer if I wanted, but at the same time, where would it have ended? In my mind, transferring was the same as running, not that I'm any braver or any more foolish than anyone else. Also, I knew if the inmates ever got wind of this, and without a doubt they would, I would never live it down, and that would have made it very difficult for me to work in any prison.

Once I had processed all the information, and it was a lot, I ended up telling them I appreciated the concern but felt I'd be safer in the SHU. I let them know I'd take as many precautions as possible. Or maybe they told me to; I can't really recall.

I didn't tell the staff about any of this, but I was much more security-conscious. I made damned sure I wasn't standing in front of a cell door when it was opened and made doubly sure I didn't stand around with my back to any inmates. I was also very careful on my way home from work for several weeks. I kept remembering that warden in Quebec, but there was not really much I could do other than try to be aware of what was going on around me. I also have to admit I never mentioned this to Sheila. Perhaps I should have talked it over with her, but I didn't think her worrying about it would help anything, and there was nothing either of us could do about it; after all, a person does have to live his or her life. But you can bet I was much more alert to my surroundings whenever I was out with the family. So I just let it ride, and nothing ended up happening. Whether that was because I was careful, I don't know. I guess it's just another 'who knows'?

One day I received a phone call at home to tell me an inmate had escaped from Millhaven and to keep an eye out for him. As soon as they told me his name, I thought, *Hell, that's the same guy that took off from Four Block at the Bay!* I don't remember how long he was gone, but he did end up back at Millhaven. This fellow was quite a guy. I don't remember him ever injuring anyone inside or even giving staff a hard time; I know I never had a problem with him. Mind you, he was apparently willing to shoot an OPP officer during the Bay escape. I guess he just didn't like being locked up. Or he liked the challenge.

Shortly after this escape, we briefly thought we had had an inmate take off from the SHU! During a count we came up one short. Even after the recount, we were still short one, but by this time, we knew who was missing and had verified that he should have been in his cell. God, the way my heart was pounding. I thought I was on the verge of having a heart attack. Extra staff poured in from the other units, and every cell in the place was checked. At the same time, staff unlocked and looked into every duct, and every area in the unit was double checked—no con! I don't know if management had notified the police, but after we had checked everywhere, we just stood around looking at each other, scratching our heads, and trying to figure out how in hell he could've made it out of the unit. We were also thinking of the repercussions this was going to cause and knowing full well they would be tremendous. You just don't have escapes out of an SHU.

I was on the first floor wandering around the servery area when I heard a loud thump and someone screaming, "Got him! I got him! Elevator; need help!"

I whipped around the corner, and there was one of my

guys looking like he'd seen a ghost, and there was the missing con crouching in the corner, looking even more scared than the officer. I can't explain how relieved I was locking that inmate up. How could I have explained an escape from an SHU? You can't!

Later, I pulled the officer aside and asked him how in hell he had stumbled onto the hiding place in the elevator. "Jesus," I said, "that place was checked several times."

"You won't believe this, but it's a good one! I just stuck my head into the elevator, and more for fun than anything, I yelled up, "If you don't get the fuck down right now, I'm going to shoot." And someone starts screaming, "Jesus Christ, don't shoot, hold on, I'm coming down!'"

I should emphasize here that there was no chance of the inmate being shot. We certainly didn't carry weapons in the units; we didn't even carry night sticks except in special circumstances. Carrying weapons was absolutely illegal. And even worse, it upset the inmates.

He continued his story by saying, "I looked up, saw a ceiling tile move, and suddenly the con jumped down and almost landed in my arms! Holy fuck, I almost pissed myself. I didn't even have time to get out of the way!"

I told him I was so relived to see that con that if he had wet himself, I would've given him my pants to wear. I can still remember how euphoric we all felt after locking that asshole up. The rest of the shift was kind of a happy blur for all of us.

Fire was one of most scary and dangerous situations a correctional officer could face. During our training, we practiced the fundamentals of fire fighting, but that was all—fundamentals. For several years after I started in the service, we didn't even have Scott Air Packs to protect us against smoke inhalation. Thankfully, that changed, and we eventually had them spaced throughout every institution. I only remember two cell fires while I was in the SHU, and neither one was serious. On the other hand, they didn't end up being serious because of the actions of the staff.

And the Haven did have its share of fires. I was told shortly before I transferred in that one of the units had had a terrible cell fire. The inmate was in the cell when he started the fire, and by the time staff realized what he had done, it was roaring. In fact, it was hot enough to warp the cell door, and the control officers couldn't open it electronically. The CX 4 in charge of the unit ended up getting a crow bar and eventually managed to pry the door open, but he also succeeded in getting his hands and arms badly burned. I have to admit I can't remember if they managed to save the inmate, but if they didn't, it wasn't from lack of trying.

I do know there wasn't a thing in the local paper regarding the staff's effort. I realize the service didn't go running to the media with information about situations like that, but on the other hand, the media didn't seem to have difficulty digging out information when it was negative—strange the way things seem to work.

"Fire!"

I was working days in the unit when I heard the scream. Needless to say, I was terrified of cell fires. By the time I whipped down to the cell, staff had the fire out and the inmate secured and on his way to ECA for the nurse to check! Amazing, considering the fact I hadn't exactly poked around on my way down. I couldn't have asked for better than that. I'll admit it wasn't much of a fire, but if the staff hadn't spotted it and reacted properly, it would have been.

Once everything settled down and we were back to normal, I thought I'd better check the cell for damage. There was that all-important report I had to write, and logging damage was a large part of it. I informed the control what I was doing and told them I'd wave when I wanted the cell opened. I reached the cell, and once I had assured myself that it was the proper one, I gave the control a wave. Just as I stepped in I noticed a few plastic bottles under the desk had melted a little, but I didn't give it another thought. I didn't see any flames or danger, so I cautiously took a couple of steps into the cell, and suddenly, *wham!*

I couldn't believe it—there was no air, not one God damned breath! I was only about four paces into that cell, and by the time I made it back out onto the range, I was staggering and had to grab the wall so I wouldn't fall over. I'd never run into anything like that before and thankfully never did again. Thank God the guys in the control didn't pick this particular time to play games. Sometimes when you went into a cell they'd close the door behind you just to shake you up a little. If they had done that, I don't think I would've walked out. Imagine the officers trying to explain that one to management, never mind to my wife!

The second fire I was involved with was in the ECA. Luckily, before it really got going, one of the guys happened to take a look down the range and gave a yell that he saw smoke. I stuck my head out of the office, and sure enough, there was smoke. I hit the alarm to let unit staff know we needed assistance, grabbed the cell door key, and headed for the cell on the run. One officer came with me, and the other ran to grab a fire extinguisher. Thankfully the door wasn't hot yet, and it opened without a problem. And there was the stupid son of a bitch squatting on the floor looking at us with a stupid-ass grin on his face. He had placed his mattress between himself and the door and set it, his bed sheets, and some clothing on fire. The CX 2 that was with me, luckily a huge, strong guy, reached in, grabbed the stupid idiot by his hair, and hauled his ass out! We didn't have to worry about fighting him, though; he was too busy trying to catch his breath and put out a couple of small fires on his pants. By then the other officer had made it back with the extinguisher, and he put the fire out. Thankfully, we didn't even need the fire hose.

This was accomplished in just a few minutes, and by that time the place was crawling with staff. Hit that emergency button in the hole and you got a response! We always had a very real fear that inmates, somehow, would grab a cell key and gain control of the place. God, I can't even imagine what a mess that would have been.

It only took a few minutes to get back to normal. That is, except for all the yelling and screaming the inmates always did. As usual, this carried on for twenty minutes or so but then thankfully quieted down. But in the back of our minds we knew that just a couple more minutes and it could have been a lot worse—maybe even deadly!

A few weeks later, Smith from the Bay came back into my life. He had only been there a few days when a psychologist that I knew quite well came into the ECA to see me. He told me Smith was due for release the next day and he was worried about him. "I have visions of him sitting somewhere by himself and starving because no one brought him anything to eat. I just can't get it out of my head."

"I tend to agree, Jim. The first time I saw him was at the Bay. He was lying on his bed staring at the ceiling; he does have a real fascination with ceilings, and I think starving is a real possibility."

I had known this particular psychologist for several years; I first met him when I was at Collin's Bay, and we got along really well. I suppose part of that was because he was not what we called a "con-lover"; he did his job to the best of his ability, and that was that.

The next day Jim came down and gave me the good news that he had found a place willing to take Smith and that it was all set up. I must admit the news made me feel better about Smith being released. And that was the last I ever saw or heard of inmate Smith.

You can meet a lot of interesting people in the prison system, both staff and inmates. Eventually, I'll probably mention some staff, but right now, I am more interested in writing about inmates. I must admit it's easier to write about inmates than it is the staff.

One such interesting person was an inmate I'll call Progie. I could call him a lot of things, but they wouldn't be very polite. This character was around thirty and had lived in northern Ontario; in fact, he was from my home town. And in all the time I knew him, he was either in the SHU or the hole; there just wasn't anywhere else to put him. You have likely heard the phrase "strong as a bull." Well, that saying was invented for Progie. He was squat, heavy, and all muscle—including his head, both inside and out. Progie and I always got along relatively well. We could speak to each other fairly politely—unless he was really upset about something, that is. Hell, I even managed to reason with him at times.

One day I came in to start the night shift in the SHU, and I could tell something was seriously wrong. Most of the staff were just standing around the office talking. One glance told me they were stressed, upset, and had been in some kind of a physical confrontation. And the CX 4 proceeded to fill me in.

Progie had been out in the yard, and when he came in he refused to go to his cell. This happened fairly often and usually there was no reasoning with him, so they had to wrestle him in. It was six officers against Progie (that made it almost an even match, with Progie still slightly in the lead). Eventually, they got him down and cuffed. I can't remember if they had leg irons on him or not, but as usual, he refused to walk. That meant staff had to pick this bull moose up and carry him to the hole. It started out as usual: one guy on each arm, one on each leg, and one following along with a nightstick. These night sticks are well made. They were about three feet long, and if I remember correctly, they were made out of hickory wood just like in the movies.

So there they were, struggling down the range to the hole and lugging this oversized asshole. Naturally all the cons were banging on their cell doors and screaming at the staff to stop kicking their buddy. You'd never have known they didn't like him any more than we did—maybe even less. Up to this point in the story, I was on the verge of chuckling, because this was standard procedure with Progie. Ain't that a great way to earn a living? But then I realized there was more to the story, because no one was grinning. The four continued on and said everything was going along as usual until the guy holding onto Progie's left arm got a little careless. Progie cranked his head to the side, managed to get the officer's thumb into his mouth, and chomped down on it, and he wasn't about to let go!

So there they were: an officer screaming in pain and the cons laughing, banging on the doors, and hollering to their buddies to let them know what was going on. The staff yelled and cursed while they tried to pry Progie's mouth open. In short, it was nothing but a God damned chaotic mess. The officer with the nightstick started whacking and jabbing at Progie with absolutely no effect. We had always believed this guy's pain sensors didn't reach up to his brain, and this proved it. And then to the shock of everyone, the nightstick actually broke, and Progie was still chewing on that officer's thumb. If I remember correctly, someone took a swing to Progie's crotch area, and that was the only thing that made him let go. They finally got him to a cell in the hole, shoved him in, and locked the door. The officer was injured badly enough to go downtown to the hospital to get fixed up and have the usual shots. The four said the thumb looked like it had been chewed down to the bone.

Eventually, like almost all inmates, Progie's time was up, and he was turned loose on the public. I would hazard a guess that he did every minute of his sentence. I can't imagine he would have been let out on an early parole; however, you could never be sure, so I probably shouldn't say something like that. I do remember us all praying he'd be out west somewhere when the police picked him up or shot him, and there was no doubt one or the other was going to happen.

I'm not sure how long Progie was out, but I was working days when they brought him down again. And to top it off, I knew he hadn't managed to get caught out west, because I was standing there looking at the idiot! At least he did say hi to me before informing me he wasn't going to any fucking cell.

"You know fucking well you're going be put into one, so why cause yourself and us the pain?" I said.

He kept insisting that he shouldn't have been there, because he had only been sentenced to provincial time. I told him all I could do was phone the sentence administrator and get a verification of his sentence, and then come hell or high water he would be going into a cell.

He just looked at me and said, "Not fucking likely, Thibedeau. You can stick that cell up your ass!"

Oh God, here we go again, I thought

I went into the office, phoned the administrator, received the answer I imagined I would, and then immediately phoned N area and told them to send in some extra staff. There was no damned sense in fooling around. As soon as I heard the barrier open and close, back out to the hallway I went. I looked at Progie and told him that one way or the other he was going into a cell. I tried to talk him into going peacefully and told him he could iron out his problem the next day. Oh no, not Progie; he hadn't changed one damned little bit. Luckily, it wasn't nearly the mess it had been the last time we tangled with Progie. Of course, this time there were extra staff, and it only took a few minutes to get him into the cell and no one was injured, including Progie. Another successful operation with just some torn shirts and a lot of muscle stiffness. But that's not the end of this story. Oh no, not by a long shot!

The next morning, down trooped the sentence administrator with some guy in a suit, both wearing stupid, shit-assed embarrassed grins. And with a sudden flash of insight, I just knew it; Progie had been right! I didn't know who in hell to blame, but believe me, I felt like dropping those two idiots. That fight we'd had yesterday had been for nothing, and someone could've been badly injured. And I was right; they told me Progie was a provincial prisoner and their staff would be there shortly to take him to Millbrook.

Millbrook, as far as I knew, was a maximum-security jail, and I knew Progie hadn't said anything about going there. Now these idiots were telling me they wanted him out of his cell to sign some papers. Once I had given my head a shake, I made it very clear that I would take them down the range to get their papers signed, but there was no way in hell he was coming out of his cell. I also insisted that they not tell Progie he was going to a max and just let him know he was going to a provincial jail.

Well, they didn't think that was the proper thing to do. They thought they should be fair to the inmate and insisted on telling him where he was going. That's when I kind of lost it! I told them they were both fucking idiots, but if they wanted, they were welcome to go down, and I would even tell the control officer to open the cell door for them. "But there is no way in fucking hell I'm sending anyone down with you. We're sick of fighting that asshole, but if you insist, just go right ahead and have fun. When you're finished we'll pick up the fucking pieces and shoot the son of a bitch if we have to. And if you don't like it, get your ass up and see the God damn warden about it!" I guess there are times when a person has just had enough bull shit.

I guess that was enough for them, because they took off out of the unit. I went down to the cell with an officer and gave Progie the news through the food slot. I told him he was right, handed him the papers to sign, and ordered him to pack up his stuff, because some provincial guys were coming to pick him up. I made a joke about it and told him the next time I would listen to him and not to the idiots up front. He gave a bit of a laugh, said it had been fun, and then asked me where he was going.

"Christ," I fibbed, "I don't know. That's up to the province."

His reply was just, "Okay, I'll be ready when they get here."

Next I phoned T control and told them to make sure they phoned me when the provincial guys made it in. A short time later T control phoned, and I went out to N area to meet the escorts. I briefed them on the type of con they were collecting and then said, "Let's get down and get him out. Oh, and one other thing—for Christ's sake don't tell him where he's going until you have him locked in your vehicle."

After my little spiel, they looked at me as if I were nuts or something. It was easy to tell they were thinking, *Hell, we work in a max and handle cons like this all the time. What the hell's this federal guy all excited about?*

I didn't really give a damn what they thought; all I wanted to do was get his ass out of the unit and as far away from me as possible.

Once Progie and the escort left, we just stood around looking at each other and grinning. We even made bets on how long Progie would be staying in a provincial joint. I forget exactly how long he was away, but eventually we had him back. From what I understand, when he came back, he had something like six assault charges against him. I have often wondered what those tough guys on that escort thought of Progie after a few weeks.

I don't remember anything earth-shattering happening for a while, so things must have been relatively quiet. Of course, in this line of work, *relative* was the operative word, and quiet didn't last forever.

One afternoon I was on my way in for a night shift, and once again the guy in the ID building asked me to hold on for a minute. With a sinking stomach, I turned and headed back. "Just want to let you know a con was killed in your unit. A lot of the work's done though, and the body's been taken out. But the OPP are on the way in for the search. But don't worry," he said with a grin, "You'll have extra guys on overtime to help you out."

Naturally, all this was said with a laugh. Guys just loved to see other guys doing extra work.

"You're just a barrel of good news. I don't suppose you know who was killed?" I imagine I was hoping it was the con who had killed the guys in the Bay, but no such luck.

Shortly after I got down to the unit, I was informed that the OPP would be in shortly, and as per normal routine, I was to pair up one police officer with one correctional officer. Each inmate would be taken out of his cell, frisked, and locked in a common room while his cell was searched. Depending on how many search teams were working, we could have up to five inmates locked in a common room at the same time.

Sad to say, I don't remember what precipitated this particular murder or even if anyone was ever charged for it. There were just too many similar episodes to remember them all.

A week or so after the murder, I was asked if I would do the keeper's job again. I told them I would for a couple of reasons. For one thing, I thought it would be good to get out of the SHU for awhile; I was really thinking I could do with a change. There was also a rumour going around that there was going to be a CS competition, and I had definitely made up my mind to write the next one. Supervisor competitions didn't come around very often.

Anyway, I went up acting again, and it was a fairly quiet time for me. However, one shift wasn't quiet for one of the keepers. A couple of days later, John filled me in on what had happened. He said he'd been doing a tour of the units and was called over to J unit. When he arrived, the staff waved him over to one of the ranges where the CX 4 was having a discussion with an inmate who was standing at the top of some stairs. John said he walked around the corner, looked up at the inmate, and then took a second look when he saw him holding a razor blade! As soon as he told me the inmate's name I could place him. He'd had been around a long time and had slashed up several times, and most of his slash-ups had been quite serious.

During our discussion, John said he didn't do a very good job of talking the con down. "Christ," he said, "the con looked me straight in the eye and yelled, 'Hey goof, watch this!' And he started slashing at his arm and blood started spurting up! Hell, that's the first time I've watched someone actually slash, and I was damned near sick. In fact, the four heaved his guts up all over the place."

"I gotta tell ya," I interjected, "better you than me."

"Anyway, we get this guy to the hospital and the doc starts working on him. And then he looks right at the con and says, 'There's so much scar tissue the stitches may not hold, and if they don't, you're not going to make it. If they do hold, please be aware there's no way we can put any more stitches into these arms of yours. If you do it again, you'll bleed out and that'll be it. It's up to you.'"

And I don't remember him ever slashing up again. Ain't that something? Shortly after I went back into the SHU, the competition poster for a correctional supervisor position was posted. I was encouraged to write it by several higher-ups and a couple of keepers, and I must admit that made me feel pretty good. On the other hand, I was thinking, *Jeez, what if I don't make the list? I'll look like a dumb jerk.* I think these competitions tightened my stomach up as much as the incidents did. If I remember correctly, a couple of our supervisors, including my boss, teamed up and held study sessions for a few of us.

Eventually, I received the date to report to RHQ for the written portion, and down I went, sweating all the way. Even after eight years in the service, these things still made me nervous. I must admit, once I finished the written section, I felt pretty damned good, and while walking out I was telling myself that I'd aced it. Then I remembered that was what I had thought at the Bay, and I hadn't even made their God damned list. Well, you can imagine what those thoughts did to my sense of well-being—sent it right into the toilet, that's what.

The next day, back to work I went. Of course everyone wanted to know how I had done, and they asked all kinds of questions. But other than that, everything was normal. All I could do was wait and hope I had made it to the next stage. And sure enough, eventually I received my notice to report for the oral portion of the competition. And off I went. Once again, when I finished the oral section I felt really good about it. Within a month or so the results came out. And I had done really well. I forget if Jack was ahead of me or behind me, but we were close. Now it was just a matter of waiting in case there were any appeals against it.

I don't really remember if there were any, but eventually I received notice that I had been successful and was being offered a CS position at Joyceville Institution! This place was also known as JI or The Ville. As usual, there was a phone number to contact to confirm my interest and receive my reporting date.

I must admit I was quite proud of myself. But I really wasn't sure about leaving Millhaven. It was an excellent place to work, and the staff were really close, both uniformed and nonuniformed. This decision was much more difficult than the one I had had to make at the Bay. This time I really wasn't sure if I wanted to leave.

I haven't really mentioned a lot of the physical stuff that happened at Millhaven. Most occurrences I have forgotten, and I imagine they would sound repetitive anyway. But there were many such incidents, and several of them were serious. Once again, most of the injuries seemed to happen to staff. Fortunately, when it came to injuries, I was rather lucky.

Eventually, my papers came through. I wrapped everything up at Millhaven, completed my last shift, and headed home. And once my rest days were finished, I headed for JI to begin the next step in my career!

Chapter 15

Attempted escape from the SHU.
Promoted & transferred to JI.

The promotion from correctional officer to *senior* correctional officer was a stepping-stone and gave me some authority over staff. But going from senior correctional officer to correctional supervisor was a much larger jump. The CS was in charge of the prison on weekends and back shifts and also had the responsibility to award disciplinary actions that could be relatively severe. A disciplinary award could be anything from a verbal reprimand up to a three-day suspension or fine. A supervisor could also recommend consequences up to dismissal from the service, and in addition, a CS was also responsible for a squad of officers. This included ensuring their training was up to date, completing yearly performance evaluations, and, if an officer was having difficulties, possibly performing quarterly evaluations or even recommending release from the service. When in charge of the prison, a CS also had the authority to place an inmate into segregation and call in the IERT if necessary during an emergency. All in all, it was a lot of responsibility.

I pulled into the parking lot and suddenly realized how differently one tended to look at an institution as a supervisor. I have to admit to being apprehensive; this was a huge change for me. On top of that, I'd only been to Joyceville a couple of times on escort duty. Hell, I didn't even know if I was in the proper parking lot. I had to get directions to find the keeper's hall, and once there, I was taken to the deputy's office and introduced. After we had completed our little chat, I was shown around the units and told I would receive a week or so of training and then I'd be on my own.

Joyceville was a medium-security institution and operated under the living unit concept, which was a little different from what I was used to. Each living unit had one LU 2 in charge of it, and they were paid at the CX 6 level. Because the Ville was a medium-security institution, I was being paid at a CX 5 level, but I was in charge of the institution on back shifts—strange. So the LU 2 was paid more than me yet he had to have my permission to even put an inmate into segregation. Once again—strange.

Because LU 2s covered the living units, there were only six CSs working at JI. This meant we had to work more back shifts and weekends. I must admit that didn't make me overly happy, and several months later, the regional office decided that number was going to drop by one. Naturally, that meant more back shifts for the rest of us—whoopee.

I got along well with everyone and still did trips to the units even though there was an LU 2 on duty in each area. Unfortunately, I didn't have time during the day shift, because it was busy and I was usually tied to the keeper's hall. When I did get manage to visit the units, the staff were friendly and said they were glad to see me and to visit anytime.

I had been at the Ville for a month or so, and one night the LU 2 phoned to tell me he had to put an inmate into segregation. He explained what was going on, and I told him to get started and I'd be right down. I was thinking they might need another person, and also I was used to being present when something like this was happening; after all, it was my responsibility. By the time I made it to segregation, it was almost over, and there hadn't been any difficulties anyway. But the LU 2 thanked me for coming down and said it was unusual for a keeper to show up. I must admit I found that a little strange. Actually, I found a few things strange. It was certainly different from what I was used to.

One evening not long after that, I received a phone call from the officer at the main entrance. The call was a bit of a shocker, but after eight years in the prison system, it shouldn't even have been a surprise. Anyway, Ed phoned to tell me there was a guy waiting to pick an inmate up and take him out on a temporary absence. I told him it was okay; I had the permit in the office, and he went out once a week for an AA meeting.

"Oh," he said, "I know that. The problem's with the guy picking him up. He's an ex con from the Bay!"

"Well that's not okay; I'll be right there." And I took off to the main entrance. Sure enough, there was the inmate that used to operate the radio room at the Bay; Christ, I would have recognized the asshole from a mile away. I had a chat with him, and sure enough, everything was authorized. He had papers to prove he was out on parole and papers allowing him to regularly pick this other inmate up and take him to the meetings. *Boy*, I thought, *that's just great; a pervert taking a convict to AA. You just never know.*

I went into the control and explained what was going on, and all he could say was, "Holy fuck, where in hell are the brains of the people who authorize this shit?"

"I know how you feel, but it's not up to us," I said. "We can only go with the flow and hope it's not serious when something goes wrong." Unfortunately, it was going to be serious when this one went wrong!

A few years later, I ran into the same inmate at KP. And when I looked at him, I couldn't help thinking it would've been great if I could have had his parole pulled that evening at JI. It would have saved a family in the area a great deal of pain.

I had been at JI for a couple of months before I ran into my first staff problem. We were told we were going to have seven or eight new officers in for a visit. They were in the induction training course and would be with us for a week for on-the-job training. We were also informed that some of them were female. *Well*, I thought, *no big deal; this happens quite often.*

When they showed up, I was working days in the keeper's hall, and I had a 2 I/C that was really good at his job. The idea with this training was to put the trainees in posts with the regular staff. Normally this would have been a simple job. I just assigned each new officer to a post with regular JI staff and switched them around after each half day or so. I drew up a list of new staff and where they were assigned, but before giving it to their instructor, I handed it to the CX 3 for a final perusal. I was just about to head out with the list when the three said he would recommend moving a few of the new staff around. He pointed out who was on a couple of the posts and said if I sent a female to those posts, two of the JI staff would likely be on the phone to tell us they were going home sick. I had a difficult time grasping this nonsense and told him so.

"I tell you, Vern, I agree. Everyone with half a goddamn brain knows we're going to end up with female CXs, but some of the older staff are having trouble wrapping their heads around it. In fact a couple told me they'd quit before working with a female."

"Jesus, that's crazy. They'd be out of a job and the female staff would be working here anyway—in fact, that would open up more positions for the women. Christ, they'd better grow up and smell the roses."

Once again he agreed and said the decision was up to me. Part of me thought I should bring this nonsense to a head, but I chickened out and rearranged the roster. I really shouldn't have taken the easy way out, and it still bugs the hell out of me that I did.

The time rolled along, and by the time I had been at JI for five months or so, I was getting to know the place. However, I still wasn't used to not being involved with the units or with the inmates.

Hell, I couldn't even get used to having fewer staff evaluations to complete, and I should have been elated about that. But I really didn't care for the extra back shifts, and then we were told we were going to lose a supervisor's position. That meant more back shifts and more weekends, and that really made me unhappy.

Around this time I received a phone call from Jack. He had accepted a supervisor's position at KP at the same time I was transferred to JI. Jack asked if I would be interested in transferring to Kingston Pen. He informed me there was an opening and it was mine if I wanted it. He also told me I had a few days to think it over but I had to let him know by the following week. There's no doubt in my mind Jack had talked it over with the deputy and likely with the warden; that made a guy feel important. In any case, it gave me something to think about, and to be honest, I was finding the Ville boring.

KP had a lot of history, both good and bad. After all, it had been built in the 1830s or so, and it was one the first penitentiaries built in Canada. It even had once housed both male and female inmates at the same time, and I'd been told it was still old school. Routines were strictly adhered to, and a keeper might have been classed as a correctional supervisor, but he was still a keeper. Jeez, the cells didn't even have hot water in them yet! When you drove past the place, it had an aura around it that, to me, seemed dark and ominous.

On the way home that day, I thought about the pros and cons, and once I made it home, Sheila and I talked it over quite extensively. There were several more supervisors working at KP, so that meant fewer weekends and back shifts, but on the other hand, KP had a hell of a lot more problems than the Ville. But the last major riot had been 1971, which was about ten years earlier, so I figured they must have things, relatively speaking, under control. The major item causing me to hesitate was that KP was now a PC institution. Those inmates were not nice people to be around. I don't necessarily mean they were any more dangerous than other inmates; actually, they were less so. My concern was dealing with them while knowing the type of crime they were in for. They still had to be treated like any other inmates, and I could envision myself having some difficulty in that area. Little did I know that at times I would have more problems with the staff than with the inmates.

After much debating and thinking, I decided to put in for the transfer. I contacted Jack and told him my decision. I also said I would speak to my deputy and asked Jack not to say anything until then. I also told him I had no idea how long it would be before I could report. His reply was to not worry. The main thing was for KP to know I was coming. In fact, Jack seemed really pleased about my decision.

Now came the awkward part of this little episode, and that was informing my deputy that I had decided to transfer. I knew he wouldn't be very happy. I don't usually blow my own horn, but I was doing an excellent job for him, and we both knew it.

As soon as I was back at work, I went to give him the news. I was right; he wasn't happy, and that certainly increased my discomfort level. He reminded me about having three supervisors close to retiring and told me that would mean more responsibilities for me. He also said he had been planning to have me act for him whenever he was away from the institution. In fact, he said I was about the only one he felt comfortable leaving in his position. He didn't have to tell me how that would have given my career a boost, but he did anyway.

Eventually, we reached an agreement. He would sign my papers as long as KP would allow me to stay at JI until he could get someone in to take my place. He said he would contact Don, who was the deputy at KP, and let him know what we were doing. He would also find out how quickly they wanted me to transfer. I let him know I really appreciated his cooperation and, at least in my mind, I left his office on good terms. I really believe that, because I ran into him several times at meetings and other places, and I never felt any stiffness between us.

I forget now how long it took, but my transfer to Kingston Penitentiary finally came through. As usual, I was apprehensive about transferring from a comfortable environment, especially since I was going to KP. But when I compared it to the way I had felt when I was on my way to MI, this transfer was a breeze.

And that's where I headed after my rest days.

Chapter 16

Transferred to KP. Union conflicts. Union president ordered off property.

On my first day of work at KP, it was winter and I was on the day shift. I pulled into the parking lot, climbed out of the car, and looked at the place. In some ways it reminded me of the Bay—high walls and towers. But these walls were much higher, and there were five towers rather than the four at the Bay. At that time, it struck me as very dark and forbidding. As a matter of fact, the word sinister came to mind. Even with my feeling of apprehension, I thought, *Boy, the history here—if only walls could talk.*

While I was walking down the sidewalk toward the north gate, I had to keep reinforcing the thought that I was a supervisor and belonged here. I walked and walked for what seemed like ages, and kept saying, "I'm a keeper; I'm a keeper."

Eventually, I made it to the gate and entered through that huge, thick wooden door with a sense of awe, and I noticed a couple of pock-marks in it. I found out later they were from a firearm. Apparently, someone who didn't care for Kingston Pen very much had driven by and fired a few shots at it. Once I was inside, though, I have to admit my sense of awe didn't last very long; I soon came crashing back to reality and realized it was just a prison, albeit a very old one. The CX 4 at the gate told me that I was expected and that I might as well go on down to the keeper's hall. He informed me that a couple of keepers were in, but it was still a little early for the deputy. I knew where the hall was, so at least I didn't have to ask directions, and that was a little bit of a relief. I headed down, and a correctional officer unlocked the barrier and let me in.

This hall was different from any other hall I'd ever been in. It was huge. There were two large desks with a keeper sitting at one and a CX 4 at the other. In addition to the barrier I had come through, there was one on the other side of the hall that I assumed led to the wing and cells area. An officer ran, well actually walked back and forth with a key letting people in and out of both barriers. The next thing I spotted was the count board, and it was bigger and older than any I'd ever seen. Behind the desks and securely attached to the wall was an extremely large steel safe with two heavy-duty doors. There was no doubt in my mind that it was full of firearms. And just then, as if to justify my thought, the keeper took a key, opened it up, and handed a shotgun, a bandolier of ammunition, and a .38 in a holster to an officer. For a sharp second I thought I had arrived just as they were having a problem, but it was just the normal routine, and my stomach settled back down to its normal queasiness.

After several minutes, the traffic through the hall slowed to a stop, and the keeper taking the roll call looked in my direction and said, "That's about it. Come on and we'll head up to the duty keeper's office and slip in and see the deputy at the same time."

He introduced himself as Cecil as we headed out through the barrier and started walking toward a large building off to the left. He told me that in the old days this building had housed the female cons. Now it held the warden's office, the deputy's office, the duty keeper's office, and several other offices. "It's just a hive of activity," Cecil jokingly informed me.

We entered the nearest barrier, which was open, climbed a narrow set of cement stairs to the second level, and we were there. At the head of the stairs he waved toward an office and said the two security clerks worked out of it, and we headed across the hall to the duty keeper's office. As we entered a large office, Cecil told me the deputy was just down the hall and the warden was upstairs. Cecil mentioned that we had one CX 8, and his office was also in the area.

Cecil started to explain the duty keeper's job to me, and it sounded mind-boggling. He told me that we took turns doing the job a week at a time, and it was one busy job, and before a long weekend it was nuts. Then, being a smart-ass, he said, "You'll just love it. Hope you like paperwork." He explained that the guy in this position did just about everything. He made sure the roster was full for the next day, set up the escorts, authorized annual leave, made sure any sick leave was covered, and pretty much anything else that popped up. And to top it off, he said, "Everybody and their goddamn fucking dog phones this office for information or to find out why things aren't going the way they should be. It doesn't matter if it's a security issue or not; we're supposed to know the answer and should be able to straighten it out and straighten it out immediately!"

I was hoping he was exaggerating, but I was to find out he wasn't; if anything, he was understating. Cecil told me he would be tied up in the office all day and introduced me to another keeper and suggested I just hang around with Marv for the day. And that's what I did. Marv basically did his job with me in tow and at the same time gave me a tour of the place. He also introduced me to numerous staff, most of whose names I wouldn't remember for quite some time. That was one of my problems with transferring around. Like a lot of people, I have difficultly remembering names, and as a CS, it was never too long before I ended up doing roll call. Just try that when you're in a new prison and don't know most of the names—lots of fun!

All in all, it was an extremely interesting day. The wing and cell area, commonly called "the wing," was one huge, domed, circular area. All ranges exited into the wing, and inmates had to pass through the wing to go anywhere. Basically this was the same idea as the strip at the Bay and N area at Millhaven. To exit the hall into the wing, the correctional officer working the hall had to unlock the barrier and let us down. When we reached the bottom of the stairs, another two had to unlock a barrier to let us into the wing. And there I was—a keeper and standing in the wing at Kingston Penitentiary. Who would've ever thought!

The place was huge! I stood there and counted fourteen barriers. Signs posted on the wall next to each barrier told me eight of them led to ranges. The ranges were named A through H. but C and D were closed and had been for years. There was also a barrier leading to dissociation, one to the kitchen, one to the south passage, one to the radio room, one to the recreation area, and of course the one going up to the keeper's hall.

All inmate traffic had to use the south passage to exit or enter the wing. There was even the familiar metal scanner. Inmates had to use A range to reach the institutional hospital, and just past G was a small office sticking out from the wall used by the four in charge of the wing. I was also informed that each range had two tiers. *Ha, just like the Bay,* I thought. To denote an address for an inmate sleeping on, say A range on the upper tier in cell number 10, you would say 2A10. Nothing to it; just a little practice did the trick. To reach the upper ranges we had to use stairs in the wing area. Marv told me there was another range above each of the existing ranges. These ranges also had two tiers but had been closed for years. However, he said there had been rumours floating around that they might be reopening them, and C and D ranges as well.

E range housed inmates like Clifford Olsen who were deemed to require long-term segregation for their own protection. In other words, it was for inmates that had to have protection from the protected. I was to discover we also had a few inmates in the dissociation area for protection. I guess they were being protected from the inmates being protected from the protected inmates.

Figure that one out. And people wonder why some correctional staff are half-crazy at times! In fact, shortly after I transferred out of KP, they received another notorious killer. Naturally, due to the nature of Paul Bernardo's crimes and subsequent notoriety, he had to be locked up on E range, and eventually Williams came along as well. However, in my mind, at least, Bernardo and Williams's crimes were not much more horrendous than crimes a few other inmates had committed. In any case, Bernardo's notoriety also necessitated his protection from the protected who were being protected from the protected, or something like that. A person begins to lose his chain of thought after a while.

KP had open-faced cells, and cell bars do not stop spit or God knows what else from entering a cell when thrown by a passing inmate. Bernardo was frequently the recipient of spit and possibly other materials until the staff installed a plexiglass cover to fit over the front of his cell. I was even told there was a camera placed in his cell for his protection. Just imagine the poor guy having to live under the eye of a camera twenty-four hours a day—well golly gee.

The events regarding Bernardo occurred after my transfer back to MI, so I wasn't around to witness them. However, I find it difficult to believe I would've been overcome with sympathy for his position in life. But by now, I'm sure his notoriety has worn off, and I imagine he's just another con housed at Kingston Pen; that is, if he hasn't been transferred somewhere else.

I'll take this opportunity to explain where that officer with the shotgun was heading that morning. As soon as I stepped into the wing, it was one of the first things I noticed. Looking up from the floor you could see a catwalk enclosed with heavy-gauge chicken wire. This position, called twelve cage, was patrolled by a CX 2 on both the day and the night shifts. In addition to observing movement in the wing area, he was responsible for backing up staff when they were on the ranges. This certainly made the staff, and I don't doubt even some of the inmates, feel a lot safer.

We hung around the wing and cells while Marv ironed out a few problems. Once that was accomplished, we headed out the south passage to the shop dome so Marv could have a chat with the CX 4 in charge of that area.

We went out the south passage and headed over to another large building. Marv said it was the shop dome, and naturally, it held most of the shops. We entered through one of the entrances, and you could sure tell it had been built several years ago—actually, about 140 years ago. The first few times I entered this place, I was overwhelmed by its architecture. But like everything, once it was familiar, I hardly noticed it any more. It was an enormous, round, high-domed building, and once again several barriers and doors opened into individual shops.

During our walk around that first day, Marv told me KP was presently having problems with the hours of work. It had started out with staff coming in early once in a while to relieve a post. Originally, this was an agreement between the two guys and only happened if someone had to get away early. That wasn't a problem as long as the keepers knew about it. "The problem now," Marv informed me, "is that almost everyone's doing it, and half the fucking time we don't know who's here and who isn't. Now it's even worse. A few of the jackasses have started leaving before their relief's even in. Christ, if anything ever happened later in the afternoon, we couldn't even be sure who in hell was in the prison, and if someone was missing, we wouldn't know if he had gone home early, was a hostage, or had been killed and hidden somewhere! Wouldn't that be a great fucking situation to try and explain?"

There ended my first shift at Kingston Penitentiary, and it was an interesting day. Little did I realize at the time that I would be staying at KP longer than at any of the other institutions. And I would like to add here that KP is one unique institution.

Sheila was certainly interested in the place. To be honest, she was interested in every institution I worked in, but especially Kingston Pen.

Over time, and without trying, an officer, especially at the keeper rank, became aware of why certain inmates were sentenced and, as I mentioned, some of these crimes were sickening. However, these people still had to be dealt with on a day-to-day basis, and most of them were very needy individuals; in fact, you could say some of them were clingy. Most of the inmates firmly believed they had done nothing wrong and were always on the alert for anything negative directed at them by a staff member. We often heard them say, "It wasn't my fault boss; I'm sick!" That was enough to almost make me sick. If an inmate saw or heard what they perceived to be a negative action or comment directed at them, by God, in went the complaint! I want to state here that in my opinion, PC inmates are much more prone to complaint writing than 'normal' inmates. The problem was that now I was one of the people who had to deal with these asinine complaints and submit written replies. So there I'd be, listening to this guy whining and sniveling and demanding his rights. At the same time, in the back of my mind, I'd be thinking that at the very least he should be locked in a cell somewhere and fed once or twice a day through some type of laundry chute. Then I would shudder and think, *God, some day this asshole will likely be back out on the street!*

I want to stress here that there were a lot of inmates in KP that were not in for sex crimes. I've mentioned that some were sent to KP for debts they owed over one thing or another, and a few had helped the police or correctional staff. Naturally, there were also some former police officers and, believe it or not, even former correctional officers (once again I'm being a little facetious). But no matter what, you couldn't get away from the high number of sexual predators in Kingston Penitentiary.

Even given the type of inmate at Kingston Pen, I was never

sorry I had transferred to the place. Supervisors were given a huge amount of responsibility, and I learned a lot. I ended up acting as the IPSO a couple of times, I was the coordinator of the institutional emergency response team for a while, and I was also coordinator of the dog handlers. In fact, to do that job, I had to take the dog handling course, and that was interesting. I was even trained as a range officer. In fact, my whole stint at KP was interesting. While I was there, I had a very good deputy warden, and I respected every warden except one, and that wasn't bad by any stretch of the imagination. At any rate, it only took the one day, and I was pretty sure I was going to find my time at KP interesting, and I did; I even enjoyed a good part of it. And believe me, you couldn't say that very often when you worked in these places.

So the next day, I was actually kind of eager to get to work; I was hardly apprehensive at all. I went through the north gate, said hi to the staff, and continued down to the hall.

As near as I can remember, one of the first items of any importance I was involved in at KP was the matter of staff leaving early. The keepers had a meeting with both the warden and the deputy the week after I arrived. It was also the first opportunity the warden and I had to meet each other. The meeting carried on for some time, and I came to realize staff leaving early had evolved into a serious problem and would likely be difficult to correct. I've discovered that most problems reach serious proportions because they're not corrected at the very beginning. After much discussion, it was decided we would hold roll call for each shift, except the mornings, in the staff lounge. All staff were going to be directed to report for roll call and would not be allowed to leave the lounge until the duty keeper or the keeper in charge of the night shift released them. And we decided not to release them until ten or fifteen minutes before the start of the shift.

And don't doubt for a minute this wasn't a huge change. The staff at KP had been doing their roll call, such as it was, the same way for years. Also, in my profound experience, I've learned most humans do not appreciate change; in fact, change, as a rule, is hated. This seems to be especially true of correctional officers. And you can multiply that hatred by at least two when it came to KP staff. I heard over and over at KP, "Christ, we've been doing it this way for twenty fucking years or more; why change now?" This may have been because most of the staff at KP were older, and a large percentage had only ever worked at KP. That did tend to narrow one's point of view.

I don't recall anything about my first back shift, but I remember pulling into the parking lot and thinking, *God, this is old Kingston Pen, and here I am in charge of the place.* I don't mind admitting I was more than a little nervous. I was also hoping like hell nothing out of the ordinary would happen. I was lucky. I don't think anything major really happened until I had been a KP for some time, at least not while I was on duty. But boy oh boy, over the years, I paid for that quiet start!

Everything at KP just ticked along without any major problems, and I settled into a regular routine. I managed to get familiar with the staff, and they grew accustomed to me. I took my turns at the duty keeper's job, met the two security clerks, and became familiar with the institution. And I wasn't bored—not one little bit.

The keepers started having meetings every morning. Apparently, this order came down from 'on high' and affected all institutions. As far as I remember, we were never officially informed of the reason, but I don't doubt it must have been a good one; after all, it did come from Ottawa (I'm being facetious again). And since the deputy, assistant wardens, and more often than not the warden were present, we just figured it was for better communication. During one of the meetings, we were informed that a senior correctional officer from RHQ was transferring in. I had never met the man, but some of the guys at the meeting knew him or at least knew of him. I was told he had worked at Millhaven and had been transferred to RHQ just before I transferred to MI.

Once I heard his name, I recalled hearing several stories about him. I was told he was one of the guys management had used as a 'heavy'. Apparently, when there was a problem with inmates, he was pulled off his post and, one way or another, he helped settle things down. This became a problem when things changed at MI and he wouldn't or couldn't change with the times, and eventually, in management's eyes, he became a liability. From what I was told, this was unfortunate, because he had been a good officer with a lot of potential. But once the system changed, they didn't know what to do with him. Eventually he ended up at Region in some out-of-the-way office. While he was at Region, he had written a senior correctional officer's competition and had been successful.

I met him shortly after he arrived, and he was one huge guy. I certainly had to look up when we were talking; he was well over six feet tall and had the weight to go with the height. I also discovered that he was very pleasant and personable. I can also emphatically state that he was one of those people who are natural leaders, and I honestly believed, at least for the first little while, that he was going to be an asset to KP.

And for a while he (I am going to call him Barry) did do an excellent job. He worked well with staff, and most of them really looked up to him. I know I didn't have any problems with him, and in my opinion, we got along just fine. Eventually he was elected president of the local union at KP, and after that it didn't take long for things to start changing.

At first everything kept moving along. Barry settled in as union president, and naturally, at times, we had a few difficulties with the union. Sometimes the union was right, and sometimes they were wrong. But we did have several work-to-rule situations.

One thing I could never understand was the union using work-to-rule. The only people it inconvenienced were staff. It meant they only had their legal half hour to eat, and there certainly was no leaving their posts early. But on the other hand, it made a lot more work for us keepers, and maybe that was the idea; I honestly don't know. I do know it started causing tension between Barry and me and I would imagine between Barry and a few of the other keepers.

One day Don, the deputy, called me up to the office and told me Barry had been in with a complaint. My first thought was, *Oh Christ, here we go again*. Don said Barry was complaining because the supervisors usually called in another supervisor on overtime if we were short on the day shift. Barry stated that in his mind, when we were short a keeper and had a spare CX 4, the spare should be put into an acting position. Once Don explained the complaint to me, he asked what I thought about it.

It wasn't very often I agreed with the union, especially with Barry because of some of the stunts he'd been pulling, but surprising even myself, this time I did agree, and I told Don he had a point. I didn't see any harm in putting someone in an acting position, especially since it would only be on the day shift and there would be other keepers around. At the time, I didn't realize this was going to lead to the biggest rift Barry and I would have.

We'd been having serious union issues for about a week, and with my luck, I was duty keeper. One afternoon we noticed that the next morning Barry was going to be a spare four and we were short one keeper. We knew Barry would be extremely unhappy about being an acting keeper, but there was nothing we could do about it; after all, he was the one who had originally filed the complaint.

So the next morning rolled around, and I went in a little early, hoping a four would be out sick. No such luck. There was Barry's name on the spare list and one vacant keeper's position still open. I was sitting in the lounge taking roll call, and in walked—actually, strutted—Barry. He was well aware of the situation and headed right for me to check if he was still spare. At the time I was willing to bet a day's pay that he knew damned well he was still spare. Before he had a chance to ask, I told him he would be filling in for a keeper. He said he didn't think it was fair to expect him to do that because of his position in the union. I reminded him that the acting thing had been his idea and that keepers were still in the union. During all this back and forth, I tried to make sure the staff could hear me. I really wanted them to know I was doing my best to be reasonable. At the same time, I realized nothing was going to make a difference to a few of them, but I was hoping the majority would take note.

During our conversation, I could see staff watching us, and I knew this had been thoroughly discussed among several of them. I didn't really know what their feelings were about the issue, and to be honest, by then I didn't give a good God damn. I told Barry this was now procedure, and I was giving him an order to act as a keeper for the day and that was the end of it. By this time I must admit I was getting a little stressed, but not nearly as stressed as Barry; he was actually quivering! I completed our little talk by telling him to sit down until the shift left and then we'd finish our business. Just as he turned to sit down, he gave me a prewritten note explaining why he wouldn't act. I was a little surprised at the note for a couple of reasons. First of all, it was hand written and almost illegible; second, it proved I was right and this whole issue had been planned. Barry and his followers had been waiting for just this opportunity. And it was just my luck to be duty keeper.

Once roll call was completed, I gathered my paperwork and headed toward Barry, very thankful that one of the keepers had hung back. I was beginning to think I might need a witness, because Barry was certainly agitated enough to deck me! We met in the middle of the room, and he was still vibrating. I realized he was under a lot of stress, but he'd brought it all on himself; certainly no one else had caused it. Regardless of his condition, there was absolutely no way I could or would back down. I looked up, way up at him and asked him one more time if he was going to obey the order.

"No fucking way, Thibedeau; stick it up your ass!"

I told him I was going to charge him for refusing a lawful order and he was to leave the property immediately. For a minute or so—at the time it felt like ten—he stared down at me and continued to vibrate while I thought, *Oh God, I'm going down again, and this time from a staff member.* I had already decided that if I did get assaulted, I was going to lay charges against him with the Crown. Then he gave himself a shake and asked if he could have ten minutes to consult with the union before leaving. I told him ten minutes was fine, but then he was to be off the property. He was actually gone before the ten minutes were up. I really think, in my whole career, that was the nearest I ever came to being attacked without it actually happening.

Barry had a right-hand man in the union. This senior correctional officer, I'll call him Mark, had transferred to KP from Millhaven about a year after I had arrived at MI. I honestly can't recall anyone at MI being sorry Mark transferred out; I know I wasn't. Of course, at the time, I didn't realize I would have to deal with him at KP. Oh well, such is life. I don't exactly recall when I had my run-in with Mark, but once again, I was duty keeper at the time, and as usual, there was a work-to-rule going on. This time my problem had to do with the outside barrier at the end of the south passage.

Post orders stated it was to remain locked except during major movement, and among other responsibilities, the four in the yard was to control the barrier. In real life, this barrier was never locked during the day shift except during emergencies. With all the other duties the four was required to carry out, it wasn't feasible to be running back and forth locking and unlocking that barrier. In fact, if we'd insisted on keeping it locked during the day, I'm sure the fours would have revolted.

On this particular morning I was at the desk trying to sort out the usual mess when I started to receive phone calls about the south barrier being locked and people lining up trying to get in. Mark was the yard officer, and I contacted him on the radio and asked him why the south passage was locked. He said he would give me a phone call. My immediate thought was, *Christ, the assholes are at it again!*

When Mark phoned, he reminded me about post orders stating that the barrier was to remain locked. There was a lot of back and forth conversation, which I ended by telling him the post orders were only a guideline and he was to unlock the damn barrier and leave it unlocked until he was told differently. Silly me, I thought the problem was solved, and I went back to my paperwork. Within several minutes, the phone calls started again: the south barrier was still locked; can't get in; what the hell kind of game's going on now and so forth. Once again I contacted Mark. I must admit I was a little frazzled by this time. I asked him, rather politely, I thought, why the damned barrier was locked after I had told him to leave it open. Once again he started in about the post orders. Part way through our conversation and while I was doing the talking, he hung up on me.

I couldn't believe it. I sort of flipped and tore out of that office like the devil was after me. I think I made it down to that yard shack within seconds, and once there, I spotted Mark sauntering over to unlock the barrier to let a handful of people in. Christ, he was acting like he was having a day at the beach, and that certainly didn't improve my mood any! There's no need to get into the conversation we had; suffice to say I ended up ordering him to give me his radio and keys and to get the hell off the property. I also informed him he was going to be charged for refusing to obey a lawful order. Just like his buddy Barry, he asked for ten minutes to speak to the union. I gave him the ten minutes and told him if he wasn't gone by then I would add a charge of trespassing. Believe me, I really can't stand having anyone hang up on me, especially in a situation like that!

Back to the office I went to write another report for the deputy, and I was still steaming. This idiocy was starting to get to me and, I would imagine, to the other keepers as well. By the time I made it to the office, the security clerks already knew what had happened. In fact, one told me when I first stormed out they thought we were having another hostage situation!

I headed into the deputy's office with another report. "Boy," he said with a grin, "this is getting to be a habit, isn't it?"

No one from management ever spoke to me about those episodes, so I just assumed they were satisfied with my decisions. I'm also not aware of the results of any disciplinary actions. Since I was directly involved with the situation, it wasn't up to me to have the hearings, and I wasn't interested enough to find out. One thing I do know was that I never had anyone else ever refuse one of my orders again!

Several months later, Mark caused another incident. Luckily, this time it had nothing to do with me; it was strictly a union thing. Mark had to report the theft of his union briefcase. He claimed that he had brought it into the institution, left it on the coat rack at the officer's mess, and gone in for lunch. And lo and behold, he was absolutely shocked to find it gone when he came out! He claimed there were union papers and quite a bit of money in it. No one could ever figure out how anyone, even Mark, would be dumb enough to bring in a briefcase, especially with money in it, and not keep it clutched in his sweaty little hands. You can bet that was a hot topic for a while. It didn't matter who you spoke to, no one could figure out how anyone could be that dumb. Hell, there were inmates, visitors, and all kinds of staff going in and out of that area. Everyone thought that it was really stupid, or at least strange. A short time after the case of the missing briefcase, rumours started drifting around that the union finances had been in a mess and there was a shortage of money. However, once the money that had gone missing was added in, the books balanced—strange!

Chapter 17

Inmate and a knife. Hostage negotiations. Two suicides.

My time at Kingston Penitentiary kept rolling along. It was still interesting, busy, and anything but boring. Even with the staff problems, everything usually operated more or less efficiently.

Ever since I'd come to KP, I had heard a rumour about one of the sex offenders having pictures of his victim. This guy was in his forties or so and was a short, scrawny son of a bitch who had murdered at least one young girl. I imagine he'd been sentenced to life, but who knew? At various times, staff had searched his cell for these pictures but hadn't had any luck. One day, I was in charge the wing, and my old buddy Barry caught up to me. He told me one of his informants had whispered that he had seen this inmate in his cell with the pictures we had been trying to find. I told Barry to grab a couple of officers, get to the cell, and give it a toss and just maybe this time we'd be lucky. I continued with what I was doing but kept an eye on that particular range.

A few minutes later I saw Barry clutching something in his hand as he hustled out of the range with the inmate in tow. He gave me a wave and pointed to the hole, so I beat it in and told the staff we had a con coming in. I waited for Barry and the con to show up, and when they came in, Barry told me we had what we'd been looking for. Barry appeared a little tense, and while staring at the con, he handed me a binder.

I opened it up, looked at a picture, and immediately felt sick! I only took a quick look at the one picture, and that was enough. It was a shot that I assume had been used in court showing a young girl around sixteen or so lying on a metal table without any clothes. Someone had used a marker to draw circles around several bite marks on her body. I looked at the con and thought, *God, I'd love to just squash you like the dirty little bug that you are*, but instead I told him he was going into a cell and to strip. He started to say something, and I remember warning him to keep his fucking mouth shut and get his clothes off. And then the stupid idiot, with wide-eyed innocence, said something about it not being his fault because he was sick!

Right about that time everything went black, and the next thing I recall is the inmate running down the range to a cell, and he must have been clutching his clothes, because he was buck ass naked! I wasn't sure what was going on, but when I glanced at the staff, they were looking at me with a strange expression. To this day, I don't know what I said or did, and I never asked, but guessing by the shocked looks, it must have been something. I guess I kind of lost it for a short time.

Once the inmate was locked up, I thanked Barry, took the binder, and headed for the deputy's office. I went in, told him what we'd found, and dropped the binder on his desk.

"How in hell could he get these?" was about all he could say.

They were all official pictures, and we figured they had to be from the trial. We just couldn't imagine how he had gotten his filthy little hands on them.

Don asked me to hang around while he phoned the Mounties to see if he could get an answer. While he was doing that, I told him I was going for a coffee. Actually, what I had to do was get away and be by myself for a while. I was still shaken up and on the verge of being ill. I had seen a lot since I started in the service—suicides, several slashings, a few stabbings, and God knows what else, but this one really got to me. Once I settled down a little, I went back to the office and Don told me a Mountie was on his way in. It didn't take very long for this young officer to show up, and I think he must've just finished his training. At any rate, he couldn't believe what we had and said he'd take the pictures with him and find out whatever he could.

It didn't take him long to get back to us. The next morning Don called me up to his office, and there sat the Mountie with that God damned binder. And what he told us just about floored us both! The pictures had been used in the trial and that somehow made them public property, and the inmate was legally allowed to have them. There wasn't a damn thing we could do about it. If I hadn't been sick about the mess before, I certainly was then. Don said we'd have to give them back. "But," he exclaimed in no uncertain terms, "the puke is not going to have them in his possession. Take them down and have them put into his effects at A&D." And that's what I had to do; well, that and release the little bastard from the hole. And that I did by phone. There was just no way I trusted myself to so much as look at him.

This episode has been on my mind ever since. I just wish to hell I had shredded them. I'm not sure what bothered me the most, the inmate having the pictures or the legal system that allowed him to have them. I know I couldn't get it out of my mind. I kept thinking about the parents and what it would do to them if they ever found out. What made matters worse for me was that our daughter was roughly the same age as the little girl at the time.

This particular episode kept eating at me, and I just couldn't shake it! Seeing the little prick running around happy as hell and not bothered by anything eventually got to me. About two weeks later I had an appointment with my doctor over something and ended up talking to him about those damned pictures.

He told me I was nuts to work there, and he wanted me to stay home for a while. I ended up taking two weeks off, and during that time I wasn't sure I'd be able to go back in. The doctor wanted me off longer, but I figured two weeks was long enough, and for better or worse, I headed back in.

So there I was, back in old KP.

Naturally, we continued having staff problems. But in between, supervisors were still responsible for their normal duties. Staff evaluations had to be completed, inmate problems had to be solved, inmates committed self-injuries, staff had injuries, all the normal stuff. But for all the difficulties with staff, it goes without saying they almost always pulled together when it was required. And then just to ensure things didn't calm down, a rumour started making the rounds that Ottawa was going to put female correctional officers into maximum-security institutions. Well, you wouldn't believe how that stirred the pot. I've mentioned before that a large portion of the staff at KP had been in the service for years and most of their service had been at old KP. Talk about change—this was Change with a capital C! And most of the staff were not happy about it.

Whenever I was chatting with staff about female officers, and there were lots of conversations, I told them I really didn't think they had to worry about females at KP. My line of thinking was that due to the type of inmate we had, women would be much safer in a place like Millhaven. Well, that just goes to show what I knew; I must have forgotten this place was run by the government. KP rather than Millhaven ended up with female staff, and as expected, the number of hostage-taking incidences shot right up!

Staff actions had sort of quieted down, but then the union became aware of the Health and Safety Act. I don't know if the act had just been changed or if the local union had happened stumble onto it, but it was sure used in Kingston Penitentiary. Part of the act more or less stated that employees could refuse work if they believed it was or could prove dangerous. It went on to say that employees could not be sanctioned for refusing to carry out such duties. Well, did the union ever grab onto that.

Imagine working in a maximum security institution with a bunch of murderers and being allowed to refuse work if it was deemed dangerous! Jesus, where did they think they were going to work when they joined the penitentiary service? This section of the act was implemented several times at KP, but the time I remember the most was when the staff decided it was unsafe to have more than one barrier open at a time. This started at breakfast and continued all day, and what a day that was. And of course, with my ever-present luck, I was in the wing. It took so long to feed the inmates we had to skip the noon meal. Breakfast didn't finish until almost noon, so we decided to leave the inmates in their cells and start the evening meal around two or three in the afternoon. Needless to say, the inmates were not happy.

Every time there was a refusal to work because of a health and safety issue, an inspector had to come in from Ottawa. I'm not sure how many times one or more inspectors had to come in to make a ruling, but they started to get pissed off. Eventually, the union received a report stating that these actions had been frivolous and that if it continued the union would be subject to a fine. I forget now how large the fine would have been, but it was several thousand dollars. Suddenly, this type of job action came to a screeching halt. But it certainly took a long time for this to occur.

The staff problems were serious and caused a lot of friction among the line staff. I know I was keeping a close watch in my rear view mirror, especially on my way home after a night shift. And then when a couple of supervisors had their cars badly marked up in the parking lot, the warden had us park across the road with management.

One day in the middle of all this, a notice was posted informing staff of a union meeting. I was standing reading the thing, and one of the guys I knew quite well came by and asked if I was going to go. "Yep," I replied, "I believe I will."

"Christ, Vern, don't even think of going. It's going to be pretty rough."

After hearing that bit of information, I must admit I had second thoughts. Later, I discussed the idea of going with two other supervisors and eventually decided to attend. After all, we were dues-paying members even if we didn't want to be.

At any rate, we met and went into the meeting together. And it was hot and heavy. We stayed together near the back of the room, and we certainly had some looks tossed at us. If looks could kill, I wouldn't be writing this now. Shortly before the meeting was over, an officer walked by us to use the bathroom and in a low voice suggested we leave before the meeting ended. He didn't say much other than there was talk about trouble on the way out. We figured there was being brave and there was being stupid, so we took off. We couldn't think of any reason to push our luck.

Eventually things became a little quieter for a short time, and then we were told we were to receive several women from the next induction course.

It was strange seeing female staff in uniform inside KP. We did require more staff; the upper ranges had been opened, so naturally we had more inmates. But like all changes, it wasn't as bad as everyone had dreaded it would be. The staff realized it was a sign of the times, and they either had to work with it or resign.

But I must admit I enjoyed observing the male staff's reaction to the new officers. A few staff tried to stay as far away from them as possible, a few younger ones couldn't seem to get close enough, and a few older staff took them under their wings and helped them as much as possible. But what tickled me the most was watching a few of the staff suddenly start to clean themselves up. Their uniforms improved, they were cleanly shaven, and I had to chuckle at the way they suddenly started to strut. It really was comical; they walked around with their shoulders thrown back, their guts sucked in, and a couple of buttons on their shirts undone. God, it was fun to watch!

Ah, yes, the female gender. As all males know, females think differently than males. And I would think that's *usually* a good thing.

The inmates weren't sure how to handle it. Some were actually shaken up. I even got the impression a few were scared of the female staff. After all, no matter what Ottawa thought, we did have sexual perverts locked up in KP. However, once a few inmates had been charged by the female officers, things eventually settled down somewhat. I think that was when the inmates realized the women were correctional officers.

I did note that not one female came to me with a complaint about a male officer acting inappropriately. By inappropriately, I don't mean being overly friendly or trying to get a date. I was concerned about a few staff being hostile or even attempting to set a female officer up so she would look bad. It's a sad fact that I even thought something like that could take place, but it was a very rough period. I would have been willing to bet money we would get complaints of harassment, and there may indeed have been a few, but I never heard of them. And there is no doubt in my mind there would have been plenty of opportunities to lay a complaint!

In the end, as expected, everything more or less worked out. Most of the females ended up being good officers, a few weren't suited for the environment, and a few were mediocre officers—just like any new staff.

The first physical incident involving a woman took place in the hole. As usual, disassociation was 'manned', oops we had to stop using the terminology 'manned' and switch over to 'staffed,' by three officers. There was the CX 4 in charge and a couple of CX 2s working for him. On this particular day, the four had one male and one young, very quiet female with him. She was one of the officers who, in my mind anyway, wasn't really suited for this type of work. I was in the wing area when the emergency alarm for disassociation started to scream! I grabbed the spare key from the key safe and several of us headed in at a run. When we made it in, the first thing we saw was two male staff fighting an inmate and the con screaming like a banshee. Staff piled on, got him under control, and locked into a cell. During the fight, I noticed the female officer was standing in the office looking extremely apprehensive. I must admit that concerned me somewhat; actually, it concerned me a hell of a lot.

Once things settled down and the four had caught his breath, I took him into the courtroom for some privacy to find out just what had happened. While he was getting himself together, he told me they had been getting the con out for a shower and everything was going okay, but suddenly the inmate had just started to scream and jumped them. Once he finished his story, I asked about the officer standing in the office and why she didn't seem to be helping any.

"Oh, she's okay. I yelled at her to get into the office and hit emergency buzzer, and it's a lucky fucking thing she did, because we were losing him!"

That's when I first realized the women had been accepted. I knew damned well he was covering up for her; that's what the staff did for each other.

I continued the conversation by saying, "That's all well and good, but by the time we made it in, she should've been out giving you guys a hand. God, if the con had won the fight, we would've been in big trouble."

So there I was, knowing I had to talk to a female officer about the situation and knowing she was still shaken up. I hung around for a while, and we all had a coffee and talked everything over. I made sure I told the staff they did a hell of a good job, and I complimented them on hitting the emergency buzzer. I emphasized that if it hadn't been hit God only knew what could've happened. While we were standing around chatting, I noticed the girl had her hair in a bun. That wasn't a bad idea—less hair for an inmate to grab—but she had a wooden stick four or five inches long and sharpened at both ends holding the bun together, which was not a good idea.

Just when I thought I couldn't wait any longer, I finally had an opportunity to speak to her privately, and I was very gentle. Hell, I didn't have a clue how to handle the situation. She still looked like she was going to cry at any moment, and that concerned me more than fighting with the inmates. I didn't even question why she didn't help out after she'd pressed the buzzer. I just told her it was a damn good thing she had hit it and that any time we all walked away from an incident we were ahead of the game. Then, pretending that it was just an afterthought, I suggested she not use that method to hold her hair up. I explained that it could be used as a weapon and then stressed again that she had done a good job.

In all honesty, I should've discussed her staying in the office, but I decided to wait until the next day when I assumed she would be calmer. I was still scared silly that she was going to break down and cry, and if she did, I didn't know what the hell I was supposed to do. I certainly couldn't hug her and tell her everything would be okay—sexual harassment, you know.

When we were first told female officers were coming to KP, I was deeply concerned. First of all, naturally, I was concerned for their safety. We had some very sick individuals in that pen. Then there was the harassment thing. It had been drummed into the supervisors' heads that harassment would not be condoned in any government department. And there was the worry about interviewing females privately. That was a major concern for supervisors. We were well aware it would only take one complaint about a supervisor acting inappropriately, and right or wrong, he would be finished. And then we all knew females reacted differently than males to criticism. God, what would we do if one broke down and started to cry? I asked one or two management types if we were going to receive any training regarding female staff prior to their arrival. About all I received was a 'look' and the enlightened words, "You just treat them like any other staff member!"

Sure, I thought, *just pretend we're all office workers; just fucking great.*

The next day rolled around, and I didn't have that chat with her after all; she never came back to work. I guess she was more upset than I had realized. But it did take a load off my shoulders.

A couple of months later I was in talking to the deputy and he asked me if I would be willing to be the coordinator for the dog handlers. I told him the only dogs I was familiar with were the house pets Sheila and I had had at different times.

"Ah, you'll love these guys. They're just overgrown house pets."

I'd been around a few guard dogs, and I didn't believe a word he said, so I just replied, "Oh sure, it may even be fun."

Several years later, one of the dog handlers at MI got into a fix with a dog, and it was a miracle he got out of it. Whoever it is up there looking after correctional officers was certainly watching over this guy on that day. The dog handlers at the Haven were armed with revolvers during their shifts, and thank God for that. Apparently, Bard had completed one of his patrols, and just as he got into the sally port, the dog turned on him! Bard had been a dog handler for a hell of a long time, and that particular dog had been at MI for ages, but for whatever reason, the dog latched onto his elbow and started yanking. Unfortunately, the dog grabbed the right elbow, and where do you carry a side arm? On the right side, of course. To this day I can't imagine how Bard did it, but eventually he wrestled the revolver out of the holster and shot the dog in the head. I was told it took three rounds to put him down.

Everyone felt badly both for Bard and the dog. No one could figure out why the shepherd had turned on him. He was sent away to be examined (the dog, not Bard) and of all things, he had a brain tumor. I was always kind of glad it was something like that. At least it wasn't the dog's fault, but Bard was very lucky he was armed.

But guard dogs and dog handlers also had their lighter side, and I just have to mention an episode that, although not to the handler, was extremely comical to everyone else. One evening the yard officer took a dog up a fire escape to check a door. Well, the dog bounded up the stairs without a problem, but there was no way in hell he was coming back down those stairs on his own four paws. You can bet the handler tried everything, but eventually he just gave up, picked that huge guard dog up in his arms, and carried him down the stairs like a big baby. Well, so much for instilling terror in the inmates.

I would have given a day's pay to have snapped a picture of the officer lugging that big four-legged baby down those stairs; it would have been appreciated in institutions far and wide. And then whenever there wasn't much to chuckle about, staff would have been able to glance at that picture, and life would suddenly have appeared in a much better light. Mind you, I don't imagine the guy carrying that huge dog would have done much chuckling; staff could be unmerciful when they had something like that to chew on.

Seriously, though, the dogs were a great tool for controlling inmates. I think they worried more about the dogs than they did about firearms.

One day I was working the wing and cells. E range had just come back from their yard, and it was quiet, so I thought, *What the hell, no sense in hanging around.* I should've taken off as soon as that thought entered my head, and if I had known I was going to end up a hostage, I certainly would have!

A few minutes later I was getting up to head for the gate and one of the guys working E range stopped and said an inmate wanted to see me. Thinking it would only take a couple of minutes and maybe save the night shift some aggravation, I headed over to E range.

Because E range was segregation, there was an office right on the range. Actually, it was a converted cell holding a desk and a couple of chairs, and that was about it. Anyone doing an interview had his or her back to the wall and faced the door; the inmate being interviewed sat with his back to the door and faced the desk. I was never at ease having an inmate between myself and that door, but sometimes there was no choice about it.

An officer escorted the inmate into the office and with a wave of his hand said he was on his way home. I'd had several dealings with this con and knew he had spent a lot of time in the RTC and that he was a bit of a needy individual and maybe even a little nuts.

And what were the first words out of his mouth? "Mr. Thibedeau, I want to be transferred to the treatment center. I can't stand this place any longer."

I said, "Don't tell anyone, but there are times I feel the same way, but you know as well as I do that I don't have the authority to do that. You'll have to talk to your case management officer, and then you both can write up a transfer request."

"You don't understand; I want to go right fucking now." And then the son of a bitch pulled a knife and started waving it around!

I have to admit, it wasn't really a large knife, but at the time, it looked pretty damn huge to me, and my immediate thought was, *Jesus Christ, why me again? I always seem to step into it.* And there went my old stomach again, heading south. My mind flashed back to Three Block office and the advice I had received from Don several years earlier about getting the hell out. Maybe he had been right; I just might not get out of this one!

Speaking in technicalities, this was a hostage situation, and as far as I could remember, it was the second one that had taken place in E range.

The first episode involved a young, quiet female correctional officer. The inmate had dragged her into his cell and tied the door shut. It was a sad state of affairs, but for a while we had so many hostage situations, I can't really remember them all or in what order they occurred. I do know I went down to the cell to speak to the inmate and thought he was rather an inadequate sort of individual. He also appeared to be deeply concerned about the officer's well-being and assured me he wouldn't harm her. Kind of a polite and caring hostage taker! However, she did complain about her arm being injured when he grabbed her. As soon as she mentioned an injured arm, the inmate became agitated and insisted he hadn't hurt her and reiterated that he had no intention of doing so. Once again, tough hostage taker, but it was good to hear just the same. I don't believe this one lasted very long and thankfully force was not required to end it.

Naturally, the officer was shaken up. In fact, I don't think she ever came back to the institution. Apparently, her arm was too damaged to continue in this line of work, and I believe she ended up with a position in Ottawa.

That was certainly one benefit of having female officers. Well, perhaps it was a combination of the female staff and the precious charter our prime minister had put into law a short time previously. I'm not really sure, but in any case, there was much more emphasis on assistance with post-traumatic stress problems. Before women entered the service, at the conclusion of an incident, you just stayed home for a while if it was necessary and then came back in to work and went about your business.

So there I was with my stomach in the basement and this joker holding a knife and wanting a transfer to RTC, and me not having the authority to do it. Also, uppermost in my mind was the fact that there was no way in hell I was going to be dragged out to the wing area by a con holding a knife. I wasn't sure how the staff would react, especially the guy up in the cage with the shotgun. And at the very least, it would have been embarrassing as hell. To be honest, I'm not sure which I was more concerned about.

One of the first things I told him was to put the knife down before someone saw it and kicked the shit out of him. I was hoping he would drop it and this would be over. But oh no, not him; he looked surprised and just lowered it out of sight. So we just sat and chatted for a while, and he eventually calmed down a little.

And then I had a bright idea, or at least I thought it was. I told him I'd phone the treatment center and see if they had a cell. My idea was to phone the CX 4 and insist that I was going to bring this Perkins over from E range and admit him, knowing full well the four wouldn't go along with it. After all, this was a government-run operation, and believe me, if nothing else, there were procedures on top of procedures that had to be followed no matter what. But I figured, if nothing else, the four would know something was wrong and hopefully would pass the word along. Hell, I even told him where we were. However, you know what they say about the best-laid plans—. I still don't understand why he didn't pick up on it after all the crap KP had been going through.

Eventually, I realized my great plan hadn't worked. No one came busting in, so I knew it was just the con and me. I knew I had to come up with something different to get my ass out of this one, but I had no clue what. During our conversation, I'd been watching him, and I realized he'd relaxed a little, at least compared to when he'd first pulled that damn knife. He held it in his right hand and was keeping it down between himself and the desk so it couldn't be seen. But more importantly, he'd also shifted to his right a little, and his right leg was in plain sight, so I quietly moved to my left a little at a time. Eventually, I had myself in a position where I could take a kick at him and hopefully smash his knee—emphasis here on the *hopefully*. At the same time I realized if I took the kick and missed there'd be hell to pay. I decided to try it only as a last resort. I ended up wishing to hell I had taken the chance. Once again, hindsight is great.

Finally I had him talked into going back to his cell on the promise that I'd take the matter up with the warden and the deputy. I also told him he was almost guaranteed a transfer. I must admit, though, I neglected to mention the transfer was likely going to be to the SHU. Hell, why push my luck? As he was getting up to leave, I told him to leave the knife on the desk. I tried to make him realize that if anyone saw it, the shit would hit the fan and he might very well get himself shot! Not that there was anyone out on the range to see it—or so I thought. But there was no way he was leaving without the knife.

He walked out of the office, and my adrenaline started sinking to a normal level, and I thought, *Thank God that's over with*. Little did I know it was just beginning!

I'd calmed down a little and was getting up to leave when I heard a commotion on the range. I tore out of the office to see what the hell was going on, and there was the con with an officer and that God damned knife! She'd just started her night shift and was checking the range when Perkins stepped out of the office, and they had practically bumped into each other.

My first thought was, *Oh no, here we go again*, and my adrenaline immediately went sky high. I was beginning to have an idea what a yo-yo must feel like. He had her in front of him and was holding the knife up to make sure she couldn't miss it. The officer, I'll call her Dianne, looked back at me, and I still remember her eyes; they were huge and seemed to be silently begging for help, and there wasn't a God damned thing I could do!

I was about twenty feet from them, and they were heading up the stairs toward his cell. I thought about yelling for her to fight but realized I could never clear that distance in time to help. So I signaled her to go with him, and as calmly as I could I said, "Try not to worry, everything's going to work out okay. Perkins and I've been talking, and we have a deal." Then I looked directly at him and asked, "What the hell are you doing? You're making this mess a fuck of a lot worse, and now I'm going to have a hell of a time explaining our deal to the warden!" I didn't hear his reply, but they kept on heading up to his cell.

One lucky thing about E range was that it was segregation, so at least all the inmates were locked up. And by God, they stayed quiet until the situation was resolved. And that was certainly different from the other ranges and other prisons I'd been in.

I tore out of the range and told the four in the wing we had a hostage situation in E range. I also told him to make sure he posted someone at the range barrier so nobody, and I emphasized *nobody*, could go in. "And don't forget," I hollered as I kept going, "have the staff lock everything down; no inmate movement anywhere!"

I heard him say something like, "Jesus Christ, not again."

I made it up to the hall in record time, told the night keeper what was going on, and advised him to phone the deputy before he got away for the day. If the deputy had left, that would mean the night keeper was the crisis manager until the deputy made it back, and I didn't think he really wanted that too badly. Once that was done, I beat it back down to the Wing to make sure things were under control in that area.

I really wasn't sure if I should go up to the cell or not. But my concern for Dianne overrode any doubts I had, so I headed for the range. I reinforced the order to the officer at the barrier about making damn sure he didn't allow anyone onto the range. I also told him that once things got organized, he was to write the name and time of anyone entering and leaving the place. I ended the conversation by instructing him to start the sheet with my name and the time.

I entered the range, and the first thing that struck me was how quiet the place was. Once I was about half-way up to the cell, I made sure Perkins knew it was me coming up and that I was on my own. Once I got there, the first and most important thing to me was Dianne's well being, and I found she was fine. He had her sitting at the back of the cell, and she signaled me that everything was okay. She wasn't even tied up, at least not yet. When Perkins informed me that he had no intention of harming her, I must admit I felt a rush of relief. I had a feeling he was being honest; at least, at that point he was. But in these situations, things could and did go south in a hell of a hurry.

One of the concerns in a hostage situation was the hostage becoming agitated and causing the hostage taker to become even more hyper. This could cause him to do something that even he might regret. Of course, by then it was too late; you sure as hell couldn't go back and undo an action. Hell, if I could have gone back in time, I would've taken the kick at that damned knee. I was immensely grateful that Dianne was a mature, cool-thinking person. Her temperament certainly gave us a head start.

I chatted with both of them for a few minutes and made sure things had calmed down. I emphasized to Perkins that my main concern was to ensure no one was injured and to get Dianne out and back to her family.

It never hurt to humanize a hostage and make sure the taker realized the hostage was a real person with loved ones. Perkins assured me once again that he had no intention of harming anyone other than maybe himself. I told him I was glad to hear that but I also insisted that I didn't want him harmed either. I informed Perkins that someone trained in these situations would soon be up to speak with him.

"Oh no," he said. "The only person I'm talking to is you. You make sure they don't send any other fucker up here!"

Believe me, my stomach and heart sank when he told me that. I'd been thinking I was out of this part of it. But all I could say was, "I'll see what I can do, but right now I have to fill the deputy in on what's going on, and I'll be back as soon as I can."

As I was leaving I spotted some material lying on the desk. Once I saw what it was, I was pretty sure by my next trip up he'd have the cell door tied shut. I also knew I didn't want the responsibility of negotiating, because I had very little training in that end of this business.

After updating the staff in the wing, I beat it up to the hall and headed over to the desk to discuss the situation with Don. He hadn't left yet, and that made him the emergency coordinator. Luckily for the keeper, they'd caught him at the gate on his way out.

That's the way it was laid down in our Bible. When an emergency started, the highest-ranking officer took over as the EC. If someone higher on the totem pole came in, he or she could take over, but to do that, the person had to officially notify the emergency coordinator and note it in the emergency logbook. On the other hand, the new arrival didn't have to assume control and could remain as an advisor; it was his or her decision. Staff just hoped whoever was in charge knew what they were doing; lives usually hung in the balance!

I was going to be in that position at Millhaven in the future. We were having a major problem on a range one evening, and when the warden finally walked in, I was exceptionally happy to see him. I even felt my chest and shoulders lighten right up. *God, I thought, he finally made it in; I'll be able to relax a little.* Then, in front of witnesses, he said, "You're doing just fine, Vern; you might as well remain the emergency coordinator." It was nice to have his confidence, but at that particular time I wasn't really sure I wanted it!

I explained everything to Don, and he brought me up to speed on his end. Then, as I knew he had to, he told me whether I wanted it or not, I was stuck with the negotiations.

I'm not sure how often I traveled back and forth to that range, but it felt like I covered about ten miles. I'm not even sure of everything Perkins and I talked about, but my main concern was to keep him calm.

There was one time shortly before the situation ended

when I really became concerned. I was talking to the inmate and he appeared to be getting really edgy and Dianne was extremely nervous. Jesus, this really had me worried. You could only do so much to keep things relatively calm in these situations, especially when it dragged on like this one. I didn't stay very long and got my ass up to see Don. I'd been wearing a bomber jacket because it was chilly, and Perkins had never asked me to open it up so he could check for a weapon. I told Don about him being agitated and that I thought I could hide a revolver in the back of my belt. We chatted back and forth about it, and Don decided I should go back and see if things had settled down. He said if Perkins was still excited, I'd take a .38 with me on the next trip. He followed that up by saying, "Hopefully, you won't have to use it!"

Down I went and immediately noticed everything had calmed down. It was around 2230 hours when it finally ended. The agreement was for me to come back with three or four officers, and Perkins would hand out his knife, allow us to remove the ties on the barrier, and step out. We'd handcuff him, take him to RTC, and place him into a cell. I'd also instructed Dianne to stay at the back of the cell until we had the inmate out and cuffed.

And that's exactly how it happened. To my eternal relief, it worked like a charm! Once the inmate was cuffed and taken away, Dianne came out of the cell and gave me a big hug; and then she thanked me! I couldn't believe she thanked me. I was feeling responsible for the whole God damned mess. In fact, it had been eating at me the whole time, and then Dianne came out, gave me a hug, and thanked me! But no matter what she said, to this day I still feel responsible. If anything had happened to her, it would have been the end for me. I would have resigned on the spot. But it was over and everyone got to go home. I don't know about rest of the staff on the shift, but it took me a while to settle down and get to bed. I would guess that I even had a few drinks! After all, I had to get ready for the day shift. The one downside to this situation was that we lost Dianne. She either transferred out or resigned; I'm not sure which.

After that episode, things settled down. It had been relatively quiet for a few weeks, and I was in doing a boring morning shift when I had the crap scared out of me! Some time around three in the morning, I decided to take a trip down to the wing. I stood around and chatted with the staff for a while, and when they had to do their walk, I headed back toward the hall. As I sleepily made my way over to the hall barrier, I noticed that a female officer was going to do the walk on E range and thought no more of it. That is, until I reached the hall barrier. I was just about to stick the key into the lock when a scream emanated from E range! My stomach dropped, and I'm positive it hit my knees, and I swear to God my heart stopped beating for several seconds. When something like this hit the fan, I couldn't help wonder how my poor old body kept on going. I took off racing for the range. The screaming continued, and I just knew a con had made it out of his cell and had either taken her hostage or was in the process of killing her. I made it to the range in what must have been record time, and there was the four; he wasn't exactly laughing, but he was awfully God damned close to it. Once he had himself under control, he explained what had happened.

Apparently, when the officer opened the barrier to the range, there was a rat (the type with four legs) sleeping or walking on the bar above the barrier. When the barrier swung open, it caused that poor little thing to fall. Luckily for the rat and unluckily for the officer; it landed on her shoulder! Well, I don't blame her for screaming one little bit. I would have done the same thing. We could chuckle and joke about it, because the rat just jumped down and galloped away, but if it had bitten her, it would have been a different story. I don't recall if she wanted to go home or not. But if she had requested to leave, I'm sure I would have let her go with my blessings.

I am not sure exactly when it started, but we ended up being tested for TB every year. This disease became a real concern in the service, and we were well aware of the problem at KP because we ended up with an inmate from India who was infected with TB. The real problem started when, for some reason, he refused treatment. I was never sure if it was something to do with religion or that he just didn't like prison; I just know it put the institution and the staff in a hell of a spot. Heaven forbid you would ever try and force medical treatment on an inmate! Remember the charter.

So there we were with an inmate who had a highly infectious disease and who was refusing treatment, which was his right. To hell with everybody else's right to stay free of the disease. Oh oh, what to do? Why, just spend several thousand taxpayer dollars and remodel a couple of cells in our hospital. That will solve the problem!

And it must have been expensive. They punched out a wall to enlarge the cell; he did have to be comfortable, you know. Then they put in some kind of an air exchanger that gave the oversized cell an inverse airflow. The inverse airflow enabled staff to open a food slot and pass him his meal. Apparently, when the slot or the door was opened, the air would rush into the cell and not out, and that would keep staff safe, or so we were told. As far as I know, he stayed there until he died.

But by God, he had that right, and the taxpayers had the right to spend the money.

And life went on. I'll say it again, if nothing else, Kingston Penitentiary was an interesting place to work; in fact, at times it was even fun.

During one morning shift, the supervisor in charge received a phone call from the police. They wanted to know if we had a husband and wife team by the name of Potter (name changed again) working for us.

"Oh yes, we sure do."

"Well," the officer continued, "we thought we should let you know that we attended their residence on a domestic call. We also thought it serious enough to remove all firearms from their residence!"

I imagine the supervisor's next phone call was to the deputy or the warden.

We could always laugh at such things, but usually not until the situation was settled and no one was injured. One such episode happened in the hall at the end of a night shift. I can laugh my head off at the stupidity of it now, but at the time everyone in the hall, including me, was scared to death. Believe it or not, but we even had a couple of staff on the floor hiding under desks.

I was coming in for the morning shift, and as usual, the night keeper was sitting at his desk and the four was beside him at the other desk. The count had come in, so as usual, the twelve cage officer came down to the hall with her shotgun, revolver, and ammunition, but this time things worked out a little differently. I was innocently standing by the desk getting ready to take over the shift when I saw the supervisor and his four literally dive under their desks! I didn't know what the hell was going on. Then I glanced over at Shirley, who had just come down from twelve cage. Holy God, I couldn't believe my eyes. She was standing there with the twelve-gauge shotgun underside up and pointed toward the desks and was using her fingernail to try and pry the shells out of the loading chamber! Jesus, when I saw that, I swear to God my blood ran cold. No wonder the guys had dived under their desks, and there wasn't another desk for me to dive under. Strange as it seems, for some reason it popped into my silly head that she was going to break a fingernail! I honestly don't have a clue why I thought of something stupid like that. But I remember she had very long nails and they were painted a bright red.

Very gently and quietly, I shuffled toward her, reached over, eased that barrel up, and then hung onto that shotgun for dear life!

I'm not sure of the outcome of that little episode, but I did find out later that, interestingly enough, it wasn't really all Shirley's fault.

As you can imagine, this went around the institution like wild fire. A day or two later, I was speaking to an officer that had been on the same induction course, and he mentioned that he wasn't shocked something like that had happened. In fact, he said he was really surprised it had taken as long as it did.

Well, I thought, *this sounds interesting,* so I pressed him for the whole story. And did I get a story. Honest to God, there were times all we could do was give our heads a shake and wonder how in God's name we survived.

He said he had started the service about the same time that they had begun to put women into the maximums. He also stressed that staff in the institutions didn't have a clue about how much pressure was put on the college to get the women through the course. He continued by telling me that one day his class had been out on the range, and Shirley had been having a hell of a problem with firearms. Apparently she was really scared of them, and every time she had fired a round, she had closed her eyes and jerked the trigger. "Naturally," he continued, "she never did hit the fucking target.

"Eventually, the instructor said it was time for a coffee break, so we all headed up to the shack. We were about half-way up when the instructor yelled at Shirley to hold on. So the rest of us just kept trucking up. We were all inside having a coffee and shooting the shit for five or ten minutes, and then the two of them walked in. Once we finished our coffee, the instructor told us everyone had passed the weapons training and we were heading back to the college! We just looked at one another and knew it was bullshit. Christ, we were all right there having our coffee and none of us had heard one goddamn shot being fired!"

Something like this sure made you wonder what was important in this life. But I'll never forget Shirley trying to dig those rounds out with those long red fingernails and those two big guys quivering under the desks!

But the female officers did put the supervisors and fours into a bit of a fix at times even though it wasn't always their fault.

At KP, during a shift, one correctional officer was responsible for each range. Among other duties, he carried the keys for the range barrier and the cells. He ensured the cell doors were locked for each count and then unlocked for meals or whatever. He was also responsible for solving any problems on the range. In short, the range, within reason, was his responsibility.

Therein lay the problem. If you had an agitated, possibly violent inmate, did you send two women down the range to settle him down? If there was a male and a female in the area, this was not usually a problem. In fact, quite often, a female officer was able to calm an irate inmate down much more easily and quickly than a male. However, what did you do if it was two females in the area? It wasn't proper to take one female out of her area and send a male in when there was a potential problem. First off, that singled out the woman and she got pissed off at you; second, the male would be asking you what the hell was going on. "After all," he would insist, and rightfully so, "she makes as much money as I do." However, at times, it was beneficial to have the strength of a male and political correctness be damned.

Sometimes it was a tough call. You wanted to be fair, but also, you didn't want someone injured if it could be helped. It was another damned-if-you-do-and-damned-if-you-don't situation, and that didn't even take into account an officer who happened to be pregnant.

In this job, it only took seconds for a major incident to rear its ugly head. We had an inmate living on A range that was somewhat mentally challenged or possibly even a little crazy; we certainly weren't qualified to tell the difference. There had been a problem simmering on the range for several days. As near as we could tell, some inmates were giving this guy a really hard time, and naturally threats were thrown back and forth. But all we could really do was try to make sure the situation didn't become serious. Unfortunately, we failed on that point!

I lucked out and wasn't at work when this incident went down, but I was told the inmate who had been acting strangely was out in the wing, and an argument of some kind developed. The inmate pulled a knife and intended to gut one of the cons that had been giving him a hard time. A CX 4 automatically jumped in and tried to stop it from happening; it didn't work. Gerald, who was the four, was stabbed in his chest! I wasn't there, so I can't say exactly what happened, but the con ended up in the hole, Gerald was rushed to the hospital by ambulance, and the son of a bitch that agitated the whole thing was back on his range relaxing. The inmate who did the stabbing even apologized for injuring Gerald. In fact, the wound was in the chest area, and he was very lucky he was overweight; the knife didn't reach his heart, and he got to live through it!

Spitting: it's a horrible, filthy habit. But in a penitentiary setting, it's also a serious insult, and one night a spitting incident almost forced me to gas a whole range!

I was working the night shift and received a phone call telling me I'd better get up to upper E just as fast as I could. I'll tell you, it didn't take me long to get up there.

And Christ, what a sight greeted me. The ranges, both three and four E, were full of inmates who were stalking around and threatening all kinds of mayhem. Luckily the staff had the range barrier locked, because the cons were not in a happy mood.

I asked the two in charge of the range what the hell had happened. Short answer—a con had spit on an officer. Oh, Christ, I'd only heard of this happening once or twice, and one of those times, it had been an accident. I looked out at the bunch of milling cons and knew there was no way in hell I could let this pass. One way or another, the spitter had to go to the hole. Once that was accomplished, it was up to the officer if he wanted charge the inmate with assault downtown or within the institution. But in any event, I was going to put the con into the hole!

I spotted the range representative looking at me and waved him over. I informed him an inmate had spit on an officer and there was no way in hell I could allow that, and one way or another, the spitter was going into segregation. The more I talked about it, the more pissed off I managed to get myself. I ended up telling the representative that they had five minutes to turn him over and that if I had to, I would gas the whole God damned range, but he was going to the hole. I even looked at my watch to give my speech a little added emphasis. After that, I just stood there watching them scuttle around in groups, yapping, waving their arms, and making all kinds of dire threats. At the same time I was thinking, *Boy oh boy, this could quickly become one hell of a mess!*

Just about that time the officer who had been spit on, I guess he would be the spitee, came up to me and said he wanted to talk to me. Into a side room we went, and I just stood there looking at him, knowing something was up. He finally opened up and said that before I made any decision, I should be aware that he had also spit on the con.

I just looked at him and said, "What the hell are you talking about? Officers don't go around spitting on the cons, for God's sake!" Well, apparently this one did.

He told me he was on the range and had had a little confrontation with the inmate, and the con had spit on him. "The thing is, I spit back at him."

Well, what the hell do I do now? I was walking back toward the range and saw the range rep waving at me. I headed over to him, and the first thing out of his mouth was, "You're not going to believe me, but the officer spit on the inmate, and that's the fucking truth!"

"Yeah, I know, he just told me that little fact. But," I continued, feeling like a little kid, "that buddy of yours spit first."

He looked at me and with a bit of a grin and said, "I know, but what in hell are we going to do now? I don't think either of us needs a fucking riot over this!"

"The only thing I can think of," I replied, "is to call it a wash."

Both the range rep and the inmate involved agreed. I ended up feeling like an idiot, but it could have been a hell of a lot worse. Luckily for me, the range rep was one of the reasonable inmates.

I told the officer I appreciated him owning up to his spitting, because it undoubtedly saved us from a serious problem. Then we had a few more words. It must have been a good lesson for him, because eventually he ended up being promoted to supervisor.

Life at Kingston Pen kept rolling along; some days were good and some were bad. Over all, the union problems had settled down, although at times they still jumped up and bite us on the ass.

Naturally, like any institution, KP had to deal with suicides. I'm not sure how many happened on my shifts, but I can specifically remember two and both, as usual, happened on the morning shift.

One was on the second tier in H range, and Nelson, the new CX 4 I had met at MI, was in charge of the wing. I'm not sure what time I received the phone call, but it was short and sweet: "Get down to H range; we've got a 'hanger'!" By the time I made it down, the staff had the cell door open, and there was no doubt he was dead. I told staff to check the range while I went up to make the phone calls. The nurse had already contacted the coroner's office, so I only had to notify the police and the deputy.

There was only one tiny little glitch to this suicide. Just as I made it back to the wing, Nelson signaled that he wanted to talk to me. I walked over, and together we strolled away from the other staff and then I just stood there wondering what the hell was up this time. In a quiet voice, Nelson told me the staff had found the cell next to the hanger unlocked. "To be honest," he said, "the con in the cell pointed out the unlocked door to the staff. Do you think, to save things from getting any worse, there's any chance we could just forget about it?"

I knew why he wanted to forget about it. The cell being unlocked meant the night shift had locked up, done the count, and missed it. It also meant our shift had done at least one count and I don't know how many walks without noticing that unlocked cell. It also meant the police had to take a second look at this thing. I knew damn well the inmate in the unlocked cell hadn't gone next door, made it through a locked cell barrier, done the guy in, and then relocked the cell on the way out. But one thing I had learned in this business was that you had to cover your rear end.

And that's what I told Nelson. "What do you do," I questioned, "if we let it go and don't report the cell being unlocked, and next week the con demands a favor? If you say no and he rats on you, then it really hits the fan. I don't want to be a prick about things, but it's much better to be up front, take the flack, and get it over with."

As far as I know, it didn't end up being a big deal anyway. The police came in, I explained about the unlocked cell, and as far as I know, that was the end of it. After that it was just a matter of waiting for the coroner to come in and pronounce him dead so the wagon could take him away and we could get back to normal. And as far as the open cell goes, I don't remember anyone even asking me about it. But I do know you don't cover things up. It just doesn't work out.

I don't remember how much time passed; it could have been a month or even a year, but I was on mornings when once again I got a call about a hanger. I made it down to the cell just as the staff was dragging him out so the nurse could work on him, not that it would do any good. I looked down at him and saw that it was the asshole from the radio room at the Bay. This was the same sex offender that had come into JI to pick up the inmate for the AA meeting. I watched as the staff dragged him out by his arms and, for some reason, noticed that his T-shirt had pulled up above his stomach and you could see that oversized belly flopping around. Once again, I didn't need medical staff to tell me he was dead. *Why in hell,* I thought, *didn't he top himself before he attacked the little girl?* But he hadn't. He had waited until he had done the damage, and then I assume he felt sorry for himself. Who the hell knows? I know I don't.

Anyway, that ended another shift, and we all got to go home to our families and maybe even thought to give them a hug.

Chapter 18

Escape attempts. Hostage situations.

Escape: a dreaded word in the world of corrections! And no matter how secure a prison is, it does happen. The mandate of corrections, loosely stated, is the humane care and control of offenders sentenced by the court. You cannot humanely lock people up and not have escapes every once in a while, and believe me, the emphasis, especially once the charter came into effect, was on *humanely*.

Almost every institution has had escapes. In fact, just before I joined the service, Millhaven had six inmates get out at the same time, if I'm remembering correctly. Now that was an escape and, thankfully, very unusual. I don't know if they were all recaptured or not, but I would expect they were. I also imagine this escape caused a major search of the Kingston area.

In any case, escapes do happen. And KP certainly had its fair share.

The west tower was a very popular tower for these attempts. It was close to a couple of buildings, and while I was at KP, there were two or three attempts to use it as an escape route; however, none were successful. You have likely guessed by now that the west tower was not staffed on all shifts; maybe it should have been.

One winter night, an inmate thought he would give it a try. I don't know how long he had been planning it, but he had to wait for a stormy night with snow blowing around. Finally one rolled around, so he figured he'd give it a shot. His idea was to get under the tower, throw up a rope and grappling hook, climb up into the tower, and then climb down the outside and take off. He managed to get the hook caught and was about a quarter of the way up when the wind suddenly died down. Naturally, when the wind died down, the snow stopped whipping around, and there he was, hanging onto a rope with his ass swinging in the breeze! Naturally, a tower officer spotted him, and he ended up in the hole. Also, during this episode a guard dog came in very handy; like I said, the cons were scared to death of them.

There were two escape attempts while I was on duty at KP, and they were not at all humorous.

On one night, we were doing the 1600 hours count and came up one short. Even before starting the recount, I felt my stomach start its quivering. And at that point, the chances were very high it was a miscount. It wasn't. It didn't take long to figure out which range was short one inmate, and once that was known, it was only a minute or so before we knew who was missing. I found out where he worked during the day and sent a few staff to search the area. A CX 2 gave a locked barrier a good yank and almost fell over when it swung open. I received a radio call about it and hustled down to take a look, and sure enough, the lock had been doctored. This barrier, at that time, led into the change room, and it only took a quick look around to notice a set of large shears were missing. That told us the inmate was likely armed, and this situation had suddenly become even more dangerous!

I told the staff to get out of the area and onto the range. Once we were all out, I had a four and a two come up to the hall with me. I issued the four a revolver and told him I wanted them to go back to the area and do a search. I also instructed him to make damn sure at least three staff worked together, and they were to yell out that they were armed before entering an area. Firearms were very seldom carried inside an institution, but I must admit Collin's Bay was on my mind. There was no way I wanted any staff injured or killed—not on my shift, or any shift, for that matter.

And definitely not because they were unarmed!

Luckily the incident ended when staff spotted him hiding between two barriers and he just gave up. On the way to disassociation, the inmate told me he had the rope and everything all set to go, but the officer in the west tower was too alert, and he never got the chance.

The second attempt was much more straightforward and didn't take nearly as long to come to a conclusion.

Once again the 1600 hours count was short, this time by two. There went my belly again; it just shriveled right up into a ball. During the recount, we figured out who was missing. This time it was the canvas repair shop, and I really started to sweat; I could just visualize them going out through the sally port in a load of mailbags!

I told the 2 I/C to look after the hall, and I took a .38 revolver and tucked it into my belt, and several of us headed for the shop. As soon as we entered the shop, we found the two inmates, and they claimed they'd fallen asleep and missed the count. That was absolutely a load of crap. They knew it, and they knew I knew it. I don't know what happened, but something screwed up their plans, or they wouldn't have been sitting there waiting for us. I had a jacket on and zipped up far enough to hide the revolver, because I didn't really want to be seen waving it around, but on the other hand, I wanted to be sure they knew I was armed. When it came to situations like this, inmates weren't stupid. So I just hung back and didn't take my eyes off them. Both of them gave me a look, and they knew damned well I was armed; I didn't have to say a thing.

In fact, a few days later, one of them complained to the deputy about me running around with a weapon. Don mentioned it to me, and I reminded him about the two officers being killed at the Bay and that was the end of that discussion.

I don't know how the instructor missed the two inmates when he closed up his shop; instructors were supposed to count inmates in and out. But I'm willing to bet he heard about it from on high, and that never happened again.

Rumours: There were always rumours in the penitentiaries. I think I may have mentioned earlier that pens are worse than the military for rumours. Usually they just died out, but for a couple of months there was a persistent rumour regarding a nun being involved with an inmate, and it just refused to die.

One night around 1900 hours or so, I received a phone call from an officer regarding this nun and the inmate. He was emphatic that something had to be going on between them, because they were just too cozy—way too cozy.

I decided to sit in the wing office and watch the inmates and the civilians come up from the recreation area. The inmate I was interested in came up and headed for B range. The officer looking after the range unlocked the barrier, and in went the inmate and a few of his buddies. But once the barrier was relocked, this particular inmate just hung around the barrier. And sure enough, the civilians come up, and the sister headed right over to B range; in fact, she almost ran over. She practically hung off the barrier, whispering and holding hands with the con, and I have to admit, I was flabbergasted! I was just heading over to send her on her way when the officer said something to her and she left for the hall.

What I'd seen was enough for a report, so up to the hall I went. The first thing I did, just to be safe, was to phone the north gate and make sure she had left. Once I was assured she was gone, I sat down, wrote the report, and stuck it into the deputy's mailbox.

The next afternoon there was a message to see the deputy before going down for roll call. He told me the nun wasn't allowed into the institution for the time being and the inmate was locked in segregation. He also said he had authorized a phone call for him later that evening and wanted me to supervise it. The inmate phoned the nun, and among other things, he told her if she was stuck she could go to his mother's place and his mom would help her; there were even some tears. Jeez, I didn't know if this guy was still with his wife or not, but he had two kids.

As you can see, you just never knew what you were going to bump into in these places.

Around this time, for several reasons, the population of the federal institutions shot up. Ottawa had no choice but to decide we had to implement double bunking. Christ, what a mess that was.

One of the jobs of the supervisor in charge of the wing was to assign cell locations to the inmates. Once double bunking started, we had to be extremely careful not to put a couple of guys that hated each other into the same cell. To say the least, it would have been embarrassing if they had pounded one another other while they were locked up together. On the other hand, we also had to ensure that anyone refusing to share a cell had a legitimate reason, and at times that was a fine line. So rather than enemies, we had to try and put two friends into the same cell, but we also had to make damn sure an inmate wasn't being coerced into double bunking because of a sex thing. It didn't take the inmates very long to understand what was going on, and eventually several approached us and requested to be bunked together. It's difficult to believe, but I ended up with a list of inmates requesting to be double bunked. I wonder why.

One of the problems that reared its ugly head was that at times a couple of inmates would have a spat and demand to be split up. Sometimes that could take a while to sort out, and we usually had to shift a few inmates around to get everything settled down again. There were times we didn't have so much as an empty cell to play around with. I have to admit, sometimes when I was doing the wing I felt like a damned pimp. And to rub salt in the wound, pimps made a hell of a lot more money than we did; some of them even had nice fur coats.

I did run into one problem around this time that could have had serious consequences for me. At the time we used a restraint procedure called hog-tying. Staff had to obtain a supervisor's permission to use this technique, and speaking for myself, I only allowed its use to prevent an inmate from harming himself. However, I ended up having two inmates attempt to lay excessive use of force against me with the police. That ended the use of that procedure for me. As far as I was concerned, an inmate could run his head into his cell wall or do whatever he wanted to himself. This was the only job I had, and I wanted to keep it.

One day the deputy asked me if I would be willing to act as the preventive security officer for a month or two. This certainly took some contemplating. It was a completely different job from the supervisor's responsibilities. But it was steady days, I could wear civilian clothes, and I would have no line authority over other staff. The IPSO just reported to the deputy and to RHQ. I talked it over with Sheila, and the next day I told Don I'd give it a shot.

And it was different. I must admit it took a while to get used to being an IPSO. Not that I even came close to learning the job. I knew that would take a lot longer than the one or two months that I was filling in.

There was really only one thing of any consequence that happened while I was doing the job. And that was half serious and half comical; at least, my part in it was comical. And thank God it ended up the way it did. It could have been extremely serious! We'd received word that a vial of cyanide was coming in or was already inside. At first I didn't put much stock in the tip; I had been told a lot of weird things, but cyanide? Also, I was thinking *For God's sake, how the hell could anyone get their hands on cyanide?* Well, lo and behold, we found out it was not all that difficult.

The tip told us the cyanide was going to be used to poison specific staff members and several inmates. Hey, no sense in just picking on staff. On a Friday afternoon, two of us headed down to where this vial was supposed to be hidden, and sure enough, there it was! Thank God for informants; police and corrections would be in a terrible fix without them. But we weren't sure what to do with the vial. So far, all we really had was some white powder. For all we knew, we were being set up to look like fools and it was baking powder, and believe me, no one was willing to sample the stuff. We finally decided I should lock it in the IPSO's safe for the weekend and then take it to Ottawa on Monday for testing. So I tucked it into the safe and went home for the weekend. We big shots almost always had weekends off.

As usual, Monday morning came around, and in to work I went. I checked with the garage and found out there were no service vehicles free, which meant I'd have to take my own car. That didn't break my heart; my car was in much better shape than the joint vehicles. So I told Don that I was heading for Ottawa and was going to take my car.

"Okay, but don't forget to keep track of your mileage."

Eventually I made it to Ottawa and found the RCMP lab, and so I wouldn't forget to mark the mileage down, I tripped the dash over to mph, wrote the figures down, and never gave it another thought. In I went with the vial. After about two coffees' worth of time, the lab tech came out, handed me the report, and said, "This is definitely cyanide. In fact there's enough in the vial to kill several people!"

Well, I thought, *ain't that something?*

I jumped back into the car and headed out for Kingston. Several minutes later, I was still in the Ottawa area and on a four-lane highway that, luckily for me, had a wide, grassy median. I was just bombing along, passing everything and thinking, *Jeez, do they ever poke along here.* I even checked my speedometer to make sure I wasn't speeding by too much, and according to the reading, I wasn't. After a few minutes and passing several more cars, I noticed an OPP car on the other side of the median. I also saw him turning his head to give me a good look. *Well*, I thought, *that's kind of strange.* Then I took another look at my speedometer

239

and thought, *Holy crap, I left it in mph; no wonder I'm passing everything in sight.* I slowed down and even debated getting off the highway but thought, *Aw, what the hell.* Luckily I never saw that officer again.

Once I made it back—very quickly, I might add—everyone was a little excited about the cyanide, and we found out it was quite easy to get hold of the stuff. I don't know what became of it, but it certainly was an interesting episode.

I finished my stint as an A/IPSO and went back into uniform just in time to work on my squad's personnel evaluations. Also, the deputy asked me to take on a fairly new correctional officer by the name of Stubbs and try to help him improve a little—well, actually, help him improve a lot. He told me two other supervisors had given it a shot and Stubbs hadn't changed one iota. He also added that if his job skills didn't improve, they were going to release him. What could I say? I told him I would give it a try, and I honestly did try.

I don't think any of the supervisors enjoyed doing those evaluations. They were a lot of work, and I had something like twenty-eight officers on my squad. Almost all of them were on yearly evaluations, but even so, they were lengthy and time consuming.

Most of my interviews went okay. Naturally not everyone was happy, but once I explained my reasoning for a lower rating in an area, staff members usually agreed.

One officer wasn't happy with his evaluation. He was very good at the security part of his job, and I graded him as such. His one problem was that he viewed everything in black and white with very little variation in between. As you can imagine, when dealing with people, especially convicted felons, this caused a few problems. It seemed every time I was in the wing when Ron was working the area, I spent a great deal of time settling difficulties between him and inmates. During our interview, I tried my best to explain the problem. I was very diplomatic, my justification was well written, and I really believed he had accepted the criticism in the manner it was intended. At least that's what I believed for a couple of days.

I guess Ron must have gone to the union regarding his evaluation, because I was called up to see the deputy. He told me Ron was extremely unhappy about his evaluation, and the deputy and I had a lengthy discussion about it. I explained my reasoning for the grade, but the long and short of it was that Don wanted me to redo it and ease up on the one section. I told him I really wouldn't be comfortable doing that, so Ron was transferred to another squad. I figured that was the end of it, and it was, at least until the next time we had union problems and Ron, Barry, Mark, and I believe Melville tried to set me up. But what the hell, I guess it was all part of the game.

But Stubbs was a different ball of wax. I knew him fairly well and realized he had problems working in an institutional setting. But once I was told I'd have to do his evaluations, I took a lot more notice of how he went about his duties, and he did need some guidance.

My first opportunity to offer guidance came during a noon meal. I was working the wing, and Stubbs was in the kitchen passage supervising the meal line. I forget what he did or didn't do, but he really screwed up. I walked over to talk to him about it, and he politely listened to what I had to say. He more or less agreed and said he could see my point and it wouldn't happen again. *Well*, I thought, *that was easy*. I couldn't understand why the other guys had had a problem with him. I figured I would have him sorted out in no time and back on regular probationary evaluations.

About two days later I was still in the wing and I saw Stubbs pull almost exactly the same stunt. I beat it over to talk to him, and I doubt I was as polite as I had been earlier. It only took a couple of minutes to realize everything I was saying was just going over his head. He just looked at me as if he didn't have a clue or didn't care what the hell I was talking about. I really tried everything I could think of to sort him out. I acted like a coach, a disciplinarian, and even an uncle, but to no avail; some people just shouldn't work in a penitentiary.

Shortly before I transferred back to Millhaven, the deputy and I had a lengthy discussion regarding Stubbs. The upshot of our conversation was that I told him I had given up and in good conscience could only recommend that Stubbs be released from the service.

Several months after transferring back to MI, I bumped into an officer from KP, and we had coffee together. After catching up on the gossip for a while, he suddenly asked if I remembered a guy named Stubbs. Once I replied in the affirmative, he asked if I'd known he was a native. I told him this was the first I'd ever heard of it.

"Yep, no one knew he was, and you sure couldn't tell by looking at him. Anyway, he was transferred out to another institution and into a different job, and did he luck in. I was told Ottawa sent a directive down to the deputy commissioner telling him to transfer Stubbs over there."

Naturally, the guy I was talking with didn't know about the difficulty the deputy and I had had with Stubbs, but the job he went into must have pissed a lot of people off. It was a promotion plus steady days. Christ, I knew guys that took courses on their own time just so they'd be qualified to apply for that position! But what bothered me the most was that this job had a lot of responsibility, and I really had to wonder if he was up to it. I certainly hope he was, because staff would be counting on him, especially during emergencies. One thing for sure, he wasn't fired. Oh well, that was life in the service.

One day in the wing, something happened to set off a dozen or so inmates. I'm not sure what it was, but they were pissed! To make matters worse, they were in the wing area, very agitated, and milling around like a bunch of cattle. Happily for me, the deputy and one other supervisor were there keeping me company. Oh, and an idiot officer I'll call Melville was in twelve cage. It took quite a while, but we finally had the inmates more or less settled down, and they were just about to head back onto their range when a booming voice echoed from twelve cage, saying, "Go ahead; make my fucking day." At the same time we heard a round being pumped into a twelve gauge!

Believe me, that sound is something you never forget. Christ, I didn't know if I should hit the floor, run, or just stand there and wet myself. We spun around and looked up to see what the hell was going on, and you won't believe it, but I swear to God this is true. That idiot Melville was standing up there in the cage with a bandoleer of ammunition hanging over his shoulder, two or three buttons of his shirt undone (don't ask me why I remember that), the revolver on his hip, the shot gun pointing out at us, and a thin cigar hanging out of his mouth!

Well, things sure quieted down; for a few seconds you could have heard a pin drop. I was thinking he'd cracked up, and I didn't like the idea of being between this idiot and the inmates—not a nice feeling! Then the inmates realized the same thing, and I guess they figured he wouldn't shoot, because they got stirred up again. The deputy looked at me, and I looked at him, and for a couple of seconds that was about all we could do. Finally he shook his head and said, "Vern, get up to that fucking cage and get that stupid son of a bitch out of there before he gets us all killed!"

And that's what I did. And I accomplished it just as quickly as I could. I don't recall what happened over the episode, but there's no doubt something was done. Thank God he wasn't in my squad; I had enough problems of my own. I did end up having another run-in with him, though. He was another one who worked with Ron and the two union guys when they tried to set me up.

After I left Kingston Pen, Melville got himself into a real tough spot. Someone reported him removing construction material from the institution and his vehicle was searched. Because some stolen material was found, officials searched his house and found a large amount of stolen material. Naturally he was fired, and of course the union appealed the decision. Six months later an adjudicator ruled the firing was excessive and changed the disciplinary action to a six-month suspension without pay. So, there you go. Management received an asinine ruling and the service ended up with a thief guarding other criminals.

I must state here that I was not involved with this situation and am repeating what I was told. I also don't know if this person ever did come back to work.

I'd been at KP for about four years when we had a major hostage situation in our hospital, and as luck would have it, I was in the Wing and Cell area. Shortly after work up, I noticed an officer escorting three inmates down A range to the hospital. Once they were about half-way down, I forgot all about them. I'd witnessed this happening dozens of times, and this particular time certainly didn't make an impression on me. I was still in the wing area when I heard scuffling and yells from the hospital area and a door slamming. Shocked, I looked down the range and saw that same officer racing back toward me!

Once again my physiology knew exactly what it was supposed to do; my insides immediately tightened up, my stomach started its flipping around, and it was difficult to get my breath. Hearing the scuffle was bad enough, but when you saw an officer running, you knew damned well that whatever had happened was serious. One of the things you didn't do in a prison was run unless something earth shattering was taking place. He hadn't even made it off the range when he started yelling, "They've taken over the hospital; they've got the fucking hospital!"

Oh God, I thought. *That's bad.* At the time I couldn't remember how many staff or inmates were in the place. But I knew there had to be at least three nurses and a senior correctional officer.

Once the officer reached me, between deep breaths he said he had escorted the inmates to the barrier, and as soon as the door was unlocked, one of the inmates had pushed him aside while the other two stormed in and grabbed the four. "The last thing I saw was a con yank the key from the four, slam the door shut, and lock it. Jesus Christ," he said, almost crying, "There wasn't a goddamn thing I could do!"

Before he had even finished filling me in, I told the four to have the wing and the shop dome locked down. Then I radioed the CX 4 in the yard and told him to lock the south barrier and not allow anyone in or out. Once that was done, I took off for the hall and contacted the deputy and duty keeper.

I have to say that the staff handled everything very professionally, asking very few questions and just doing what they were told. You could tell they'd had plenty of experience with this type of situation—in fact, too much experience.

After I contacted the deputy and filled him in as best I could, everything took on a life of its own. I still remember thinking that if this had to happen, thank God it was during the day shift when there was an abundance of staff. Mind you, on the night shift, there would never have been three inmates going in at the same time anyway.

I didn't have much to do with the actual hostage situation. I ended up staying in the wing and trying to keep everything as normal as possible. Inmates in the shops had to come back in, they still had to eat, inmates due for release had to be released, reliefs and lunches for staff had to be arranged, and it seemed like hundreds of items had to be sorted out. There was no doubt this was going to be a long one.

I also had to release a few of the staff from their posts because they were on the ERT. One of the first things we had to do was get a team suited up and on standby. When something like this first started, there was no guarantee it was a hostage situation. There was always a possibility the inmates were high or just flipped out and were on a rampage. Actually, in these situations, you kind of hoped it was a hostage-taking; that was usually the lesser of the evils that could take place! At the time, for all we knew, the officer could be injured or worse, and God only knew what other things could be happening. It didn't take long to get things settled down and for someone to make contact with the hospital and find out it was a hostage situation. I must admit that was a relief. Christ, what a job, relieved because it was only a hostage situation; can you imagine? There were times you wished to hell you could go back to being bored.

Communication! There's always a lot of talk about the importance of this subject. However important communication is normally, it was a hundred times more important in these situations. If staff weren't kept up-to-date, rumours started immediately. You could hear anything from "I hear the situation is over" to "Oh Christ, staff have been killed, and the team is going in!"

Negotiations with the inmates were ongoing, but I didn't even know who was involved; I was busy enough carrying out my job in the wing. But I was told the IERT was set up in a building close to the hospital. I had also been informed that staff were locked in a room and tied up next to several oxygen tanks. That didn't sound very good.

Stress tends to wear a person down, and after a while there was always an urge to just get in and end it, but stress also had a good side. If anything, stress weighed down the hostage takers more than it did the good guys. We got to relax a little, and if it went on long enough, we were able go home for a while. Not the cons. They stayed right in the middle of the situation, and they didn't get a chance to relax at all. Unless they were complete idiots, it had to prey on their minds. They never knew what we'd planned or when we might decide to charge in. They were also well aware that IERT had the equipment to go in—everything from gas to flash-bang grenades to firearms. And I don't care who you are, that's a hell of a lot of pressure to constantly have sitting on your shoulders.

Stress and tiredness tend to cause humans to make mistakes, and that's how this particular incident ended. I forget how long it went on, but the calmness was suddenly shattered by banging and screaming! A couple of the hostages stuck their heads out a window and started waving and screaming at us to get the hell in! We didn't know what the hell the inmates were doing, but it was enough to give the team the word to go. They had their plan ready, and it was just a matter of getting authorization to implement it, and that only took seconds once the screaming had shoved our adrenalin up about a hundred points!

To make a long story short, they made it in and had the area secured in a matter of minutes. And seconds after that, word came down that no one was injured. I say it only took minutes to secure the area, but it literally felt like an hour. Speaking for myself, I was just vibrating. We didn't know if the inmates had gone on a rampage or what the hell had happened. Believe me, when a situation deteriorated to that extent, it was much easier to be on the action end of the business rather than sitting around and waiting for word to drift down.

Apparently the break came when an inmate left the room where they were holding the staff. He was the only inmate in the room at the time, and when he left, the idiot left the key sitting in the lock. The four, being a sharp officer, jumped up, grabbed the key, and locked the door! Then the hostages started screaming for help. And help came sure enough. I wasn't involved with the negotiations, so I don't know what the inmates were trying to get out of it. They must have realized they weren't going to get out of prison. All inmates know, or they should know, they can't negotiate their way out of a prison.

Several days later, word started to circulate that one of the nurses had been infatuated with one of the hostage takers and had even given him a gold necklace of some kind. Whether this was true or helped to instigate the situation, I don't know. I do know that no one was physically injured, and that was the best we could wish for in these situations. As far as the rumour about the nurse, after several years and four different institutions, nothing surprised me anymore.

Once the hostage episode at the hospital was resolved and the inmates were shipped out, likely to the SHU, things settled down for a while. I don't remember if the nurse that supposedly set the thing off ever came back, but I seem to remember she was either transferred or left the service.

Anyway, once again everyone got to go home.

Chapter 19

Three CX killed. Inmate Olson and phone calls.
Back to MI.

By now I had been at Kingston Pen for several years, and everything, on the whole, was going pretty well. I knew the staff and respected most of them, and I hoped most of them respected me; however, there were a few staff members I didn't give a rat's ass about. I was also very familiar with the emergency routines; God knows I'd been through enough situations to be familiar with them!

On one particular day, I was working days and everything was just floating along; in fact, you could even say it was a little boring. That is, until I received a call to go up and see the deputy whenever I had a minute. I headed up as soon as I could get away, went into the office, and was invited to sit. Then he said, "I've got a good deal for you that will take two weeks."

Well, when the boss said something like that to me, I started to get a little edgy—in fact, quite nervous. Don told me there was a national supervisor's course starting up in a week or so, and he wanted me to go on it. He said there'd be a supervisor attending from almost every prison in Canada, and this was the first time something like this had ever been attempted. "If nothing else," he said, "you'll have an opportunity to discuss our problems with supervisors from across the country for two whole weeks."

This sounded really good to me. I was even getting a little excited about it; then he lowered the boom.

"The course is at the staff college in Quebec!"

That was when I halfheartedly tried to get out of it. "Christ, remember when I took the guys there for the funeral and how pissed off I was when we got back? I'm not really sure I ever want to go back there."

While I was reminding Don of that trip, my mind slipped back several years and reviewed it a little more fully.

During 1982, a prison in Quebec had a riot and staff lost control. I had never been inside that particular prison, but I knew the layout because it was an exact mirror image of Millhaven's. I wasn't sure what all had happened in there, and to be honest, I didn't really want to know. There wasn't much information about it in the papers or in the news, but three officers ended up being killed. I did learn a little more about the incident while we were at the funeral, and I'll tell you, it would have been hell inside that place.

One day not long after the riot, I headed out for Quebec early in the morning with five or six correctional officers in a CSC van, and everything went fine until we hit Quebec. Shortly after we entered the province, we had a mechanical problem with the van and pulled into a garage. They did a good job, and everything was fine until I went to pay the bill. I had a federal government credit card, and when I presented it, the guy looked at it and informed me in broken English that they didn't accept "that thing," and I ended up having to use my personal credit card.

Eventually we got on our way, found the church, parked the vehicle, got out, and just stood there gawking around. I had never seen so many people milling around for a funeral. A lot were in civilian clothing, but what really caught our eyes were the uniforms. The Mounties, provincial police, police from several municipalities, some military, and dozens upon dozens of correctional officers were present. I have to admit to feeling a little lost. The next thing I noticed was the church. It was immense. I didn't feel lost anymore; now I felt overwhelmed. There were so many people attending the funeral, even this church wasn't large enough. Once the pews were filled, everyone still outside, both police and corrections, filed in and stood in the aisles. We ended up standing in the middle of three columns of uniforms that started at the entrance and ended almost at the front of the church. That enormous church was packed. I'm not sure who was standing on my left, but a file of QPP was on my right.

The service was extremely long, and to be honest, I couldn't understand much of what was spoken; I assume it was a combination of French and Latin.

When the service was completed, a correctional officer started making his way up our aisle. Once he reached us, he spoke in French, and since I didn't have a clue what he was saying, I looked over at the QPP officer beside me and asked him what we were supposed to do. He looked back at me, shrugged his shoulders, and said something in French. It wasn't really a big deal, because we just turned around and walked out of the church. Once we made it out, about all we wanted to do was get down into the parking lot and have a cigarette. Believe it when I say it was a long service.

We were standing around talking with each other and wondering if we should take off, find a coffee shop, and then head back to Kingston. While we were chatting I was looking around, and wouldn't you know, there was the QPP officer who couldn't speak to me in English. The thing is, he was speaking English almost as well as I could! Just as I was staring at him, he glanced toward me, and he knew I had heard him. When he saw me his expression changed, but I honestly couldn't tell if he was mentally telling me to fuck off or if he was embarrassed. I always hoped it was the latter. This was not the ideal time to be acting like an asshole. To this very day, I could give a detailed description of that jerk. It's not something that's easily forgotten.

I did find out a little of what went on during the riot though. The inmates managed to capture the eight in charge of the prison.

In fact, he was working his last shift before retirement, and he was one of the guys who didn't make it out!

Once the inmates had control, a number of them frog-marched one of the officers up the corridor toward what we called T control. They dragged him almost all the way up to the control and then screamed at the staff to open the barrier. The officers hollered back that they were not allowed to do that. The cons told the officers if they didn't open the barrier they were going to kill their buddy. And that's what happened! The staff tried everything they could think of, which really wasn't a hell of a lot, but to no avail. The inmates dragged the hostage back down inside, and he was also one of the ones who didn't make it out. The staff couldn't even shoot. The officer was between them and the inmates. All they would have been able to do was watch. There is no way on earth I can envision what those guys went through. But I can imagine the screaming and crying that went on. How could they be in a situation like that, see what they saw, and stay sane? I doubt either of them ever went back inside again.

I never did hear how the staff regained control of the institution. But one thing I do know is that it must have been a God-awful sight once they did get in! Another sad statement is that the cons involved in this slaughter were almost certainly considered heroes among most of their peers. Oh well, what can you say? Things happen, and you hope you survive and get to go home to your family.

With a jerk, I came back to the present and thought, *Christ, do I really want to go back to Quebec?* Don and I covered the subject quite extensively, and I did realize it was an unusual opportunity and I really didn't want to refuse. I told him I'd have to talk it over with Sheila and make sure we could make arrangements for the kids and I would let him know for sure the next morning.

The next morning I told him I would be happy to go on the course. He informed me that he had received a phone call from

Jerry. Jerry was the officer from the Bay who had passed the CX 3 competition that I failed, and since then he had been promoted to a supervisor. Jerry was wondering if he could hitch a ride with me to Quebec, so I ended up with company on the trip.

This course was extremely interesting, and the staff at the college treated us exceptionally well. The course was well worth the effort. Unfortunately, it was the first and only time the service ran that type of training; money problems wouldn't allow it, you know.

A few weeks after returning from the course, Don asked if I would be interested in becoming the emergency team coordinator. He told me it wouldn't be a case of me actually taking part in any assaults or actively participating in the training. Apparently, the wardens had been instructed to have a management representative involved with the teams, and I really couldn't argue with the idea.

The next step was to speak to the four who was running the team; in fact, I believe this was same guy who had originally gotten it up and running. As far as I knew, he had been doing an excellent job, and I wanted to make sure he realized I wasn't coming in to circumvent his authority. During our chat, I stressed that I was just a buffer between the team and management. I also made sure he understood that the warden was just doing what he had been ordered. Once our conversation was completed, he seemed to have accepted the idea, and then he asked if I was going to volunteer to be maced.

"Maced! What in hell are you talking about?"

He explained that every new member of the team was required to be maced. This was a requirement so all members would understand how it affected the inmates. So there I was, between a rock and a hard place. I certainly didn't have to be maced, and I damned well didn't want to be. On the other hand, if the team members had to go through with it, I felt I should also bite the bullet. I drew a set of equipment but never intended to use any of it except the boots and coveralls. In fact, I still have the boots and the IERT hat.

The next training day was at the staff college, so off I headed with the team. I honestly think they were really looking forward to using that stuff on a supervisor. Me? I wasn't looking forward to it at all. I'd been involved in the use of mace several times, and usually there was some blow-back. And believe me, the stuff is potent!

We had the gym reserved for half the day, so in we went. I changed into my coveralls, and there I happily stood—very close to the showers, I might add. I had a team member standing on each side to lead me to the shower. I was told to just let them do their thing and everything would be hunky-dory. So there I stood like a damned idiot.

And then, bang! I was squirted right on the forehead, and within a couple of seconds I would have been willing to kill someone if it meant I got help! I had always known that stuff was powerful, but I had no real idea until this happened. God, you can't see, can't breathe, and you know damn well you're going to die! However, once I was guided into the shower, it didn't take long to wash it out and get back more or less to normal. It was a rough way to get involved with the team, but I think it was worth the effort. Part of the procedure in the use of mace had always included getting the inmate to a shower or at least to some water as quickly as possible. I could now appreciate exactly why we did that. Being maced was not an uplifting experience!

Around this time more than half a dozen of us got involved with the Human Rights Commission. If you want some free advice, stay the hell away from those people, just as far away as you can get! I didn't know anything about it until one day I was told to go up to a certain boardroom. Off I trotted, and when I entered the room wondering what the hell was going on, I spotted a couple of strangers and seven or eight correctional staff shuffling around. A couple were supervisors, a few were CX 4s, and several were CX 2s. Everyone except the 'suits' seemed a little nervous. Once everybody involved had made it, the strangers introduced themselves to us. I forget their names, but they were government lawyers from Ottawa!

They calmly informed us we had been named in a complaint sent to the Human Rights Commission by an inmate at KP. They also told us they had been given our case but thought everything would work out okay—emphasis here on the word *thought*. But then he concluded by saying, "If the good of the service deviates from your personal best interests, we suggest you retain your own lawyers."

I don't know how in hell he figured any of us would ever be able to afford lawyers to take on the Human Rights Commission! Christ, they had more money and more power than God. Another thing I found out was that if there was a complaint, it would appear the investigator's job was to prove you guilty, not to prove the facts of the case! And I kid you not! This thing dragged on for several years, and I still don't remember ever being told what I was supposed to have done that was so horribly wrong! You can bet we would never have been allowed to treat an inmate the way we were treated. But I knew the inmate who laid the complaint, and it's amazing how much hate he had eating at him.

I dealt with hundreds, maybe even thousands, of inmates, but very few were like this one. He just hated all staff. And he could pick many ways to let you know how he felt. One thing he loved to do was to stare at you and then spit as he walked past. He always (or almost always) missed, but one way or another he let you know exactly what he was thinking. I won't talk about his crime, because it was sickening, but I do know an officer would never, ever have wanted to be a hostage with him in the area!

He even laid a separate complaint against a nurse and me. According to him, the nurse went into segregation one evening to deliver medication, and when she came to his cell, she unbuttoned her top and waved her breasts at him! And then to make matters worse, he claimed I was in charge of the prison and was standing at the entrance to the hole watching her do it and laughing about it! When I was first told about this complaint, I thought they were joking. Even if this story had been true, with the physical layout of segregation, he wouldn't have been able to see me. But they weren't joking, not by a long shot. I think this was about the most farcical thing that ever happened to me in the service. But I still had to make a trip to Toronto, find a particular building, and go in front of a board to explain how stupid this whole thing was.

But that human rights complaint hung on for several years. I know damn well I never did anything wrong, and one of the other supervisors involved with this mess was Jack, whom I knew from both the Bay and MI. Believe me, if anyone was on the straight and narrow, it was Jack. Just accusing him of racial discrimination or threatening an inmate or anything similar was enough to tell me the whole damn system had gone crazy! I ended up being questioned by two or three different investigators. I still didn't know what the hell I was accused of, but I was worried. I knew damn well Sheila and I couldn't afford a lawyer over this crap. We did talk the problem over, though. Sheila had taught me to do that while I was still at Millhaven.

I had walked in the door after a shift in the SHU several years ago, and Sheila had said, "Vern, I want you to sit down, we're going to have a talk."

That was scary! My stomach must have thought I was back at work, because it just dropped. At the same time, my mind was racing all over the place trying to think of what I had done wrong and I didn't have a clue. But I did exactly as I was told; I sat. Sheila asked me if I realized I hadn't gone to bed sober during the last couple of weeks or so. I was flabbergasted; I didn't know what she was talking about. Hell, we used to buy booze for Christmas and still have some left for the following Christmas.

I guess Sheila could tell I was having a problem digesting that bit of information, because she asked me to just sit and think about it for a minute or so. And I did. And by God she was right. I'd started coming home and having a drink, and I guess it escalated from there. The really scary thing was that I hadn't even realized it! And that really did scare me. It scared me enough that I didn't have any booze in the house for some time.

The long and short of this story is that it's really wise to talk things out.

If I'd been on my own, Lord only knows where I might have ended up.

I also learned that once the human rights people sunk their teeth into something, they were like pit bulls; they just wouldn't let go. I'm not sure how many years passed, but I was back at Millhaven when Robert, who was also involved in this mess, received a phone call. I handed the phone to him, he identified himself, and then there was nothing but silence. A minute or so passed, and then he exclaimed, "Listen, I've had enough of this bullshit, and I'm finished talking to you people; from now on you contact my lawyer and leave me the hell alone!" Then he slammed down the receiver!

He just stood there for a couple of minutes collecting himself and then looked at me and said, "It's those goddamn human rights fuckers again, and I've had it. Jesus Christ, they just never stop; all this over that fucking asshole who should've been put down anyway. It's disgusting!"

And I agreed whole heartily with him. Law-abiding people should have defenders like that. I swear to God, they didn't believe their job was to find the truth; it was to prove a complaint was valid whether it was or not.

Eventually the warden at KP or a higher-up caved, and the inmate did receive money. I imagine he must have laughed all the way to the bank with that cheque from the taxpayers!

There was a long stretch at KP when we just couldn't seem to shake staff problems. I don't know what benefit staff thought they could earn from pissing everyone off, but they went ahead and did it anyway. This particular stretch was rough enough that the night shift had two supervisors on duty. So there you go, the union pissed everyone off and still managed to get the supervisors some overtime; wasn't that nice of them?

On this particular night I was working overtime in the wing area, and the regularly scheduled supervisor was working out of the keeper's hall. My job was to try and keep the wing's routine as close to normal as possible.

I'm not sure what caused this problem, but I had to actively urge staff to open the range barriers to facilitate movement, and they were slow. This was something else that always mystified me at Kingston Pen. There were approximately seven officers assigned to the ranges in the wing area, and to unlock a range, an officer had to go down and individually unlock each cell. That put one or two staff locked on a range with anywhere from forty to sixty inmates that they had pissed off. Figure that one out; I can't. And on top of that, once the cells were unlocked and the staff were off the range, the inmates were allowed out into the wing.

So in effect, you had sixty or so loose inmates being controlled (you hoped) by seven or so officers. These were the same officers who were doing their damnedest to piss off the inmates in the hope the cons would give management a hard time. Naturally, all management personnel were at home relaxing. Now didn't this show a lot of very deep thinking? And we talked about inmates pulling stupid stunts! Granted, these inmates were mostly PC, but there were still some tough cons in KP, several of whom were not quite right in the head. And there is lots of proof for that statement.

In fact, here are a few items to prove that claim.

One night I went in to relieve Jack, and he told me they'd had a problem in the exercise yard and one inmate had been killed.

Jack told me the attackers had used a weight bar and, among other brutalities, had driven the bar straight through this guy's head a few times. As usual, several inmates were milling around, and the tower officer couldn't get a shot off. God forbid you ever hit an inmate and couldn't prove he had been taking direct part in the assault.

Here's another little item: It hadn't been very long since we'd had a hostage situation, and the hostage taker had had to be shot and killed by a member of the IERT. It was either that or let the hostage risk a good chance of being stabbed or having his throat slashed. Remember Collin's Bay; it can happen.

Another item: A couple of our brave residents had taken a girl into the bush and tied her to a tree. Then they used her as the target for bow and arrow practice.

Another item: One of our heroes had tied a girl to a chair and, among other things, broke all her fingers. I was told this girl lived.

These same inmates, and a lot more like them, would go to staff whining and sniveling about their human rights. And it was always "gimme, gimme."

Staff working in penitentiaries deal with people like this, and worse, on a daily basis. Then at the end of their shifts, they go home to their spouses and kids and have to act like they are coming home from a normal day at the office. Christ, at times that's difficult!

One other time we were in a hostage situation. I vaguely remember it was in an office, and as usual, the hostage was a female. The usual negotiations took place, and eventually we got her out. The thing was, between negotiations, otherwise known as talk talk talk, the inmate was going into the back and raping the hostage. I really don't remember anything more about this particular situation; my mind just draws a blank. Sheila reminded me that this incident seemed to bother me much more than the others, and that may be why it's so hazy.

Okay, back to the staff problem. As I was saying, you had a few officers controlling or trying to control hundreds of inmates, and at the same time, the staff was hoping to hell the inmates would go into their cells at night so they could go home. But then the staff did stupid things like unnecessarily making these same inmates late for meals, recreation, visits, and so on. All this was so the staff could get back at management for some perceived wrong. And then to top it off, the same guys got upset when the cons got pissed and made comments to them or acted out! Figure that one out; I never could.

So there I was, going through this nonsense, and the other keeper was in the hall trying to run the prison. Ron—the guy who was so upset with his evaluation—was assigned to F and G ranges. Melville, the twelve cage idiot, was also working in the wing somewhere. Boy, didn't I luck in. I had to get after staff several times about not doing their duties properly, but Ron was giving me an exceptionally rough time. Finally he wore me down, and I must admit I was a little frazzled; actually, *pissed* would be the appropriate word. I went over to him and told him, and not very politely, that I wanted him up in the hall for a chat.

Just as we were heading up, I heard Melville yell to someone, "Thibedeau's taking Ron up to the hall! Let me in, I have to use the fucking phone!"

As we went through the hall to the spare office, I told the keeper Ron and I were going to use it for a chat. I don't remember exactly how the discussion went, but eventually we ended up talking about his stress level.

Within five minutes or so, in strutted Barry with his intelligent sidekick Mark in tow! That certainly broke off any discussion Ron and I were having. I'm still not sure if he really wanted some help or if he was putting me on to kill time, but I tend to think it was the latter. But by then I really didn't give a crap, because I was well aware I'd been set up. I found out later both Barry and Mark had been sitting over at the staff college waiting for the phone call. I ended up sending Ron home after telling him if he was as stressed as he claimed, he should contact a doctor. As far as I was concerned, that was the end of it, and I didn't really give a damn what happened with him.

I must admit, though, I was a little upset that Cecil had allowed those two idiots into the institution. We were of two different opinions: he believed he was obligated to because they were union officials; I thought otherwise because there was union representation on site. But in the grand scheme of things, it wasn't really a big deal.

A few months later I was asked if I would do the IPSO position again. I didn't even contemplate not doing it; anything to get away from staff problems for a while. I sort of felt I should pay them for asking me. Well, I guess that's a bit of an exaggeration. Once again my session as an IPSO was relatively quiet. I guess I was kind of lucky, because when I acted as the preventive security officer at Bath Institution, I was busier than hell.

There was only one major occurrence while I was IPSO at KP; however, that one episode was terrible—another hostage-taking. I wish I could remember how many KP had during the seven or eight years I was there.

This incident took place in the RTC during 1988 and involved one female nurse and, I think, two inmates. They grabbed her, dragged her into a cell, and as usual tied the cell door shut with wire. The usual procedures were put into place. I've mentioned how KP staff had experience in this end of the business. And as usual, the negotiations started. I'm not sure how long this situation lasted, but I was doing the preventive security job and I was still the team coordinator, so I know I was rather busy. Thankfully, I wasn't involved with the negotiations; I never did have any training in that area. During these situations, management, as a rule, couldn't afford to lose supervisors to any duties except supervising.

As usual, we had a team in the area suited up and all set to go if they were needed. The team had submitted a plan, which had been approved, and all that was required was the word *go*. Once a team was prepared, all they could do was wait and wait and wait, and that was one of the most difficult requirements demanded of a team—waiting. The *go* was also something everyone hoped didn't come down; usually it wasn't pleasant if they had to go in. This time, because the cell door was wired shut, one of the tools the team planned to use was an electric hand grinder. The idea was that if they had to rush in, the grinder would be used to slice through the wire holding the door shut—a good plan, you would think.

And the word did come to go. I don't know what precipitated the charge, but the order wouldn't have been given lightly. I was standing on the range down from the cell, and all I could do was watch the team rush toward me, and even though I was on their side, it was still a scary sight. They had their gas masks and helmets on and wore their black coveralls with gear strapped on all over their bodies, and you couldn't help but see the shields and night sticks. It was an awesome sight!

While they were charging toward me, I noticed the guy in the lead had the grinder held up and all set to go. The problem arose when I looked down and saw the end of the electric cord. Christ, it was way too short to reach the cell, and all I could do was watch the power cord and its plug slither across the floor following the grinder. My mind immediately shot back to Collin's Bay and the case of the cut fire hose, but this was much more serious! I gave a holler to get their attention, but once they started in, there was no stopping; they had to keep going! But at least they knew the grinder wouldn't be in operation. When they reached the cell door, I saw one of the guys reach down to his boot and pull out a huge knife. That knife freed up the cell door almost as quickly as the grinder could have. But I shudder to think what could have happened if he hadn't had that oversized pig sticker. It only took a few seconds to breach the cell door and grab the inmates. Once again we were lucky. As far as I'm aware, there were no physical injuries. I do want to stress the words *physical injuries* in these episodes; I have no idea what other injuries may have occurred.

In some ways though, the IPSO position was interesting, and I certainly learned another aspect of the job. A preventive security officer dealt with inmates in a far different manner from a correctional officer. A correctional officer was usually attempting to enforce a regulation, arguing, or out and out fighting with an inmate. An IPSO was trying to get information and attempting to make sense out of that information, and naturally an inmate usually wanted a favor in return. In some aspects, it was a balancing act. I did learn more about some of the inmates in KP, though. And it was amazing what some of them told me. Some of the information was even scary.

And that leads me to Clifford Olson, one of our more notorious inmates. Before I had started doing the IPSO job, he'd contacted the RCMP in BC and told them he was willing to show them where he had buried more bodies. Of course he demanded a flight out to BC. So everything was arranged to escort him to the Kingston Airport, and it was decided he should have an armed escort. Robert drove a service vehicle and I sat beside him with a rifle. We followed the escort vehicle to the airport and then waited until the plane took off. I'm not exactly sure why I was armed. I'm not certain if it was to protect the scumbag or if it was to stop an escape attempt. I don't think it would've bothered me to stop an escape; after all, if duty called—. But I'm not sure what I would have been able to do if someone had tried to get to him. It was bad enough dealing with 'normal' killers, but when it was someone who had killed several young people, well, that sort of put a different light on things. Thankfully, I never did have to make that decision.

Olson made it out to BC, but as expected, he didn't hold up his end of the bargain. However, authorities couldn't ignore the possibility that he might have been telling the truth. The other downside was that we got the asshole back at KP. But he did get what he wanted—a trip to BC and lots and lots of publicity. Boy did he love publicity; he would have done anything for it.

Shortly after I started the IPSO job, I received a phone call from a father living in Alberta. He'd phoned because his son had received a letter from Olson, and of course Olson was locked up in Kingston Pen. As you can imagine, the father was a tad upset, and he wasn't the only one; I was as pissed off as he was. Thinking about what this inmate had done and the fact that he had then managed to get his hands on this young person's address sent chills up my back. The other thing that always worried me was how many other letters he might have sent out to young people, letters that none of us ever heard about? Scary thought.

As always happened, KP eventually received a new warden. Actually, I think there were three or four while I was there. I thought highly of every warden, but most importantly, I respected them. Respect, at least to me, is extremely important. I can understand not liking a boss. I think it's impossible to like all your bosses, but I firmly believe you should be able to respect them. The problem I ran into, and it was my problem and no one else's, was with my last warden at KP. Not only did I not like him, I couldn't even come close to respecting him.

I honestly thought I could work my way around the problem; at least I hoped I could, because I enjoyed working there. The only problem for me was the warden, and my line of thought was that you couldn't have everything, so I just had to suck it up and work with it. And I tried; I honestly did. But I eventually threw in the towel.

I don't recall just how I went about the transfer, but I wouldn't have submitted my papers before talking it over with my deputy.

I also phoned the deputy at Millhaven Institution and had a chat with him. It was a short chat. He just said something like, "Get your papers in. The sooner they're in the sooner you'll be here."

Once again, it was a good feeling knowing I'd be welcomed back.

I was really of two minds about leaving Kingston Penitentiary. Even with all the difficulties with both staff and inmates, it had been a good place to work. I had gained a ton of experience, and even though I don't remember ever being told so directly, I knew my work was appreciated. On the other hand, I had been there several years, and I must admit I like change. There was also the issue of the present warden. I was pretty sure if I stayed, my mouth would likely get me into trouble. So I thought, *What the hell; change is good.*

Chapter 20

Shooting at KP. An escape and a helicopter.
Transfer to BI.

So there I was, back at Millhaven and feeling like I was going around in one big circle. Thank God I didn't have to make a stop at Collin's Bay on the way. I must admit it was nice to be back; I had absolutely no problem settling right in. Not much had changed, at least not physically. Most institutions, including KP, had gone through management changes. Institutions now had unit managers. Each unit manager was in charge of a living unit. Of course, now all institutions had to use the term *living unit* rather than *cell block*, which apparently sounded much better to the public and to inmate rights people; it wasn't quite as mean sounding. At any rate, for good or bad, and I'm not saying it was bad, this put another layer of management into the system.

On my first day, I spoke with both the deputy warden and the CX 8 and was basically told to float around and get the feel of the place again. The deputy told me I would be assigned to A unit and he would introduce me to the manager when he returned from his course. I must admit it was gratifying just wandering around and not having any real responsibilities. I was also happy to see that I still knew most of the staff, and I had a lot of "Hey, glad to see you back" type comments thrown at me. There were several new staff, though, and most of them were female. It did seem strange seeing women in uniform at MI, but I didn't see any friction, at least not that I could notice.

Unfortunately, I was to find out there was some, but it wasn't nearly as bad as at KP.

One of the first females I met had worked in an office at MI before transferring over to the corrections end of the business. She was well liked by staff and could certainly stand up for herself. She was short, though; in fact, she had a difficult time looking through the cell door windows, and I was told she carried an empty paint can to stand on. Sarah would look in, verify the inmate was in the cell and alive, pick up her can, and move on to the next cell. So of course here nickname was "Paint Can" Sarah.

I mentioned that I didn't think there was much friction between the male and female officers. Other than a few minor issues of the sort that could crop up anywhere, I hadn't noticed any. Unfortunately, that was not to last. I'd been back for several months and was working the night shift when I ran into the problem.

During the early evening, I decided to take a trip around the living units and made E unit my first stop. The SHU had been moved from E unit to Quebec in 1984. I'm not aware of the reason for this move; I just wasn't interested enough to inquire about it. But it may have been due to a requirement for more room or possibly even for political reasons. Once again, who knows? At any rate, E unit was now a regular unit. I entered the unit office and saw the two male officers and the one female officer that were posted to the unit. As soon as I stepped in I could feel the tension, and my first thought was, *Oh crap, here we go again; I must be back at KP.*

At first I thought they were having inmate problems, but no such luck. We exchanged the usual pleasantries, but at the same time I could 'feel' them watching me, and my stomach kept sinking lower and lower. One of the male officers was a union steward, and I knew him from my previous time at MI; in fact, he was quite a vocal union representative. For some reason, this guy started using really foul language. It took me about half a second to catch on to the fact that he was doing it because of the female officer being present. I couldn't understand why in hell he was carrying on. She was a good officer, and to top that off, he was a union steward and was supposed to protect staff. Yet here he was acting like a frigging asshole.

I'd never run into a similar situation before, and I wasn't sure what to do. I hadn't been back very long, and I suspected there must be some type of history between the two of them, not that it should have made a difference. I was just about to ask the guy to step out of the office for a minute, but I spotted a slight signal from the female officer asking me to leave it alone. I almost asked him out anyway, but then I thought if I did, I was telling the staff I didn't think she could fight her own battles, and I didn't want to leave that impression with anyone. She was a very good officer, and as a person, I had a lot of respect for her. Eventually, I decided not to do anything for the moment and just to leave the unit. I have to admit, though, leaving bothered the hell out of me.

Later in the shift, the same female officer came up to the hall and wanted to speak to me privately. We went into a separate office, and I must admit I wasn't feeling very happy about this whole situation. I'd been berating myself for not taking some type of action, but at the same time I was thinking I'd made the right decision. But I was still sweating. Harassment had always been a huge issue, and ever since women had been in uniform, that issue had doubled. And there were times there was just no right answer—another damned-if-you-do-damned-if-you-don't situation.

I certainly didn't disagree with the harassment policy. At times, it went a little overboard, but it was necessary, especially if we were going to have uniformed females in this environment. And the decision to have women in uniform had been made, and in my mind, it was the only fair decision that could have been made. But these thoughts didn't help me now. Having an officer wanting to speak to you privately was not good at the best of times, and that officer being female made it twice as worrisome. And then knowing that same officer was involved with a staff problem made it ten times worse; at least in my mind, it did. And now if an official report had to go in, I was likely looking at a big, big problem.

We went into the office, sat at a desk, and started to chat; at least, she started to chat. She began by saying she knew I was aware of a problem in the unit and wanted to inform me that it had been going on for some time. I agreed that I recognized something was happening and that I wasn't happy about it. I explained why I hadn't handled it right then but told her I was going to take the guy aside and at the very least have a discussion with him. I also told her if she wanted to make an official complaint, I would certainly back her and that I had made notes in my book about the incident.

"No, no," she replied. "I don't want to make it official. I just want to make sure you're aware of it. I'm still going to try to handle it, but if I can't I'll need you as my witness."

About two weeks later I had to go to a manager's meeting taking place outside the institution. All managers and supervisors had to attend, and it was an all-day affair. Most institutions tried to have at least a couple of these events every year, and they were well worth the effort. It was amazing how much could be accomplished when there were no interruptions and no phones ringing.

This particular meeting was going along as usual, and just before it ended the warden said he had to talk to us about harassment. "As I have mentioned several times," he emphasized, "there is no such thing as not reporting anything that has to do with harassment." Going even further, he stated, "I'd hate to see a manager lose his or her job because an incident involving harassment was reported to them and they failed to forward a written report. Remember, there's no such thing as not proceeding when it comes to this subject; it has to be acted upon."

Well, Jesus H. Christ, I thought with a sinking feeling. *That's exactly what happened to me a few weeks ago!* You can bet your ass I said this silently, because there was no way I was going to tell anyone about it unless I absolutely had to. This was also the first I had ever heard about not having a choice about whether to report an incident or not. But I knew that wouldn't make any difference if it came down to the wire; a supervisor was expected to know all things. At least it seemed that way to us. However, I knew this officer and respected her, and I was 99.9 percent positive that it wouldn't jump up and bite me in the ass. But for a long time, there was always that little niggling thought picking away at the back of my mind. If she ever had a hate on for me, all she would have had to do was change her story a little tiny bit and I would have been done like a dinner. Thank God it was this particular officer and not a few other vindictive ones I could think of. And that was the last I ever heard of the incident. I never did find out how she corrected the problem, but she must have.

I think this episode helps explain just how paranoid this job could make a person. I also want to make it clear that the harassment policy didn't just involve female staff. It also, and rightfully so, pertained to everyone.

On my return to MI, I met one new officer I hadn't known before. I was told he'd transferred in from Quebec, and there was a lot of talk going around about him. The rumour was that he had been on a police force and got himself into trouble of some kind. He was supposed to have been involved with something that was on the verge of being illegal or actually was illegal, but since nothing could be proved, they got him into corrections and shipped him to Ontario. Once again I have to say that rumours could run wild, but often they had at least a hint of truth to them.

Shortly after my transfer, I had a couple of weeks of annual leave, so my family packed up and took the long drive up north for a visit. When we got back, I found out it had been a good time to be off.

We had only been back for a couple of days when I bumped into someone from MI. We were standing around having a chat, and one of the first things out if his mouth was, "Hey, did you hear about the shooting at work?" He told me there had been a fight in the exercise yard one evening and the tower officer had shot one of the inmates. "Well," he continued, "everyone thought, *Good job; did what he was supposed to do.* But after a while, word started going around that something wasn't right with the shooting, so now we don't know what to think."

The officer that had done the shooting was the guy from Quebec, and rumour claimed it had been a setup. The whispers stated inmates had planned the incident because they wanted the con shot. Rumour also said the officer was involved with the inmates and for whatever reason had purposely shot that one inmate. By the time I went back in to work, the officer was gone, and as far as I know, no one ever saw or heard from him again. Once again, I have to stress this was only talk, so who knows?

I do know it was not unusual for an officer to have to be transferred after a shooting. The other inmates took a dim view of it. They didn't mind committing mayhem on each other, but they sure didn't want the staff doing it.

Several years earlier, an officer on the response team at KP had had to shoot a hostage-taker and had been transferred to the staff college. Eventually he was told he had to return to the institution, and he did come back, but he only stayed for a short time and then left the service. It was unfortunate he had to leave; he was a good officer. As you can see, there were times when an employee of the correctional service was punished for doing his duty. There were times prisons could be crazy places to work, and not always because of the inmates.

Computers are great things, and they made the supervisor's job a little easier. Prior to computers landing, among other jobs, we used to have to do the personal evaluations by hand or type them out. I was kind of lucky, though; I had a feeling they were on the way, so I had bought a really good one, learned how to type, and become fairly familiar with them.

Now that we are on the subject of computers, I want to go back to my first one or two years at KP and talk about a day I was called up to the deputy's office. When I made it up, he introduced me to his visitor and told me he was going to put a couple of computers into the security office for the clerks. Boy, that was an exciting time!

The computer guy told us that the clerks probably wouldn't have anything to do with them at first. I guess we looked at him a little strangely, because he kind of laughed and said he had been through this several times and knew exactly what was going to happen. He explained that he'd give the clerks an idea how the computers operated, but most importantly, he would show them some of the games. He said he'd make sure the computers were on stands with wheels and leave them pushed back out of the way. He told us it wouldn't take very long and we'd notice that the machines would eventually start getting closer and closer to the clerks' desks. And by God, it worked just the way he had said it would. Imagine that—he knew exactly what he was talking about. The computers had another side benefit for the clerks. The damn things kept crashing. We finally discovered the office was too hot for the computers. So they had to put air conditioning in; did they ever luck in!

And then, hot damn, the next step was for each supervisor's office to get a computer. It meant one computer for two supervisors, but what the hell; it saved all kinds of time for us. Eventually some computer conjurer managed to install a blank copy of the performance evaluations into the machines for us, and away we went. It was great!

By the time I made it back to Millhaven, computers were a common sight.

But they couldn't do everything, and supervisors still had to patrol the institution during their shifts. One rainy night I was doing a trip around the units, and just as I walked into E unit one of the guys stuck his head out of the office and yelled that they wanted me in the ECA *now*! Well, my old stomach started its flipping and fluttering, and I took off.

For some reason my mind shot back several years to a night I had been in charge of the ECA as a CX 4 and I thought, *Oh God, not again!*

On that earlier night, I was sitting in the ECA office, and the two was down a range when he screamed at me to get down to a cell! I tore out of the office and pounded down to where he was standing and staring into a cell. By the time I got to him, he was so white I thought he was going to pass out.

"Holy Christ," he said to me with a dazed look, "Look in the cell! I don't know what the fuck to do!"

I glanced in, and I don't doubt I went as white as he did; maybe even whiter. I had never seen anything like that, and thank God I never have since. The inmate was sitting on the toilet with his pants down and holding his penis in one hand and sawing at it with a serrated plastic knife! I assume he had hidden the knife from his supper meal, but I wasn't really concerned about that. I was trying to keep from puking all over the place. There was blood and some kind of liquid spurting all over. I hollered at him and asked him what the hell he was trying to do. He looked at me, and other than the tears, which I assumed were from pain, he appeared a hell of a lot calmer than either one of us, but at least he stopped his damned sawing when I hollered. I yelled at the CX 2 to get some help and then to phone the hospital for the nurse. There was no way I was going to open a cell without more staff than just the two of us. He took off for the office, and on the way he hit the panic button, and within seconds we had more staff than we needed. To make a long story short, we hauled the con out, and as you can imagine, he ended up going downtown to the hospital in an ambulance.

I must admit, those emergency escorts always made me a little nervous. A supervisor at JI had sent an emergency escort to the hospital one evening, and the ambulance had been met by a couple of the inmate's buddies carrying a shotgun! Thankfully, no one was injured, but the inmate escaped. You can't expect two unarmed officers to take on someone carrying a shotgun. Nothing happened on this escort, but once again, you just never knew.

Anyway, it only took me a few seconds to reach the ECA, and an officer was waiting for me with the door open. Thankfully, this time it wasn't an emergency; one of the inmates had informed staff he wasn't going to eat any more meals and had given them a letter to make it official. *Oh well*, I thought, *what the hell*, it could've been something a lot worse.

Life at Millhaven just floated along. We had the usual problems but not really anything to get excited about. We even had a few relatively speaking, minor union problems.

It was somewhere around this time I had to go up and see the deputy. "Vern," he said to me, "I'm sending you to KP for a few days."

I think I just looked at him; I didn't know what to say. He explained that there had been some kind of shooting in the yard and they needed a couple of supervisors to do the investigation, and I was one of the ones elected.

The next morning I met the other CX 6 in the parking lot at KP, and Roger and I headed up to the deputy's office. I introduced Don to Roger, and he gave us a basic rundown of what had happened. Don handed us the reports and took us to an office we could use during our stay. Then he headed for the door, saying,

"If you need anything else, just give me a call," and disappeared around the corner.

Basically, there had been a fight in the exercise yard, and it had been serious enough for the southeast tower officer to fire a shot. The first shot was a warning, which didn't seem to help. The second shot was directed at an inmate but missed. As near as we could understand, the inmates more or less ignored him and finished beating up their buddy.

Roger and I read the reports and scanned the post orders, and I took him out to check the area. Just before we entered the yard, I pointed out nine cage. This cage was really a room with an outside entrance that had been built onto the side of a large building. It overlooked the yard from the northeast side. I mentioned to Roger that we used to staff the cage before inmates went out to the yard. I continued the conversation by saying, "However, I don't recall an incident report from a nine cage officer, and as you can see, if the cage was staffed, it would have cut the distance down substantially and the officer may have had a better shot."

Eventually, we found out nine cage was not being staffed any longer due to budget constraints. Surprise, surprise! (I'm being facetious again). It had become a common practice to cut posts in an attempt to save money.

It took a couple of days to complete the report, but finally our masterpiece was finished. Etiquette and fairness demanded we show it to the deputy and then visit the warden and give him an opportunity to peruse it before handing it off to region headquarters. I made an appointment with the warden, and up we went. The report wasn't a negative one, and basically we just recommended that nine cage be staffed during yard time. Even knowing the warden wouldn't be overly happy, I didn't see any problem with the report. And to be honest, I didn't give a good God damn if he liked it or not; after all, this guy was not my favorite warden. And he wasn't happy. He carried on about how he had to save money and made a few other comments regarding budgets and staffing. Oh well, life is tough; I didn't lose a minute's sleep over it.

Christmas time came, and one of the extra jobs the supervisors at MI took on was the Christmas holiday scheduling. A few months or so before Christmas, we would put a memo out to staff asking them to submit what shifts they could work over Christmas and New Year. This was done every year in an attempt to give as many staff as possible their preference of which holiday to have off. It was a lot of extra work, but we thought it was worth the effort. It usually ended up with most of the married staff off over Christmas and the single ones off over New Year. As usual, this year we revamped the schedule, and also as usual, we couldn't please everyone, so we waited for the usual bitching and whining. And we weren't disappointed. However, one guy, who happened to be a union steward and whom I knew from Collin's Bay, came up to the hall to complain and just wouldn't stop. Just yap, yap, yap.

I knew this was the way he operated; he was a large officer and had the voice to go with his size. Naturally, he always attempted to use his size and loudness to intimidate whomever he was having an argument with; it didn't matter whether it was a staff member or an inmate. I listened to him while he spoke his piece and then tried to explain the supervisor's end of it. But oh no, that wasn't good enough, and he kept at me. I finally lost it. I informed him I'd had it and he could do whatever the fuck he wanted to, but as far as I was concerned, this was the last time we were going to draw up a holiday schedule. "And," I added, "If anyone asks me why we aren't doing the fucking thing up, I'm going to tell them exactly why; to hell with it!"

As far as I can remember, I don't think we ever did formulate another holiday schedule. I know I never helped with one, and to be honest about it, I made sure a few staff knew why. There are times you just get pissed off.

Everything was going along just as smooth as silk. I kept bumping into people I knew from other institutions and from regional headquarters; it was amazing how many people I knew and how many knew me. One of the guys I got along well with had been a senior correctional officer at Kingston Pen when I was there; he wrote a supervisor's competition and was transferred to JI. I think he took over some of the tasks I would have had if I had stayed there. Eventually, David wrote a UM competition and ended up at MI for a while before going to Bath Institution as the deputy warden.

David and I always found time to have a chat whenever we saw each other and had a few minutes. One day we were chatting, and he said I should show the bosses I could handle more responsibility. He said there were always jobs that had to be done, and it was just a matter of taking them on and doing them. I knew it was good advice, but at the time I didn't really want to go any higher, so I let it slide.

Mind you, I did take several acting positions during my career. At KP, I coordinated the dog handlers and the response team, did the IPSO job twice, and was a range officer. At MI I was in charge of the V&C for a time, and I acted as a unit manager. At Bath I organized and kept the records of the inmate disciplinary board, was the urinalysis coordinator, did the job of the chief of correctional operations, and even acted as the deputy a couple of times. All in all, I think I had a pretty varied career. I know I was happy with it, anyway.

Naturally, in this job, things didn't always go smoothly. At MI, when there were serious problems, such as a whole range refusing to go into their cells, we used a type of CN gas that worked extremely well. It was highly effective; no inmate was ever injured because of it, and there was almost no cleanup required after its use. The gas was contained in a large canister, and only one officer had control of it. The gas was released by a small control knob, and the job usually only required a very small amount of the stuff. In short, it was a great tool!

I want to reiterate here that this type of CN gas was never used on individual inmates. It was only used if we had a large number refusing to leave an area or go into their cells. Another reason we appreciated this type of CN was that we didn't have to fire a gas projectile from a gas gun. Every time we had to fire one of those things, there was always a concern that no matter how careful we were, there was a chance it could hit someone. At any rate, this gas was used during a disturbance one night, and the assistant warden that wrote the report for region headquarters and Ottawa named the type of CN gas that we used. As far as I know, the normal procedure was usually just to state, "CN gas was deployed." Apparently someone in Ottawa discovered this type of gas should not be used in a confined area. This was news to us at the institutional level. We didn't realized it until management, including supervisors, received a memo stating we were not to use it except for disturbances that took place in the open air. We were not very happy about the directive; however, orders were orders. Unfortunately, with my ever-present luck, within a short time this directive was going to affect me personally.

As usual, the problem hit the fan during the last count of the night shift. When we worked the four to twelve and count up was called, the supervisor just sat in the office and hoped to hell the phone didn't ring. We just knew if one of the phones rang at count time it wouldn't be good news. So there I sat, waiting for the units to send up their counts, and that God damned phone rang! So what could I do? With a heavy heart and hoping to hell it was a minor problem, I reached for the phone and said, "Keeper's hall, Thibedeau here."

Well, of course, it wasn't a 'little' problem! I was told a whole range was refusing to go in, and they had already beaten up one of their buddies. In addition, there was the usual hooting and hollering, and naturally the blankets were up so we couldn't see down the range. I even had a difficult time understanding what he was saying because of the noise. Fortunately, I'd been through so much of this crap by now that my adrenalin hardly shot up at all, but I was sure pissed off. Down I headed to the unit to get a firsthand idea of what was going on, hoping like hell I could talk them into their cells. At the same time, I didn't really hold out much hope of that happening; once things had gone this far, there was usually no turning back. And I was right. The range representative wouldn't even come to the end of the range to talk. So back up to the hall I tramped to start the phone calls. Once I reached T control, I told the control officers to use the radio and announce that everyone was to stay on their posts. Once something like this got rolling, one of our first concerns was that it could be a distraction for some other game the cons were playing.

I entered the hall and, knowing the present staff couldn't handle the situation, phoned the first number on our contact list for the response team. Luckily, I reached him on the first try. On the other hand, I received some very unwelcome news. He told me the team had decided to use this particular evening as a night out. He figured he might be able to gather one full team, but that would likely be it. I needed one team to enter the range from the front and one to enter from the back, and crap, that added up to two teams.

By this time my relief was in, and we had a chat about the problems. After a short discussion, he patted me on the back, wished me luck, and headed down inside to sort things out. This was common practice. When a problem erupted, the supervisor on duty stayed in charge as the crisis manager until relieved by the warden or deputy, who usually assumed those duties. And I must admit, if a disturbance continued long enough for one of them to make it in, we were usually damned glad to see him!

By now the team leader was in, and after a quick discussion, he headed down to take a firsthand look at the problem.

I received several phone calls from the problem area. Actually, there was nothing new, but I appreciated the updates, because they let me know that at least so far it wasn't getting any worse. The reports said there was just the usual racket, banging, yelling, screaming, and so on. The staff did think the inmates were starting to sound a little drunk, but they couldn't be sure because of the blankets covering the end of the range. One good thing was that the staff didn't have the impression anyone else was being injured or worse. However, once again that was a bit of a guess, and that was where experience came in—you got a feel for such things. However, if they did have some brew and ended up drunk, the problem would quickly escalate.

By this time, most of the response team and the security maintenance officer were in, and I decided to change the crisis management centre to the staff lounge. The lounge had more room and was a hell of a lot quieter.

The team leader and his 2 I/C had gone down to the problem unit to try to figure out a plan and an alternate plan as well. It didn't take them very long to come back up and show me the plan. The regulations stated that the team had to formulate a plan, put it into writing, and then receive the signature of the crisis manager to show he agreed with it. This time there was a concern. They were worried about having only the one team. This ruled out the possibility of attacking the problem from both ends of the range. They were willing to enter the range from one end using shields, batons, and the usual gear, but they were apprehensive of it getting out of hand. The team leader had two suggestions. The first suggestion was to phone Collin's Bay and wait for them to send a team in to assist us. Neither one of us was very happy with that suggestion. I knew he wouldn't look forward to a team coming in from another institution, and I was deeply concerned about how long it would take. I didn't know what was happening on the range, and I was really concerned about finding inmates beaten up, raped, or killed. You just never knew what you might find once you made it back onto a range! The second suggestion was to allow them to take the CN gas that had been banned down with them. They said they just didn't see any other way out. And although I didn't say anything at the time, I had already more or less reached the same conclusion. I realized, though, that I had to impress upon them just how serious that step would be. The only way I could think of to emphasize that was to say, "Holy Christ, if I send that gas down with you and it's used, I'll likely be looking for a job by tomorrow!" I must admit, that got their attention, and that was exactly what I wanted.

We passed the problem back and forth for a couple of minutes, and I finally looked at the SMO and asked him if he would be willing to take it down with the team. He agreed, so the leader amended the plan. I insisted he put it in writing that I was authorizing the gas, but it was to be deployed by the SMO only. I did have a lot of faith in that man. I was betting quite heavily that he wouldn't get rattled easily! At any rate, the plan was drawn up, I signed it, the team started down, and I started to sweat rather heavily.

Shortly after the team left the area, I looked up, and God bless them, there was the warden and the deputy coming in! I could have kissed them both. Normal procedure was to brief them, have the warden sign a paper stating he was officially the crisis manager, and then I was officially off the hook. My first thought was that he could either cancel the team's plan or carry on with it, but in any case, it was on his shoulders. God was I ever happy—for about three minutes!

I briefed both of them and stressed the part about the type of CN gas and why I had authorized its use. Then I handed the warden the team's plan and said, "There you go. I'll head down and check things out around the units."

"Whoa, slow down there," the warden said. "I've looked everything over and you're doing exactly what I would've done. The best thing to do is leave you as crisis manager. Hell, there's no sense in changing everything over now." And with that they sauntered off down the hall. And all my happiness crashed! I didn't see them again until the episode was over.

Shortly after the warden and the deputy left, the team leader contacted me and said they were set up and prepared to go and just needed the verification.

About all I could say was "GOGo," and in they went! Of course that left me sitting there sweating bullets. I knew I had made the right calls, but at the same time, that knowledge wouldn't help if someone was injured. I also knew damned well the investigating team would likely find fault with several decisions. So there I sat and sat and sat and sweated. It felt like I sat for about two days waiting. In reality, I guess it was about forty-five minutes. In any case, once it was over, I heard the most gratifying words a crisis manager could receive in these circumstances: "The situation is contained; no injuries received; no gas used!" It's difficult to explain the feeling of elation I felt right about then! But whatever you can imagine, that's what I felt.

I don't recall how long it took to clean things up and get back to a more or less normal situation, but it did take a while. I know it was great to get home and into a normal environment. I imagine Sheila was rather pleased to see me; I only had time to make one rather hurried call home during the crisis, so all she really knew was that we were having difficulties and I had called the team in.

I'm not sure what I put into my report, but I do know I was very specific. I wanted everyone from the warden up to the characters in Ottawa to understand why I had authorized sending that particular gas into the unit.

Eventually the investigating team came around to ask all their questions. I'm not sure what they asked, but I guess everyone was more or less happy with my report and the investigation, because I never heard anything back from them. And that was a blessing!

I did hear one thing from RHQ though. Several weeks after the incident, I received a written commendation from the deputy commissioner of Ontario regarding it. One of the statements in the commendation said it was a pleasure to have a leader that was willing to go out on a limb and make a decision when it was required! This is not word for word, but it's pretty damned close. That commendation was very gratifying and certainly made me feel better about the whole episode.

My shifts at Millhaven were just rolling along, and in many ways it was quieter than Kingston Pen. Even the inmates were easier to deal with. I still can't get over the difference between what I called 'real' cons' compared to PC cons.

One morning about five years after transferring back to the Haven, I received a message that the deputy at Bath wanted me to phone him back. That really piqued my interest. David and I usually had interesting chats, but only when we bumped into each other every once in a while. The phone call did jog my memory though, and I recalled that a week or so earlier, Rick, who was a supervisor at Bath, had mentioned that I should put in for a transfer to Bath. I told him it sounded like a good idea, and I guess I promptly forgot about it. Now I was wondering if it could be about a transfer but figured it was more likely something to do with an inmate.

I gave him a call and we chatted for a couple minutes, and then out of the blue, he asked if I would be interested in transferring over. He was short one supervisor, and the job was mine if I wanted it! He said he'd already mentioned it to my boss and had been told I wouldn't be held up if I wanted to go. We talked for several minutes, and it sounded like a hell of a good idea. Before we hung up, I said I would come over that afternoon and look around.

After lunch, I headed out the gate, stopped one of the mobiles, and had him drop me off at Bath. While getting out of the vehicle, I told him I'd radio when I was ready to come back so he could pick me up. It was really strange entering Bath. There was no gate or fence to go through; you just walked in. Just that little item was a huge change. Rick was picked to show me around, and away we went. We took a tour of the place, and believe me, it was alien to anything I was used to. No cells! No walls! No fence! No uniforms! In fact, I felt a little awkward; I was the only one in uniform, and that simple fact sure earned me a few looks. Holy hell, the inmates even spoke to Rick as if they were acquaintances—not friends, mind you, but not enemies either, just kind of friendly. I couldn't get over it! It wasn't difficult to tell the place was a minimum-security prison.

At that time, Bath had two living units called unit one and unit two. Unit two was three or four park model trailers that, despite their age, were still in pretty fair condition. Rick told me they were only supposed to have been used for a few years, and that had been several years ago. So as you can imagine, security wasn't the prime consideration. The locks to the rooms were just regular locks, and shockingly to me, the inmates had keys! Naturally, staff also had keys. And that was what each inmate lived in—a room! Unit one was a little rougher. The inmates had to live in cubicles, one inmate to each cubicle, without locks or doors. There wasn't even a secure holding cell for troublemakers or drunks! At first glance, when I compared this place to what I was used to, it looked like a love fest. Well, that's a little bit of an exaggeration, but I'm sure you get the drift. Supervisors didn't even work the morning shift! I was beginning to think I had died and gone to a correctional officer's heaven!

During my tour, one of the staff that had worked at Kingston Pen asked if I remembered a certain CX 4 that had worked there. When I replied in the affirmative, he inquired if

I realized he had been promoted to supervisor. I replied that I had heard something about it. In fact, when I had heard about his promotion, I had wondered how he would fit into the job. He was a fairly good four but was exceptionally gung-ho. I've mentioned that it's a big change between the duties of a senior correctional officer and a supervisor, and when I learned this guy had been transferred to a minimum, I must admit it sort of boggled my mind.

The officer continued his story. "Well Vern, did you hear about him and his helicopter episode?"

I had to reply in the negative this time. I gave him a questioning look and said, "You got me this time. I haven't heard anything about a helicopter." "Aw, you'll love this," he said. "The camp had a walk-away one day while he was in charge, and you'll never guess what the stupid ass did. He actually took a rifle, commandeered a helicopter, and headed up into the wild blue yonder to look for the con! Christ, you can bet the stupid fucker's no longer employed by the service."

I couldn't believe it. Christ, we were nervous about using a little force on a minimum-security inmate at any time. I still remembered my episode in the tower at the Bay, and I had been concerned for staff safety with a bunch of drunken inmates. Like I said, you just never knew what you were going to hear. I've always hoped this clusterfuck was just another rumour.

We ended my tour by going to the deputy's office and having a discussion about how this job was a little different from a medium or maximum prison; actually, the jobs were immensely different. Dave also filled me in on what my duties would cover, and it almost sounded like heaven. I told Dave I'd talk it over with my wife and let him know in the morning. I must admit, though, I had made my mind up to transfer. And as far as I was concerned, it couldn't happen too quickly.

I left Bath, not even bothering to radio the mobile for a

ride, and walked back to Millhaven with my head spinning. I felt like I was walking on a cloud.

When I got home and told Sheila all about Bath, she seemed to get a little excited, especially once I told her there were no towers, segregation, mobiles, or firearms. I really believe her eyes sparkled when I told her I hadn't spotted a weapon during the whole tour.

The next morning I phoned David and told him I'd transfer over just as soon as I could.

"Well," he said, "it won't take too long. I was talking to your deputy, and he said you can come over next week!"

So after about twenty-one years with corrections, I had my fifth transfer and started at Bath, my first minimum-security institution. I didn't know it at the time, of course, but it was only going be a minimum for another three or four months, and then it would be upgraded to a medium. I've always wondered if Dave knew about the upgrade before I transferred over. Not that it would have made any difference, because there was no way in hell I would've turned it down! I'm still ashamed that I never thanked Dave for getting me over to Bath.

Chapter 21

Bath from a minimum to a medium.

Two lifers escape. Inmate suicide.

Bath Institution: little did I know I was going to spend the last five years of my working career in this place. The time was going to be interesting and very, very busy but not nearly as traumatic as my other institutions. Besides working in a minimum-security institution and wearing civilian clothes, the other major change, and a most gratifying one, was that there was no supervisor on the morning shift! Except for the few months I acted as an IPSO, the month or so I acted as a UM, and the few months I was in charge of V&C, I had always worked all three shifts. No morning shifts—*beautiful.*

I spent my first month or so just getting used to working in this environment. And believe me when I say it took some getting used to. Half the time inmates wore civilian clothing and ran all over the place, and strangely (at least to me) they were even allowed to have money in their possession. Granted, it was only fifteen dollars, but that was fifteen dollars more than I was used to. And on top of that, it was not unusual to see staff and inmates standing or sitting around having conversations. After working in those other institutions, all I could do was shake my head and say to myself, *This is one strange place.* Hell, one evening I was walking through a common room and an inmate stood up to get my attention and half yelled, "Oh Mr. Thibedeau, do you realize one of the brake lights on your car is out?"

I must admit I was a little shaken and thought, *Holy Christ, the cons will kill him. He must want to go into protection or something!* And then it hit me—I was at Bath, and this was normal.

It took a while, but once I became accustomed to Bath, it was great. As I mentioned earlier, I felt like I was in a correctional officer's heaven.

Like at other prisons, supervisors were in charge during the nights, weekends, and holidays. But during the morning shift at Bath, the CX 3 in charge of unit one supervised the institution with the understanding that he would phone the evening supervisor if he ran into a problem. So once the 2300 hours count was in and we knew the inmates were all tucked into bed, the supervisor went home. This was the difference at Bath. We just hoped the inmates stayed tucked in and didn't take off. Boy, I just loved that—no midnights.

The supervisors used a duty office in the common room of unit one, and it was a good location. We could see and hear what was happening in the unit office and in the common room. It was amazing how quickly staff and inmates forgot about you when they didn't see you.

When I first arrived, I didn't know what to do about the counts. I had been told the three in charge of unit one looked after them. I didn't think it would be proper to be the only supervisor to take over from the CX 3, so I stayed with the routine and let the CX 3 handle them. To be honest, I felt very uneasy not doing them myself, but in my mind, if you wanted to undermine someone's self-confidence, you just had to do their job for them. In short, I stayed in the office and let the three do the counts. I must admit though, I made sure the office door was open and listened to everything that went on. I certainly wanted the staff to know I trusted them, but I also wanted to make damned sure I covered my little rear end.

I'd been at Bath for several weeks and was still far from being accustomed to inmates speaking to staff in such a friendly manner. I kept waiting for the other shoe to fall, but by God, it never did.

Around this time, the deputy received a complaint about a CX 3 being in charge of the institution during the morning shift. The complaint stated that it should be a supervisor, and perhaps due to my experiences at KP, I had a sneaking suspicion it was a union thing. At any rate, there went not working mornings. We ended up having to start working all three shifts. But even that couldn't dampen my spirits. If I remember correctly, after a few months Sheila even mentioned that I was turning into a more or less normal person. Unfortunately, it wasn't going to last. So there I was on day shift, just enjoying myself and thinking this was almost like a civilian job. I was even imagining that I could do this until I retired and almost enjoy it. And then the bottom fell out!

I received a phone call from the deputy asking me to go over to his office for a chat. Heck, I wasn't even concerned about having a chat. I headed into his office and sat down, and then he gave me the news. "Vern," he said in a rather solemn voice, "Bath is changing from a minimum—to a medium-security institution!"

I have to admit, he had to repeat the news, and once he did, it sank into my very being. Christ, I couldn't even visualize all the difficulties this would entail. We had no security and no real post orders to speak of. We didn't even have weapons, and most of the staff certainly hadn't had firearms training for several years; hell, we didn't even have an armoury, for God's sake. And then there were the inmates; God, they'd flip out. Most of them had earned their way to a minimum, and as soon as they heard we were switching over, they would assume they were going be reclassified as medium-security inmates. I couldn't even imagine all the problems that would crop up or all the changes that would have to take place. *Well, at least it was nice while it lasted,* I thought. Needless to say, this turned into quite a discussion. And over the next several months there were many more discussions and dozens of meetings.

But as I expected, we managed. We had an armoury built and even managed to calm most of the inmates down by telling them they'd have the option of transferring to another institution. They were given the option of staying at Bath and retaining their minimum classification, but they were also told they'd have to adhere to any new rules, and several opted to stay.

Contractors started putting up a fence with razor wire and building a few outposts. These were just simple buildings that were used more for observation than anything else. A couple of mobiles were ordered, and the staff started their weapons training. To say the least, it was a very busy time.

A few of the meetings were somewhat intense. Eventually, it was decided that the staff would stay in civilian clothing, inmates would still be allowed to have fifteen dollars on their persons, and the inmate rooms would stay the same. After all, it would have been impossible to change the rooms into cells without rebuilding the whole damned place anyway. But we did have a couple of holding cells built just in case. There was no doubt, at least in my mind, that we would eventually need them, and of course we did.

It had been decided, I think by regional headquarters, that we would just have a single wire fence with razor wire on top. Most supervisors were on record that we wanted a double fence, but what the hell; we weren't the bosses. Unfortunately, RHQ's decision was going to affect me at a later date.

And then, with my ever-present luck, I was given the job of formulating our new post orders. I also ended up having to keep them up-to-date. This was a huge commitment. With everything going on at work, I ended up doing most of it at home. Even keeping them up-to-date over the years was a big job. Dave was really good about it, though. I just kept track of the time I spent working at home, and when I could get away, I took the time off that was owed to me. That worked out for both of us; David got the work out of me and I got to take time off without having to use annual leave.

But we also had the usual prison problems, and one afternoon, I had a tip that an inmate was in his room in unit one with some dope. Into the unit office I headed and proceeded to put my pen, watch, and other items into a drawer, and at the same time I told one of the officers to follow me and we headed down to the inmate's cubicle.

As we trooped down, I explained what was going on, and once we reached the inmate's room, I told the officer to stay right behind me, and in we hustled. The inmate was relaxing on his bed and threw one of those stupid, stunned looks at me. I told him I knew he was holding and rather than make it any worse for himself I wanted him to hand it over. At the same time I continued into the room and came to a halt next to his bed, hoping to hell my partner was right there with me.

The inmate stared at me for a second or two and then suddenly made a grab for something on his nightstand. Whatever it was, he managed to get it into his hand, and the hand was heading up to his mouth.

I made a leap, landed on top of him, and hung on to his arm for dear life! Within a second or two, he yelled, "That's enough. Here it is; you can have the fucking stuff!" He handed it over to me. To be honest I can't even remember what he had except that it was dope of some kind.

It's a good thing he gave it up so quickly, because my backup was still standing there with his mouth open. We escorted him to one of our brand-new holding cells, and eventually I had him escorted over to Millhaven.

I went into the office to reclaim my stuff, and on the way

out I overheard my helper saying to the guys, "Jesus Christ, I didn't know what the hell was going on. We went into the room, and the next thing I knew Thibedeau was on the bed wrestling with the con. Christ, it was fast!"

Other than a few minor episodes, the time at Bath continued to be good. We did have to introduce a proper urinalysis program. Bath had been operating its program by escorting the inmates over to MI for testing, but now, because we were a medium, we were informed that we had to start an official program of our own. Dave talked it over with the supervisors, and we all had a thorough discussion about it. The long and short of it was that somehow I was voted to become the urinalysis program coordinator. This also turned into a huge undertaking. It also left me coordinating our IDB. I guess that fell into place because I was writing up most of the offence reports anyway.

One of the few positive items that came out of all this was the large office I inherited; I certainly needed it with all the reading and filing I had to do. The office was great though. It was huge with two big windows, and even though they had bars on them, they were a blessing. I even had a large bathroom. The warden and I had the only two offices in the institution with washrooms. However, I had to use mine for the urinalysis program; the cons had to pee in a bottle somewhere, and I didn't really think the warden would appreciate me using his washroom. At any rate, it was nice, and I wasn't shy about telling people about my great bathroom. Although I usually forgot to tell them what I had to use it for.

I was busy! I had to figure out a filing system to keep track of the IDB, the urinalysis program, all cell searches, and a hell of a lot of things that I've since forgotten about; that computer they gave me hardly ever stopped working. And this was all completely new to me; I had never had any training in office procedures. Hell, I even ended up making my own databases. I must admit, though, I did enjoy it. And added to all this, I still had my regular supervisor's duties to keep on top of. There were times I was just spinning!

Once Bath was more or less a full-fledged medium, we ended up accepting two lifers. One was a French inmate from Quebec and the other was from Ontario. I knew the one from Ontario. Originally, I had run into him at the Bay; in fact, he had been the inmate who did up our overtime meals in the officers' mess. He had been out for a while and then ended up in Millhaven doing life for murder. I have to admit I was surprised when I saw him at MI. Rehabilitation apparently had failed again.

Anyway, they were accepted at Bath and hadn't caused any problems; at least, I had never had a run-in with either of them. That was going to change one evening, and unfortunately I was on the night shift. On that particular afternoon, everything was going along as usual—quiet. And then we did the count. I don't recall if it was the 2000 or 2300 hours count, but we came up two short.

While the staff was doing a recount, and even though I already knew it was the two lifers, I beat it over to the security office to grab the security cards. I contacted Millhaven and told them who we might be missing and asked them to have their mobiles and towers watch for them. Next I informed our mobile of the problem and told him to check the fence for any breaches. Then I tore off back to the units.

At the same time, I started keeping notes. If this was an escape, I knew everyone from God down would want to know what decisions had been made, the order they had been made in, and the exact time they were made. Jesus, what a mess! It was also hammering in my mind that they might have broken into a house to hide and could be holding a family hostage. You just didn't know what the hell was going on. By now I was half-way back to the units and hoping, maybe even praying, the inmates had been found drunk or sleeping somewhere. Even completing a suicide pact or some stupid thing would have been preferable to an escape. But at the same time I knew full well they were gone.

I'd just entered the unit when the second count came in, and there was no doubt they had taken off. I was just starting to assign staff to their search areas when the mobile radioed for me to get over to the fence near the kitchen area. I headed over, and the first thing I saw when I rounded the corner was a ladder leaning up against the fence and a coat or something laying over the razor wire and flapping in the breeze. A ladder, for God's sake. I couldn't believe it! All ladders were supposed to be chained and padlocked when not in use.

That was it; there was no doubt they were gone. I beat it back to the office to phone the police and fax the escapees' pictures to them. Then I had to phone the deputy warden and give him the bad news, and that was just about all I could do. I still had a prison to run. And they were gone; there was no doubt about that. In fact, they were gone for a few years.

That escape did a couple of things for Bath though. In very short order contractors started a second fence, and we had a detection alarm and cameras installed in and around the fence that were second to none.

But all in all, it was not a very pleasant night!

Like all prisons, things settled back down soon. The ever-present routine grabbed everyone, and we just waited for whatever the next episode was going to throw at us. I never dreamed in my wildest dreams what that next episode was going to do to me!

One day I received a phone call from Millhaven informing me that an inmate wanted to see me about something important. So over I headed. I knew this guy fairly well and had received some accurate information from him in the past. We started to chat, and he was really fidgety, which was unusual, and he also wasn't mentioning names. He started out by telling me he wanted to talk about the officer that had pushed him into the wall a few years ago. It took a minute or so before it clicked for me.

I was a CX 4 at MI at the time, and this inmate, who was extremely upset, had come to the office and said he wanted an assault charge laid against an officer in the unit. He told me that because he hadn't done something the officer wanted, he had been grabbed and slammed up against a wall. He also stated he'd had back surgery and the assault had screwed it up again. At the time all I could do was submit a report and tell the inmate to lay a complaint, and that was the last I heard of it, which, thinking back, was in itself a little strange.

The first time I met this particular officer, he was posted to KP, but we did the induction training course together. A number of years later he ended up being transferred to JI and eventually landed at MI while I was there as a four. There were some ugly rumours regarding him, a JI pastor, and his transfer to MI. The whole thing had a mysterious aura around it. As I've stated, there were always rumours circulating about one thing or another; however, rumours seemed to always follow this particular guy around.

That same officer was now at Bath, and the rumours were still buzzing.

I don't remember everything the inmate told me, but it involved this officer receiving a gold chain from an inmate as payment for something. He also filled me in on some other transactions this same officer was supposedly involved with that were definitely illegal. On the other hand, inmates were always telling stories about staff, and you had to take any information with a grain of salt. But still—this time I was wondering.

I told the inmate I would report his concerns to the appropriate personnel and if he had any more information he could always contact me. I had him taken back to his cell and sat for a while and made my notes. This information certainly had me thinking. It tied in with information I'd received from other inmates, and when I eventually left the office, I had a sick feeling in the pit of my stomach!

In the mean time, there seemed to be more inmates lined up waiting to come to Bath, but like other institutions, there was not enough room for them. Someone decided we should have more room, so another unit was built, and of course this one was to be called unit three. And with my constant luck, I was to be in charge of the unit. But to further the rehabilitation of inmates, this unit was going to be a little different.

It had been decided that unit three would actually be three or four oversized independent houses. Each house would hold, if I remember correctly, around ten inmates. The inmates would be in individual rooms and would eat their meals in the dining area of their house. They would order a week's supply of groceries and be responsible for the cooking and care of their own residence, just like living on the street. Before an inmate could move into this unit, he had to meet certain criteria, and if he screwed up, the idea was to bounce him back to one of the other units, preferably to unit one.

One morning while all this was going on, the deputy and I were standing around talking, and he asked me if I would like to take a trip for a couple of days. This would be quite a little episode and we would both learn something from it, especially the deputy, because it was his budget that took the hit.

Our Bible, otherwise known as the commissioner's directives, stated that an inmate had the right to attend the funeral of a family member. I can't remember exactly what relations *family member* covered, but it certainly did cover parents. David told me an inmate had approached him and said his mother was in a hospital and dying. The inmate wanted to know if he could be escorted to the hospital to visit her before she passed away. Before David spoke to me about it, he had phoned and verified the inmate's story. Dave asked me if I would take the escort, because the hospital was in my old neck of the woods and I knew my way around. It meant a two-day trip, but what the heck. I asked about the inmate going to the funeral, and Dave told me that wouldn't be a problem. He said the inmate wanted to see his mother while she was still alive and had promised he wouldn't ask to go to the funeral. He even had the inmate sign a paper to that effect. At any rate, I told him I'd take the escort, and we decided who would go with me.

We left early in the morning, and after a drive of around eight hours or so, we pulled into the hospital. Several family members were there, and as you can imagine, it was not a happy time. And to make matters worse, not everyone was thrilled to see the inmate. In fact, when we walked in, the inmate's sister spotted us approaching and headed in our direction. Her first words directed to the inmate were, "What in hell are you doing here? You're supposed to be in jail!"

My immediate reaction was, *Oh Christ, what have we stepped into?* At any rate, he had his visit and spent the night in Sudbury's local lockup, and the next morning we headed back to Bath.

A week or so after we got back I saw documentation for this same inmate to go out on an ETA to a funeral. I asked Dave about it and received a very short reply: "Ah hell, he asked to go to his mother's funeral and I refused; he puts in his grievance and even with the paper he signed, I still had to send the fucker. That's the last time I'll get sucked in like that!"

Oh the joys of working in a penitentiary and bending the rules. As I've mentioned, it usually just came back to bite you in the ass.

Just like other institutions, Bath had several four-legged skunks that took up residence in the area. But Bath also had an inmate who was almost blind. We found out blind inmates and skunks were not a good combination. I was lucky; I wasn't on duty this time. I came cruising in to work one morning and bumped into one of the guys on his way home. "Hey, Vern," he asked. "Did you hear about the skunk situation we had?"

"Nope, I just got in. I haven't been around for a few days."

"Well, you'll love this. That blind inmate in unit two stepped outside the other night, saw what he thought was one of the cats, bent down to pet it, and found out it was a skunk! Want to know how he found out what it was? The poor little thing had let go with a spray for self-protection. Jesus, I still can't stop laughing every time I picture it."

I have to admit it was a comical picture. I never did check out how the supervisor handled that one. I don't doubt he was more upset than the inmate—well, maybe not. The moral of the story is don't ever pet an animal that you can't clearly see.

One weekend I went in for the day shift. The place was really quiet, so I decided to catch up on my paperwork in the office. That was one thing I did have a lot of—paperwork. I was working away and thinking, *Hey life is really great—nice day, weather good, everything calm and peaceful, and I'm getting a pile of work completed. What more could you ask for?* About an hour or so before the noon count, someone knocked on the door, and in came an inmate that I knew from a couple of different prisons.

It wasn't unusual for inmates to sit and have a chat with me. Usually they wanted a favour or they had decided to give me a tip about something. As a rule, whenever I received some information, it wasn't only to help me out; usually it also helped out the informant. I always had to watch who was feeding me little tidbits. As I've said, we just never knew what the hell was going on behind the scenes. But I knew this guy hadn't come in to inform on anyone. And he hadn't. He just sat and talked about different episodes that had happened in other prisons and some of the people we were both familiar with. Eventually, he said he'd better take off, because it was almost count and he didn't want to be late. And away he went. I must admit I was a little mystified by his visit, but I just went back to my work.

In fact, things were going along so well, I went into the unit office, got a coffee, and told the three he could take the count and I'd just be back in the office. After several minutes I heard staff yell, "Count up, everyone into your rooms," and then, as usual, things were really quiet while the staff headed for the ranges to take a count. A few minutes later, the door burst open and an officer excitedly stated, "You better get to the office. We are one short!"

Oh Christ, I thought as I tore out of the office, *please let it be a miscount; please, please.* I made it into the office, and when they told me who was missing I told the staff that couldn't be right; I'd just been talking to him thirty minutes ago. Well, I was told in no uncertain terms that was who was missing. As soon as the recount came up the same, I sorted out the staff and sent them to do a search, and at the same time I got myself all prepared to phone the police and the powers-that-be again.

Just as I was heading over to the office to find the inmate's security card, a call came over the radio telling me to get over to the yard shack *now!* The back of the shack faced unit one, and the door faced out to the sports field. I took off running and tried to prepare myself for whatever the hell was going on. Still on the run, I made it the shack and tore around the corner. Just for a flash I thought two CXs were fighting a con. Once I took a second look, I could tell that they sure in hell weren't fighting; they were holding onto an inmate and trying to lift him up. I glanced up and saw our missing inmate with a cord around his neck and the other end tied to a rafter in the ceiling!

As soon as one of the guys saw me he yelled, "We don't have a knife. For Christ's sake cut the cord!"

And that's what I did; they held him up and I cut through the cord. Once that was accomplished, we lowered him down and half dragged and half carried him out of the shed. You can take my word that there's truth to the statement that a person is twice as heavy when he is unconscious or, in this case, dead! And there was no doubt too much time had passed for this guy and he was dead. One of the first things I noticed was that one of his boots didn't have any laces in it, and I knew the missing lace was around his neck. *Well,* I thought, *that should make the job a lot easier for the police.*

For a second we just stood and looked down at him, and then one of the officers asked if we should try to do CPR on him. I told him there was no point; he was definitely way past that stage.

"Well," he said, "I'm going to give it a try anyway!"

And he did, even knowing it was pointless. While he was pumping away, I used my radio, contacted Millhaven, gave them a quick rundown on what had happened, and asked them to bring the nurse over for a couple of minutes. Within a few minutes, the nurse arrived, checked the inmate, looked up at me, and said, "Jeez, there's nothing I can do for him; you know that as well as I do."

And that was about all we could do. I left the two officers with the body and took off to do the phone calls. As usual everything took on a life of its own. The police arrived, did their thing, and eventually released the body. I signed the papers, and the wagon took it away.

I've always wondered why he came in to talk to me before topping himself. We'd only spoken once in a while, and I'm positive this wasn't a 'cry for help', because I'm sure I would've picked up on it. Unfortunately, situations like this were never pleasant, and there was not much that could be said other than all staff got to go home and there was no escape. Rather a sad statement, but in this business it was true, and at times that was all that could be said.

A few days after this episode, I was chatting with an officer I had worked with in other institutions. During our conversation, he mentioned an officer we both knew who had passed away and alluded to the fact that he might have caused his own demise. This conversation shook me up somewhat. I knew the guy from the five years I worked at the Bay and thought very highly of him. He'd spent his whole career at CBI and retired shortly after I transferred to Millhaven. As far as I knew, he was enjoying life, and then suddenly I was told he passed away. Apparently shortly before his death he went into the Bay, toured the blocks, spoke to staff, and then went home. Shortly after that he was dead! If he did it himself, no one at the institution had the slightest glimmer of what was going to happen. But the tour may have been his way of saying good-bye. One thing he did though, was to leave me with some very good advice; most of which I took to heart. And I guess that's about all I can say or want to say about it.

This is a subject correctional staff never really talked about, and I don't think we ever actually mentioned suicide in relation to staff. But when I think about it, I seem to have known an uncommonly high number of officers who passed away in this manner. Once we finished our gabfest and went on our way, my mind slipped back to when I first went on the induction training course.

One morning during our first week, we all reported to the classroom. Someone we had never seen before was standing at the front with the instructor and was introduced as an assistant to a Queens University professor of psychology. The professor had been granted permission to do a two-year study of correctional staff new to the service. It was also stressed that we didn't have to participate if we didn't want to. In any event, he was going to complete the course with us and every few weeks would be interviewing the participants. In addition, if the wives were willing, he wanted to interview them three or four times over the two years. All interviews would be private; in fact, participants were given a code name, and I still remember mine. When Sheila finally moved down to Kingston, she also volunteered.

The main focus of the study was to determine what, if any, personality changes occurred over time when someone worked in corrections. Eventually the study was completed and published. Each of us received a copy of the publication, and it was several pages long; actually, it was quite thick. Unfortunately, I don't recall what I did with my copy, and I don't remember the results. In hindsight I wish I had hung onto it. I have a feeling it would now make interesting reading.

As far as I know, nothing was ever done with this study. I've been told there were several studies completed, and that they are likely sitting on a self somewhere gathering dust.

My shifts at Bath just floated along. Even though it was now a full-fledged medium, it was still an excellent place to work. I was exceptionally busy, but there were no earth-shattering experiences to worry about, the inmates were no great problem, staff worked well together, and I got along extremely well with the warden and deputy. In relation to other institutions, especially Kingston Pen, staff caused very few problems of any kind. Everything was just good!

Of course, things didn't always stay quiet. One morning I received a phone call from Jill, who was the IPSO at Bath, and as soon as I answered the phone she yelled in my ear, "Meet me by the kitchen; we may have a bomb!" This area, among other uses, was used to store items that had been sent in for inmates doing time at MI and Bath.

I tore out of the office and didn't slow down until I met her outside the building. While we were on our way inside, she explained that a staff member had phoned and said there was a strange noise coming from one of the parcels. We were directed to a screened-off area that was jammed with all kinds of packages, and sure enough, we could hear a strange sound emanating from the area. At the time, the Haven was having problems between two different biker gangs, and they really didn't like each other. So the possibility of a bomb was a real concern!

The bomb squad arrived, unloaded the robot used for this sort of thing, and went in, just like in the movies. The robot piddled around for a while and then solved our problem. The upshot was that someone had sent in an alarm clock for a beloved inmate, and the alarm was going off. Well, I suppose that was much better than finding a bomb!

That was the most excitement Bath had had in ages. It was great fun—at least it was fun once we found out it wasn't a bomb! We thanked the police and away they went.

And that was another fun-filled day in the big house.

Chapter 22

Domestic response.
A CX 4 is involved with illegal activities.

One afternoon, I was in the deputy's office having a chat before starting my night shift when he asked if I would be interested in acting as the IPSO for several months. I was a little surprised, because Jill hadn't mentioned anything about being away, but I thought, *Why not?* It was steady days, and I had enjoyed the job at KP. I was going find it quite a bit different this time around; in fact, I was going to be extremely busy and also forced into an extremely uncomfortable position. However, I still had a few night shifts to complete before spending a couple of days training for the new job.

On my last night shift I was heading to the keeper's office after completing the 2000 hours count when I spotted the yard officer galloping toward me and yelling, "Jesus Christ, Vern, you better get some guys and get over to building two; there's screaming and God knows what else going on in that fucking place!"

Building two was one of the buildings we used for conjugal visits, and I knew there was an inmate, his wife, and one four-year-old in the building and that this was their second day of a seventy-two-hour visit.

I took off running and hollered at the officer to get a couple more guys and meet me there. While I was tearing over to find out what was going on, I remembered another episode similar to this that had taken place at Millhaven. Believe it when I say that one scared the crap out of me!

Once again it was the night shift, and the yard officer, as he was walking past the V&C trailer, heard a man and woman screaming at each other and glass being smashed. He informed me of the racket by radio, and I grabbed a spare key, used my radio to tell a couple of guys to meet me at the trailer, and took off running! I didn't know what we might find. There was a woman and two children in the trailer with the inmate. I also knew the con was a miserable son of a bitch and for the life of us, we could never figure out why in hell she stayed with him, especially with kids. I made it to the trailer about the same time as three or four other staff, and he was right; it did sound like someone was being killed. I tried the door and found it locked, so I stuck the key in, and while I was wondering how in hell I would explain a civilian being injured or killed, I pushed the door open.

And what a mess greeted me. The first thing I saw was a woman with blood running down one leg screaming like a banshee, and then I spotted glass all over the floor. I also noticed the kids weren't anywhere in sight, and that really scared me! As soon as the inmate heard us, he spun around and started waving his arms and screaming about us about being in his fucking home and to get the fuck out before he threw us out. At the same time he started toward us, and I thought, *Christ, I didn't bring any mace and not even a billy.* As far as I was concerned, he was threatening us, so I signaled the staff to grab him and put the cuffs on; at least I had remembered to bring those. Two guys jumped him, and another one grabbed him from behind in an attempt to control his flailing arms. Suddenly the woman that we thought was getting the bejesus knocked out of her jumped on an officer's back and started trying to choke him! At the same time she was screaming, "Leave him alone, you fucking pigs, you're going to hurt him. God damn you people, I'll kill the whole fucking bunch of you!"

She sounded just like a con, and for all I know, maybe she had been one. Before I could get to her, one of the officers grabbed her and threw her onto the sofa. By then a couple more staff had arrived, and they took the inmate to the hole. I pushed the woman onto a chair, told her to stay there or she'd be handcuffed and charged with assault, and then went looking for the two kids. I was extremely stressed about what we might find! Thankfully, we found them in the bedroom, and I had an officer take them out of the area. Then I had another officer escort the woman down to our hospital so the nurse could do some first aid on the damaged leg. Once she was repaired and brought back up to the front, I offered to contact an ambulance and the police so she could lay charges. I was told in no uncertain terms to fuck off, so I ordered her off the property and had the mobile follow them until they were gone.

During this episode it was constantly on my mind that in 1980 this inmate had shot a Toronto police officer during a robbery and then this goof and his brother refused to allow the officer any assistance. He was on the ground bleeding while the brothers yelled comments at him, and there was not one thing anyone could do to help him; the officer ended up dying from his wounds. And this idiot hadn't changed in prison; he was still an asshole.

But that was some report I had to write. I don't remember how long it took, but I'm pretty sure it was the only incident report involving a domestic call ever handed in at Milllhaven. The only fault anyone could find with the procedure was that I shouldn't have sent the woman to our hospital. It was suggested that it would've been wiser to have the nurse come up and do a quick patch-up. So all in all, not too bad at all!

I want to add a side note here. This particular inmate and his brother were the indirect cause of another officer's death as well. Unfortunately, the original incident kept eating at one of the responding officers, and about twenty-five years later he ended his own life.

And there I was at Bath, running to another possible incident during a conjugal visit. Luckily, this time it was a television turned up much too loud, and I suggested they keep it turned down a tad.

Once I was back on days, I worked with Jill so she could show me around the office. She also gave me her institutional contacts, her police contacts, and her informants list. The master list for the informants was kind of unique; at least to me it was. Each informant was given a number, and that number was used in any documentation or reports. There was only one master list that connected the names with the numbers, and that list was kept locked up in the IPSO safe. The combination for the safe was a closely guarded secret, and that safe was built to withstand anything up to and including earthquakes. I was even shown how to test for drugs. Boy, if you gave me a type of powder, in no time I could tell you if it was a drug and what kind it was. I must admit the job was interesting; in fact, there were times I found it too interesting. One thing I did appreciate, though, was that Bath had an office administrator in the IPSO department, and she was a life saver. She knew the office procedures inside out, and thank God for that. It took a lot of the pressure off and helped free me up to do the urinalysis and IDB jobs.

One thing about being an IPSO was that you had to try to make sense out of all the information you received, and then you got to write never-ending reports about it. One day an inmate got word to me that he had to see me but wanted a guarantee no one would see us together. Was he overreacting? Who knows? I do know I couldn't take a chance and arranged to meet him in private, and that was difficult to do in a prison, especially since private also meant no staff could know about it.

Once we got together, he told me about an inmate who was receiving drug money into his chequing account on the street. He told me the inmate had several people depositing money into the account, and then to top it off, he even gave me the account number! To this day, I have no idea how he managed to get his hands on that number. One thing that baffled me was how the dealer could keep track of who was putting what into his account. Once the informant explained the system, I couldn't believe how simple it was. He told me that each person making deposits was given a number between one and ninety-nine, and when he made his deposit, he just added his number in cents to the deposit. For example, if someone was going to deposit eight hundred dollars and his number was twenty-three, he would deposit eight hundred dollars and twenty-three cents. *Well,* I thought, *pretty damn smart.* I thanked the guy, and away he went. He didn't even ask me for anything in return. Once again, though, who knows what may have been going on behind the scenes. I knew damn well I didn't.

This particular drug deal wasn't taking place at Bath; in fact, the inmate told me he had had to wait until he changed institutions before telling anyone. He informed me he didn't mind helping out once in a while, but not if it was going to cost him being beaten up or worse. And who could argue with that type of reasoning? I phoned the relevant institution, had a chat with the IPSO, and filled him in on what I had learned. I told him once I had informed the pen squad I would submit a report to region headquarters and promised to send him a copy. I never did hear anything back about the information I passed on. As a rule, we never did; it was just another need-to-know type of thing.

I did have a rude awakening one day, though, and it really shook me up! An inmate and I were just having a chat, and I noticed he kept glancing around. I wasn't sure what he was watching for but eventually, right out of the blue, he said, "Do you know that so-and-so has something going on with Devaux?" The so-and-so he was referring to was a female correctional supervisor posted to Bath, and Devaux was an inmate at Bath.

"What the hell are you talking about?" I asked with a sinking feeling. This inmate was not one that normally fed me information, but when he did, it was always factual. In an attempt to find out what he was talking about, I continued the conversation by saying, "There's just no way something like that can be going on. Christ, I'm sure it would be noticed, and I'm positive I would've heard about it."

"I'm just telling you what the fuck I know. They yap on the phone all the time when she's at home, and it's starting to cause problems in the unit."

"Hell, they can't be talking on the phone; they couldn't arrange that!"

"Jesus Christ, you guys are slow. Devaux just phones his sister; she puts him on hold and then dials his lover at her home. Christ, haven't you people ever heard of three-way calling? Everyone's doing it. Have to go, see you later." And away he trotted, leaving me standing there dumbfounded and likely with my mouth hanging open. I didn't want to believe a word of what he told me; hell, I'd known her since she transferred to Bath after Louise Arbour managed to get the P4W closed. About all I could do was give myself a shake and head for the IPSO office to write up my notes.

Into the office and to the desk I went to try and sort this mess out, and what a God damned mess it was! First I made some notes, and then I just sat and thought about it for a while, because my head was still whirling around. At the same time, I was careful to make sure that no one else could get even an inkling of what I'd been told. And that even included my assistant; it was too sensitive for anyone to know about. Christ, I had never heard of such a thing. Supervisors never got involved with crap like this, and I was still hoping it wasn't true.

I filled in my notes, and after much thinking, typing, deleting, and rearranging, I finally finished my official report. Then I sat, did some more thinking, more deleting, and more rearranging. Finally I was satisfied. But there was no way I was about to send this to region headquarters or even to the warden without talking it over with my boss. In my mind, he had more of a right to know than anyone did.

I phoned the deputy, and once I found out he was on his own, I headed over. I entered his office and he was just sitting there waiting for me. I guess when I asked him if he was by himself, he realized there was a problem. He looked at me with that expectant stare he was always able to throw at me, so I sat and filled him in. Once I completed my story, he just sat with a shocked expression and stared with me. Then to complete everything, I handed him the written report. I don't doubt he was feeling as if a train had hit him. I know that's how I still felt. We discussed the problem for quite some time and threw different ideas back and forth, but of course we couldn't solve the problem without higher input. But within a very short time we were short one supervisor; she was just gone. No fanfare, no saying good-bye, no one knowing where she went—she was just gone!

Thus ended the case of the CS and the Convict. All joking aside though, to me, this was much worse than the nun episode at KP. I had never heard of someone at that rank being involved with an inmate.

I never did hear any talk among staff regarding this episode, and believe me, I was happy about that. The only person that had any idea of what had happened was the original informant, and we just gave each other a 'look' a few times and that was it.

There were times I got stuck going to seminars. And one afternoon during a break from one, I was chatting with a couple of police officers. Eventually the conversation steered toward crooked officers, both police and correctional. It was a sad part of our life, but it did happen. A sergeant said he thought it was a miracle there weren't a hell of a lot more of them, and without mentioning any names, he told me about an incident he had been involved in.

He said a correctional officer reported the incident to his deputy warden and the deputy immediately contacted the OPP.

The correctional officer stated that an inmate approached him and said if he didn't do a patrol in a certain area at a specific time, he would find ten thousand dollars in his mail box. The officer said he didn't normally do a walk in that area at that time anyway, so he didn't think much more about the conversation. He left work, parked the car, walked up the steps and, remembering the conversation, reached into his mailbox, and sure enough, there was an envelope. As soon as he made it into the house, he opened it up and saw ten thousand dollars in hundred-dollar bills!

The officer would have had ten thousand dollars for doing basically nothing, and believe me, that was a lot of money for a correctional officer and I guess for almost anyone. However, what would be the price down the road? There was no doubt someone had snapped a picture of him grabbing that envelope, and from then on he would have been under their thumbs. It was well known that if they get the opportunity, inmates and their friends were well versed at turning the screws on someone, especially correctional staff. He would have ended up lugging in money and drugs, doing their banking, and God only knows what else. In fact, there was a husband and wife team that started at KP shortly after I left that got themselves into a real tight spot. Their problems escalated until they sorted everything out by committing suicide together.

I had been receiving information from a couple of inmates at Bath and also from another institution regarding an officer that I'll call MacLean. I did whatever I could with the information, but other than notifying my bosses and trying to get more information, there really wasn't a hell of a lot I could do. MacLean was the officer the inmate at Millhaven had wanted to talk to me about. That was the same inmate who, after our conversation, caused me to have the old sinking feeling in the pit of my stomach.

For the last couple of months or so, these two inmates had been telling me about some kind of cigarette scam. Apparently, one or more staff members (MacLean and possibly one other) were buying smokes from the inmates both for their own use and to smuggle out of the institution for resale. This definitely could have been a profitable business. Inmates could buy cigarettes from their canteen a hell of a lot cheaper than we could on the street. But to make any real money, a person would have had to take cartons of smokes out by the backpack full. My informants were telling me management should pick a prearranged time and search all packs on the way out. I put this into my report and suggested I would likely get a tip about when we should carry out the search. I was never authorized to do the search, and I certainly wasn't going to do that on my own initiative; my parents didn't raise an idiot.

I did receive information though, and in some ways maybe too much. Before I started doing the IPSO job, I got a lot of info, but after I started that job, it just poured in, and at times it was difficult to sort it all out. One piece of information was from two or three inmates who insisted there was a still in unit two. The problem was the informants didn't know the exact location, and unit two covered a large area, but each time I was in the unit, I brought up the subject. This dragged on for some time. I would drop in, have a chat and a coffee, bring the staff up-to-date with whatever I could tell them, and then mention that damn still. In fact, that's what I did whenever I had the opportunity—visit the units. I enjoyed talking with the staff, and it also gave inmates an opportunity to let me know if they wanted to talk to me.

One day I was in the office relaxing when the phone rang. As soon as I picked it up, I heard was a voice saying, "Get the hell over to unit two. We finally got your goddamn still!"

Well, I beat it over and entered the office, and one of the officers, with a grin a mile wide, led me down to a room. The inmate's bed was pulled away from the wall, and a large square hole was cut in the floor. As soon as I dropped down through the floor, there it was—that elusive still!

Staff were always finding brew. The damn stuff could be made out of anything from tomatoes to potatoes to apples, but finding an actual still was not common. But staff finally found this one, and that was due to a lot of good work and effort. And to prove it was a good job, we had a couple of very pissed off inmates who were now residing at MI; what more could we have asked for?

The information regarding the officer selling smokes had started coming to me in dribs and drabs. But now I started hearing that he was selling transfers to minimum-security camps. I took the information with a grain of salt for a couple of reasons. For one thing, I just didn't want to believe an officer would do something like that (you'd think I would have smartened up by then), and I was also almost positive a senior correctional officer could not do that without help. If this was happening, I was certain a CMO would have had to be involved, and that just made me feel a little sicker. Shortly after the informant told me about MacLean and the transfers, I began getting the same information from different sources. And the sources were completely separate; in fact, two of them were pissed off at MacLean because they couldn't come up with enough money and he wouldn't give them a break.

I can't explain how I felt about this particular situation. It's simple to say I had a constant knot in my belly, but it was really much worse than that. Christ, I had known this guy for years; in fact, while we were both in the induction course, we had gone to a bar a few times. At any rate, I found out as much information as I could, discussed it with the deputy and the warden, spent hours formulating reports, and had several interviews with the OPP and my boss at RHQ. All in all, it was not a nice time for me!

Because MacLean was believed to be involved with other illegal activities, the sergeant in the pen squad wanted to put a tail on him whenever he had the manpower. My reply to that news was, "That's a great idea. You never know what you may find out."

The more information I gathered, the sicker I felt. I was still trying to believe he wasn't really involved with this crap, but deep down I knew he was, and likely with a hell of a lot more than I knew. I was also pretty sure MacLean knew something was going on and that I was involved with that something. It was just a feeling I had, nothing concrete—but I knew.

One morning I was in a unit office talking to three or four staff when one of them asked if we'd heard about MacLean going around laughing. You can bet my little ears perked up when I heard that question. With very little urging, the officer told us MacLean was telling everyone the pen squad had a vehicle sitting down the street from his house watching him.

I couldn't believe MacLean thought this was a big joke! Christ, most staff would have been mortified if it had happened to them.

I nearly choked on my coffee. I was well aware the police had been sitting on him for a few nights. But MacLean sure as hell wasn't supposed to know about it. Once I finished swallowing my coffee, I noticed a couple of the staff glancing at me a little strangely, and I began to think that just maybe word was starting to get out about the whole mess. Just as I was leaving to head to my office, one of the guys said he had to get ready for an escort and walked out with me. Once we were well away from the other staff, he looked at me and very seriously said, "Jesus Christ, Vern, watch your back. One way or another MacLean says he's going to get you!"

Well, that statement certainly gave me food for thought. There was no doubt MacLean knew a lot of inmates both in and out of prison, and some of those inmates were heavies and likely owed him favors. You can bet I hustled over to the office and gave the pen squad a fast phone call. Needless to say, they weren't overly happy either. But it sure gave me another damned good reason to start watching my back.

The urinalysis also continued to be a big issue. But the program did cause a slight change in the inmates' diet! We'd been getting some positive test results that didn't add up. At the time, the kitchen at Bath and the other institutions had been issuing buns with poppy seeds, and they were a big hit with the inmates. However, someone realized they were screwing up the test results—no more poppy seed buns.

One morning I went to work all prepared for the IDB, and we started right on time. Things were rolling along just fine until an agitated inmate stomped in. This particular guy was black, Jamaican, and preferred to wear his pants hanging down around his ass. I can still see his red boxer shorts sprouting up above his waistline. As usual, the offence report was read out, and he was asked for any comments. The more conversation we had, the more upset he became. At the time I wasn't concerned, because he and I usually got along, but then he became exceptionally upset. Eventually, he jumped up and banged his fist down on the desk, and I thought, *Oh boy, here we go.* Luckily, the officer covering the door rushed in, and that helped settle things down somewhat.

I told the inmate to settle down or he would be on his way to Millhaven and signaled the officer to take him out. The inmate spun around and started to stomp out of the room, and that's when I noticed his pants starting to slide down even lower. And by God, I just knew what was going to happen. He had his back to us and was so hyped up I guess he didn't feel his pants slipping lower and lower. I just had time to give the chairperson a nudge and nod toward the inmate when his pants slithered down around his knees. Luckily for him, he didn't trip; he just stumbled a little before he caught them. And that's how I found out it's difficult to be huffy and indignant when your pants are down around your knees and you know damned well everyone is staring at you. I don't imagine that little episode did much for the inmate's feelings, but it sure helped to break up our morning.

The situation with MacLean kept percolating. I kept getting more information, but unfortunately nothing I could prove. One day a friend of his approached me and said he wanted to make sure I realized he had nothing to do with MacLean or with anything he was involved in. This conversation was highly unusual and certainly reinforced my belief that the situation was getting out of hand. But on the other hand, I also couldn't help wondering if he was being completely honest.

More than once I even had to arrange for an inmate to be escorted out of the institution under the pretext of a medical escort. The real intent was to escort him to a hotel room to be interviewed by the police, and we had to be very careful which staff we picked for those escorts. We had to be sure they knew enough to keep their mouths shut, and to be honest, I wasn't even sure who I could trust anymore. I know that's a sad statement, but I was becoming more paranoid every day! Even if they didn't let the cat out of the bag intentionally, it would have been very easy to say the wrong thing at the wrong time.

And then to top everything off, a completely separate problem reared its ugly head. I received a note from an inmate who was due for release shortly saying he had to see me as soon as possible. I managed to arrange a meeting that afternoon. I was hoping it was some stupid little thing that I could more or less brush off. But oh no, it was big! A con by the name of Greco had approached him and instructed him to get in contact with a hit man as soon as he reached the street.

The first words out of my mouth were, "You're crazy. What the hell are you talking about?" I soon learned that he wasn't crazy!

I was told it had to do with Greco's business on the street, his son and the son's girlfriend. Well, that took some discussion between the warden, the deputy, and me. This particular situation dragged on for a relatively short time, and naturally the police ended up being involved. A plan, including a method of extracting the informant in an emergency, had to be formulated and sent to region headquarters and to the commissioner for approval. Once again I had to arrange for escorted TAs for an inmate to meet with the police. It ended up being more than a couple of escorts, and both the inmate and I became very uneasy! Eventually, he refused to go out on any more escorts, and I didn't blame him one little bit.

Corrections and the police both had to obtain warrants, and just about the time we could see things coming to a head, my wife was notified that her father had passed away. Naturally this meant we had to take off and I would be gone for over a week. Jill was contacted, and luckily she managed to come in for a briefing and agreed to fill in for me while I was gone. I wasn't happy about missing the finale, but sometimes happenings in life can't be helped.

I returned to work a week or so later, and one of the first things I was told was that everything we had set up had worked like a charm and no one had been injured. Greco had been transferred to higher security, the one civilian that was involved was under police protection, and as far as we knew, everything was hunky-dory!

A few days later I was talking with one of the staff who had escorted the inmate, and he gave me a little more information. The officer naturally didn't know the whole story, but he knew I was involved. He told me that once they had the inmate secured in the van, he became really agitated (the con wouldn't have known he was being transferred until he was in the van). Apparently, he was mumbling and occasionally he yelled something they couldn't understand because it was in a foreign language. "But," the escort stressed, "we had no problem understanding him saying something about that 'foocking Tobedou' several times. I don't know what all went on, but he's pissed at you something fierce, so be careful!"

That told me one thing. Since the inmate was that upset, things must have worked out perfectly. But it also meant I should be careful. Anyone willing to have his son's girlfriend and even his son killed certainly wouldn't hesitate to have me done in!

Anyway, I spent a few days with Jill to bring her up to speed, and my last stint as an institutional preventive security officer at Bath came to an end.

Chapter 23

Charter problems. CX 4 suicide at Bath.
Investigation. Retirement.

Just before my time as an A/IPSO came to an end, the deputy asked me if I would be willing to stay on the day shift and fill the chief of correctional operations position. This actually didn't sound like a bad deal. Before starting the IPSO job, I had already been doing several CCO duties in addition to my regular job as a supervisor. So it sounded like I would be on steady days and maybe, just maybe, I wouldn't be as busy. Of course the part about not being busy turned out to be just a dream; it seemed like I never stopped. At any rate, I told Dave I would do it, and I never regretted my decision.

I did have to open up several new files and come up with a few databases, but other than that, I just settled into my new job in my big office that claimed ownership of that huge bathroom and was good to go! One of the first jobs I had to do was extremely unpleasant. In fact, it pissed most of the staff off. And it pissed me off for two reasons. First, it was an asinine instruction; second, it made a hell of a lot more work for me.

One of the staff's major jobs was searching cells. Unit staff were under orders, on the day shift, to search cells every chance they had and to log the searches in the unit log book. These searches were classed as random, but they also had to search a cell if they had reasonable grounds to believe an inmate was involved with drugs or anything else considered illegal. This certainly didn't mean staff were running around searching cells all day. They had other duties to carry out, so usually if they hit one to four cells a day they were doing well. And it's surprising what the staff came up with during some of these searches.

On this particular day, the deputy informed me someone had ruled that these searches were against our great charter! I've always wondered who in this great land of ours would have made a ruling like this, but of course I never did find out, and it wouldn't have changed anything anyway.

In any event, it fell upon my shoulders to tell the staff there were to be no more cell searches. However, if they did witness contraband in a cell in plain sight, they had the authority to go in and seize it. Outside that particular situation, they had to be given instructions about which cells to search, and naturally that was my job. Each day I had to deliver a list of cells to search during that day to each unit. In addition, I had to keep a record of all searches and seized articles and somehow be able to prove to a committee of some kind that the list was completely random. Boy, ain't that just great. Heaven help us if we ever went against the precious Charter or circumvented an inmate's rights!

One particular day I was in a terrible mood and sometime during the morning I headed to the unit office to grab a coffee. Once I had worked my way around five staff sitting around doing absolutely nothing, I poured a cup. I stood there sipping my coffee for a minute or so listening to them bitching and whining about how hard done-by they were. All five were sitting there complaining, and to make matters worse, there were two or three little jobs that should have been completed. After a few minutes I shocked even myself by losing my cool entirely and emphatically stating, "You know you're a bunch of lazy buggers; you just sit here doing absolutely fuck all and bitching! If Ottawa sent us a memo saying you only had to work two days a week and could still collect the same pay, you would be happy as pigs in shit—for about two weeks. After that you'd be whining and bitching about the two days you had to work and insist on changing them around!" Once I completed my spiel, I stormed out and headed for my office.

I still don't know what set me off. The staff at Bath certainly didn't cause near the problems the KP staff did, and most of these guys did their jobs and then some. I think maybe this was one of my first hints that the last twenty-five years or so were starting to eat at me.

One fine morning the deputy told me an officer from KP was transferring in and she was to report the next day. As soon as he mentioned her name I told him I knew her and was glad she was coming in. I qualified the remark by saying, "We could do one hell of a lot worse."

The next morning rolled around, and as usual I headed right for unit one for a coffee, and there was Olivia in civilian clothes. I must admit she looked a little different out of uniform. I put a smile on my face and strode over to welcome her to Bath. While we were shaking hands she gave me a disdainful look and said, "Vern, I'm still really pissed at you. I don't care how long it's been since I've seen you; I'm still pissed!"

Well, I must admit I was a little surprised; in fact, I was almost shocked. As far as I knew, we got along fine. Staff in the area froze, stared at the both of us, and waited to see what it was all about. I guess I was waiting too.

She must have seen our expressions, because she decided to let me off the hook by saying, "Don't you remember sending me over to the P4W that night to work overtime? I told you the next day I would get even with you even if it took me a life time. That place was a hell hole to work in! Arbour did us all a favor when she closed the goddamn place even though it was a bitchy way to go about it!"

Back then the P4W was often short staffed, and the supervisor would phone over to KP and ask us to try to get female officers to work overtime for them. At first this wasn't difficult, but in very short order word got around about it being a terrible place to work, and unless they really needed the money, staff wouldn't go over. KP staff that did work there came back with some horror stories. One officer told me the inmates seemed to have the run of the place. "Holy hell, they even call staff bitches and tell them to fuck off. It's crazy. Don't ever, ever ask me to go to that nut house again, because I'll refuse to go!"

The prison for women didn't have its own response team at that time, so any time things got out of control, they phoned for our team. Believe me, the team also hated going over there. Many times I saw team members come back from there really shaken up. I was told by different members that the female inmates were crazy and in some ways were a lot worse than the males. Apparently, once they got going, they'd do just about anything. The team complained about the inmates throwing all kinds of things at them including urine and feces. "Jesus Christ," one guy said, "they even strip down buck ass naked. What a sickening sight that is!"

Some of those women certainly shook up the basic beliefs our male staff had regarding the female gender.

Response teams videotaped all responses; it was just a matter of self-preservation. And that was part of what caused some serious problems for the correctional service.

One night things got really wild over there, and a team responded. As per orders, once they were deployed, everything is videotaped. As usual all kinds of crap went on, and as usual, several of the female inmates removed their clothing. And I would imagine, as per orders and once the situation was under control, inmates were strip-searched by female staff before being locked up. This was common practice in any prison; it was just plain silly to lock up inmates if they were still in possession of weapons.

But somehow that tape hit the news media! Suddenly, the IERT were a bunch of perverts taping naked females! Believe me, in those situations, the IERT was not looking at those inmates as female. They were just another bunch of crazy, dangerous convicts, but once the media gets a hold of something like that, everything takes on a life of its own.

Big investigation! In came Louise Arbour and her crew, and eventually they managed to officially close down the Women's Pen in 1999 or 2000. But before the closing, around 1995 female inmates started being slowly transferred from the P4W to five regional facilities. That was good news for KP staff. But in my mind, it was a black eye for corrections. Perhaps the place did require shutting down, but not in that manner! I spoke to several staff working there while Arbour was doing her thing, and they told me it was pathetic. Some of Arbour's staff even went so far as to bring gifts in for the inmates, and several staff told me they were treated as if *they* were the criminals. You can bet money those female inmates hadn't gone through our court system and been sentenced to two years or more for spitting in the street. This whole issue including the investigation was pathetic and a slap in the face to staff working in extremely difficult circumstances. Oh well, I guess it was just another chapter in corrections that was now closed.

The charter of rights that had been brought into law several years earlier certainly had a huge effect on the correctional service. Some of those effects were seen immediately, and some took years to filter down. Some of the changes were good, but on the other hand, some were asinine and maybe even dangerous for staff and inmates alike.

One of the changes took place several years before I went to Bath and, if nothing else, succeeded in allowing even more drugs into the institutions. At one time it was common practice at V&C to randomly search visitors for drugs. This included checking a baby's personal clothing up to and including changing the baby's diaper; hell, we even supplied a fresh diaper. It's a sad statement, but quite often these searches proved successful— drugs in a diaper! Eventually, institutions were told we had to cease these searches because they were too dehumanizing. I'm not too sure how babies felt dehumanized, but then what do I know? There was a caveat though. If we believed we had grounds to do a search and it could be justified, a search could be carried out with the permission of a senior officer, and naturally a written report then had to be submitted. As you can imagine, the searches pretty well stopped. As a rule, you don't have to kick someone in the head too many times to let them know when something has become politically incorrect. Besides, I guess in the grand scheme of things, what difference did it make if more drugs were added to what was already inside an institution?

One day I went in to work and Dave called me into his office. "Well," he said, "I have another gratifying job for you. Sorry to drop this on you, but we're no longer allowed to strip-search inmates going out on an ETA. The order states that it's against the charter; however, inmates may be strip-searched when they return to insure they're not carrying contraband."

With a sinking feeling and before David could interrupt me, I had a chance to say, "Christ, that's a great thing to tell the staff. That skin search is—"

Dave just held up his hand and told me the deputies had been to more than one meeting about this and had discussed anything I was likely to come up with.

Eventually, I ended up carrying a section of that damned charter in my pocket. It seemed like I was always referring to it for one thing or another. In my mind, the only people the charter seemed to be any good for were convicted felons. I know it was one big pain in the ass for staff!

I know this is difficult to believe, but like any institution, Bath had its share of drug problems. And because of my position as the urinalysis coordinator, I caused several inmates to be transferred to other institutions. Sometimes we even had a drug dog and its handler come in and stand in the V&C entrance. This was also kind of neat. It was surprising how many people turned around and left. The one problem with this was that I had to stay with the handler and the dog. Even though it was only for a couple of hours, it was a pain in the neck, but the dogs certainly knew their business.

One day four of five of us were standing around chatting when one of the guys mentioned the name of an officer who had retired a while back and had just passed away. He asked if any of us had heard that it might have been suicide. Everyone was just silent for a minute or so. While we were contemplating that bit of news, one of the officers who had transferred in from KP glanced at me with a speculative look. I knew we were both thinking back to an incident at KP that had taken place on a morning shift when he was my 2 I/C.

The phone call came in sometime during the morning, and I nonchalantly answered it, figuring someone was phoning in sick for the day shift. No such luck; it was a problem, and my stomach immediately dropped!

The caller was a CX 2 who had been at KP for several years, and he was really shaken up. I don't recall everything he said, but he was crying and told me he was sitting in a bath tub with a razor blade and was going to cut his wrists. As you can imagine, that bit of information certainly jerked me awake in a hurry! I'd never dealt with a staff member in this type of situation, and I wasn't all that sure what in hell I should do. We spoke for a very long time, and I was thinking that maybe, just maybe, he was more interested in having someone to talk with than anything else; at least I was hoping that was the case. He didn't do anything—not at that time anyway. Whether that was because of me or not, I don't really know, and I don't really care. I was just happy nothing happened. That was when I learned these situations were very different when it was one of your own.

During my career in corrections, I worked in five different prisons and one of those twice. I don't recall if I mentioned it or not, but I'm sure Kingston Penitentiary was the most difficult. I'm not speaking about the staff problems or the numerous hostage situations, although I suppose that was part of the problem. For me, by far, the most difficult part of the job was dealing with the type of inmate incarcerated in that place. The thought of what one human was capable of doing to another human was sickening! When one of these pathetic bastards is sentenced, most of the public can forget about them, and that's a good thing. But that's just the start of it for the correctional staff. We had to deal with the Olsons, Bernardos and Williamses of the world for years, and they all fell under our great charter of rights. There were times this could become overwhelming and an officer just felt like crying, and believe me, some do! I have to admit it was gratifying to be back at Millhaven before Bernardo and Williams were sent to KP. I tend to think that might have been just a little too much for me.

Also, in addition to the type of inmate, the age of KP was a factor; most of the buildings went up during the 1800s. While I was there, they had to seal off the top portion of segregation to remove asbestos, and then there were the numerous four-legged rats we had there. I swear to God some of those things looked as large as our guard dogs. Then there were the furry-tailed rats that some people call squirrels, plus the feces all these animals produced, and I imagine we had to have problems. Plus, most inmates weren't known for their cleanliness. In addition to everything else, Kingston Pen had pigeons—hundreds of them. I still remember an officer coming down from an upper area and exclaiming, "Jesus Christ, there must be half a foot of pigeon shit up in that place!"

I sincerely believe someone should do a study regarding staff breakdowns, family break-ups, and suicides or attempted suicides and compare KP numbers with the numbers from other institutions. I'm positive the overall numbers for the service would be much higher than in the civilian population, and I'm equally sure the numbers at KP would be higher than the other institutions. On the other hand, I tend to believe Ottawa is well aware of this and is either not concerned or doesn't know what to do about it. Part of the problem may be that if they did admit to the knowledge, it would be opening Pandora's box. Once again, who knows; certainly not me.

Again, I have to apologize if I mentioned all this earlier, but I must admit it's a pet peeve of mine.

Once again the charter and religious freedom reared their heads and caused me extra work. I forget which belief it was, but someone in their wisdom deemed it was now a recognized religion, and members were allowed to practice their beliefs. The problem arose when we were informed that part of the practice involved the use of candles. I've likely mentioned we had a great fear of fire in these places. Also, the fire commissioners had ruled there was to be no open flame in the cells, and as everyone knows, candles have open flames. Somehow, according to my bosses, I had to figure out how the few inmates practicing this religion could be allowed to have candles burning in their cells during certain times.

After several phone calls and I think at least one visit from a fire inspector, I got the okay to go ahead. The next step was to change the post orders and have a memo signed by the deputy issued to the staff, and away we went. Everything worked out, because at least up to the time I retired, we never had a fire that was blamed on candles. So that one problem was solved. Another problem was sweet grass. A directive came down allowing natives the right to burn sweet grass. This didn't cause me nearly the work that the candles did. The only problem with sweet grass was that a few inmates used the odor to cover the smell of dope. But what the hell, in the grand scheme of things…

Around this time, I contacted regional headquarters to get a printout of my pension benefits. I just wanted to get an idea of what my pension would be if I packed the job in. Several years before this, we had been told staff members, who had worked in an institution for at least five years, were eligible to receive an early pension without penalty. I had also been informed that I could buy my three years in the army back. Eventually, I received my printout. And lo and behold, it appeared to me that with the fewer deductions I would have in retirement, the pension was not too bad. I must admit that shook me up a little; you can bet it gave Sheila and me something to think about. Needless to say, I don't think the idea of retiring ever left my mind after that news.

During all this, negotiations between Ottawa and the union had been going on, and apparently not very well. There were even whispers circulating that a strike might be possible.

Eventually, even though staff had been declared essential services, they did go out on strike. Once again though, it was handled responsibly, and staff realized they had to report for duty. Management and the union actually worked together, and at least at Bath, the staff decided to work twelve-hour shifts and to give us a list of the staff that were due in on each shift. The union also promised that staff would fulfill their regular duties.

As you can imagine, management and the supervisors held many meetings before the strike. At one of them we agreed it would be a lot easier on everyone if we came in before the picket lines went up and stayed in until they went down. I must admit that sounded preferable to trying to work through a picket line every day, especially if things heated up. And that's what we did. We came in to work, brought in some clothes and other necessities, and slept on mattresses on the floor. And other than some expected problems like staff getting in late and some other minor episodes, everything worked out fairly well. Even the inmates behaved themselves. They probably realized we weren't in a very good mood and it wouldn't be a smart time to act like idiots.

One morning after the strike, I got to work and headed to the unit for a coffee. I was standing in the office, and one of the guys asked if I'd heard about Jim.

"Nope, not a word; what's up?"

"He was searching a cell and got jabbed with a fucking needle! It was deep enough to draw blood, and he had to go down to the hospital to get checked out. The fucking con, as usual, won't tell anyone if he has AIDS or anything else."

This was just another sad state of affairs we had to contend with. But what could you do? Heaven forbid anyone would circumvent the confidentiality of an inmate's medical file! I don't recall if there were ever any long-term effects from any of these incidents. But once again, who knows? That was life in corrections. But I sincerely hope something has been changed in this area since I retired.

Sheila and I were still trying to decide if I should put in for my retirement or wait a few more years. That was a lot of soul searching—it was a large decision! I think we both realized the job was starting to get to me, and I imagine I was getting a little grumpy at times, but I was also a little scared to make the great leap.

One morning I went in early to do the urinalysis and gave staff a list of inmates to be sent up. Before Gary took the urine sample, I had to read out a form to each inmate and have him sign it to acknowledge his understanding. One of the last inmates to come up was a young native guy. He sat down at the table and quietly listened while I read the form out to him. He just sat, not saying a word, and looked at me like an idiot while he listened to what I had to say. Once I finished my spiel, I gave him the sheet to sign and he just looked at me with a smirk and said he wouldn't sign it! I told him I couldn't care less; I'd just sign it and note that he had refused. One thing led to another, and I must admit, I was getting hot when he suddenly said, "That's not me. The FPS number's wrong, and I had a cell change yesterday."

"Why in hell didn't you tell the officer or me before we started all this shit? You could've buggered off and gone back to bed."

"Oh, I don't know. I guess I never thought of it."

I just sat there looking at that little shit and seeing red. I thought I'd explode. Out of all my episodes in the service, this was the closest I ever came to hauling off and smashing someone in the face! In fact, I came so close I was shaking, but I just didn't want to give the little puke the satisfaction.

That little asshole did one thing for me though. That evening I told Sheila I thought I'd better put my papers in and get the hell out while I could. And she agreed.

My next step was to talk to the deputy warden about my retirement. We'd discussed it in general terms more than once, but once I had a tentative date, the discussion became much more serious. The long and short of it was that we had to pick another supervisor to take my place, and I had to train him. It was also decided that once my replacement had a handle on things, I could use up some of the leave time I had accumulated. Believe me, that was exceptionally good news.

Naturally, my replacement couldn't just drop his duties and follow me around all day, so Berry just worked with me whenever he had a chance. But this was different and certainly a beneficial break for me. In fact, it took a hell of a load off my shoulders.

Retirement was closing in! One morning I drove into Bath in my beautiful one-ton GMC dual-wheeled diesel truck, which happened to be black. We had purchased the truck to pull the wonderful fifth-wheel RV that we were going to live and travel in once I retired. I have to admit, this idea of traveling around the country in a trailer was mostly my idea; in fact, it was all my idea.

I think—well, I know—that Sheila just agreed to do it because my heart had been set on it for the past few years. I now realize it was exceptionally tough on her.

And then I rounded a corner and saw it! A car parked in the administration building parking lot completely covered with a plastic sheet. There were only two reasons to cover a vehicle up like that—crime or a death scene!

I made it to work but wasn't even through the front when I was informed that MacLean had topped himself in his car. My first thought was, *Christ, what was he thinking?* And then, *Well, I was right all along, and he knew or suspected he was close to being arrested. Or maybe the pressure just got to be too much for him.* Also, it's sad to say, but I didn't feel one iota of sadness for him, but I did feel really badly for his family; they certainly didn't deserve this! I was also pissed at his methodology; he ended up screwing one of his fellow officers.

Apparently, on his way in to work, he stopped the mobile and told the officer he wanted to inspect his revolver. The officer wouldn't have thought too much of it, and MacLean did outrank him. As soon as MacLean had the revolver, he drove into the parking lot and shot himself! At least he didn't use a service vehicle. On the other hand, we might have ended up with a new one if he had.

The OPP came in, did their thing, and left.

A day or two later, the warden and deputy asked if I would do the investigation for the service. I've always thought I was asked to do it for a couple of reasons. First, I was due to retire shortly, and second, I had completed numerous investigations and I think I was a bit of a pro at it.

The investigation didn't take very long. It was strictly to cover how it happened, if any procedures had been circumvented, and if any changes could be instituted to prevent a similar incident. The deputy even assigned Berry to give me a hand, and I'm glad he did, because we had to interview the mobile officer at his home.

Understandably, he still wasn't back to work; the situation was eating at him, and he was having a rough time.

Even after I retired, MacLean and his crap came back to haunt me. I had been retired over a year when the OPP tracked me down on Vancouver Island. They wanted to talk about my investigation concerning MacLean, and they were hoping I could add to it. This phone call was shortly after the husband and wife team at KP committed suicide. A correctional officer I was in touch with at the time told me a rumour was going around that they had left a lengthy letter regarding their involvement with the inmates and that it had included a list of names. Apparently this situation came up in the House of Commons, and I would imagine the issue heated up for a while.

One or two years after that, the OPP tracked me down again. Once again, we were on Vancouver Island, grand place that is. This time they wanted me to go to the RCMP office and talk to a member about the incident. They also asked if I would be willing to tape the conversation and hoped I would come up with something new for them. Unfortunately, once again, I don't think I was much help.

The investigation of MacLean's suicide was my last official job with Correctional Services of Canada. In fact, Sheila and I had moved into our trailer, and life was grand. The staff at Bath had been planning a retirement party for me, and I thought that was really a nice thing to do. But I had no idea how large it was going to be! My brother and his daughter came up from Arizona, family from northern Ontario came down, and the room was full of staff I'd worked with. The party ended up being huge! Several staff, including the warden and deputy, had glowing things to say about me, and all in all I must admit I was totally overwhelmed. In fact, I had a difficult time coming to grips with the whole thing. Naturally, I had to give a little speech. I don't have a clue what I said. I was completely flabbergasted! I just hope I told everyone how appreciative I was. It was great and a hell of a lot of fun!

At the end of the night, everyone got to go home, and I was one day closer—no, I *was* retired!

A few days after the retirement party and after we said good-bye to family and friends, Sheila and I hooked up the trailer, climbed into the truck, pulled onto the highway and headed into the sunset. No, I mean the sunrise!

About the Author

I joined the Penitentiary Service, now called Correctional Service of Canada, in 1973. I was thirty-two years of age, married, and had three young children. At the time I was operating heavy-duty equipment in Sault Ste. Marie, Ontario.

It took me eight years to become a correctional supervisor, which was unusually fast at that time. During my service, I fulfilled many varied duties in five different institutions. This included eight years at Kingston Penitentiary working with inmates who required protection from other inmates. Of all the institutions I worked in, I believe Kingston Penitentiary was the most difficult and mentally challenging.

I remained with Correctional Service of Canada for twenty-six years, and then I bought back three years of military service and retired with twenty-nine years in public service.

Before putting in for my retirement, my wife and I made several discussions about that huge step. We both realized working in the prison system with all its negativity was beginning to affect my health, and we both believed it was time to get out of the business.

Once I retired, my wife and I lived and traveled in a recreational vehicle for several years before settling down to enjoy life just outside Toronto.

I still work at the odd security job as much for something to do as anything else. Other than that, with our adult children on their own, Sheila and I are just enjoying our grandchildren and relaxing.

Comments or questions can be directed to: the-door2011@ hotmail.com

Printed in the USA
CPSIA information can be obtained
at www.ICGtesting.com
LVHW090424071023
760380LV00023B/54